COMPLETE
HOME
WIRING

SUNSET BOOKS ❧ MENLO PARK, CALIFORNIA

SUNSET BOOKS

Vice President and General Manager: Richard A. Smeby
Vice President and Editorial Director: Bob Doyle
Production Director: Lory Day
Art Director: Vasken Guiragossian

Staff for this book:

Book Editor: Scott Atkinson

Managing Editor: Sally Lauten
Sunset Books Senior Editor: Suzanne Normand Eyre
Art Director: Alice Rogers
Photographer: Mark Rutherford
Illustrator: Anthony Davis
Photo Stylist: JoAnn Masaoka Van Atta
Technical Consultants: Donald E. Johnson, Brent Crane
Copy Editor: Julie Harris
Indexer: Pamela Evans

Computer Production: Joan Olson, Linda Bouchard
Digital Prepress Production: Rutherford Studios/Norman Gilbert,
    Jeanne Stack
Production Coordinator: Patricia S. Williams
Special Contributor: Bridget Biscotti Bradley
Light Fixtures: Stanford Electric Works, Palo Alto, California

Cover: Design by Vasken Guiragossian. Photography by Mark Rutherford.
Photo direction by JoAnn Masaoka Van Atta.

10 9 8 7 6 5 4 3 2
First printing January 2000
Copyright © 2000 Sunset Publishing Corporation, Menlo Park, CA 94025.
First edition. All rights reserved, including the right of reproduction in whole
or in part in any form. Library of Congress Catalog Card Number: 99-66035.
ISBN 0-376-01594-2.

Printed in the United States.
For additional copies of Complete Home Wiring or any other Sunset book,
call 1-800-526-5111 or visit us at www.sunsetbooks.com

CONTENTS

1

2

3

4

5

6

7

8

9

10

GET WIRED

To many of us, electricity seems to flow in a mysterious and vaguely scary fashion through house walls, ceilings, and floors, magically powering microwave ovens and alarm clocks before diving back into the netherworld it came from. This book was designed to help you clearly understand home electrical systems and, once you do, to harness this power neatly and safely. It's not as tough as it seems!

HOW TO USE THIS BOOK

Complete Home Wiring is arranged as a sequential primer that moves from principles to particulars. The book begins with four introductory chapters: read together, they form a crash course in electrical basics, materials, tools, and hands-on wiring techniques as practiced by the pros.

Then it's time to get dirty. Chapter Five, "Rough Wiring," presents wire-routing tips and tricks for both existing buildings and new construction. Chapter Six, "Finish Wiring," walks you through the installation of receptacles, switches, light fixtures, and appliances. Both chapters are packed with step-by-step photos and clear diagrams.

In Chapters Seven and Eight, we take another turn, venturing this time to the brave new world of telecommunications and low-voltage marvels. Chapter Nine, "The Great Outdoors," explores the specialized materials and techniques that let you take your new wiring skills outside.

The tenth and final chapter forms an easy-access reference section on electrical troubleshooting and repairs. It's located at the back of the book to help you find what you need—almost as quickly as you need it. Unsure of one or more terms we're using? See the glossary on pages 190-191.

Wiring concepts, logistics, and hands-on techniques are all interrelated. What's the moral? Unless you're well-versed in electrical basics, be prepared to move back and forth between principles and particulars—or between chapters—when planning your new project.

CODES AND PERMITS

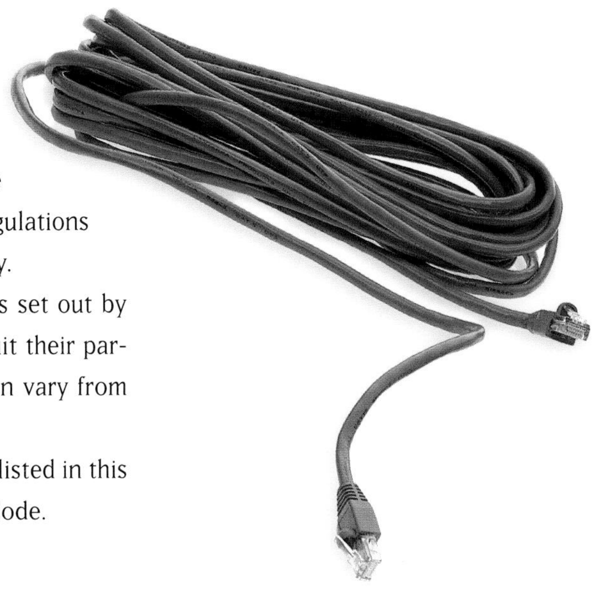

If you're thinking of doing your own electrical wiring, you should first talk with your building department's electrical inspector about local codes, the National Electrical Code, and your jurisdiction's requirements concerning permits and inspections.

The National Electrical Code (referred to as "NEC" or simply "The Code") spells out the wiring methods and materials to be used in all electrical work. The Code forms the basis for all regulations applied to electrical installations, and its central purpose is safety.

The information given in this book complies with guidelines set out by the NEC. Some cities, counties, and states amend the Code to suit their particular purposes, though, and as a result, specific regulations can vary from county to county and even from town to town.

Note: In Canada, wiring requirements may differ from those listed in this book; before beginning any work, check the Canadian Electrical Code.

SHOULD YOU DO YOUR OWN WIRING?

Doing your own electrical work may not always be the best idea. Your local building department may restrict how much and what kinds of new wiring a homeowner may take on. For instance, you may be able to do all wiring up to the point at which the circuits are connected to the service panel, but the final hookup may have to be done by a licensed electrician.

Even if your locality does not restrict what kinds of electrical work you do in your own home, you may still wish to use the services of a licensed electrician. If things crop up that you don't understand, or if there's any doubt in your mind about your electrical system or about how to proceed, it's best to call on a professional.

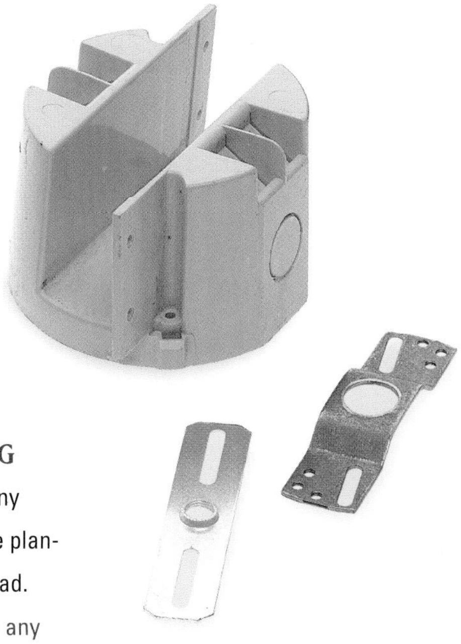

SAFETY FIRST

Electrical work is safe if you make the effort to keep it safe. Two key rules are: 1) Be sure you understand the basics of electricity, circuitry, and your own home's wiring system; and 2) Never work on any electrically "live" circuit—shut off power and test that it's off. For a closer look at safety, see pages 18-19. To shut off power to a circuit or to your entire home, see pages 170-173.

Throughout this book we'll be reminding you of important safety precautions. Each one will be presented in the manner shown at right.

WARNING

Make sure any circuit you're planning to work on is dead. Test it before making any repairs or connections.

5

AN INTRODUCTION TO THE BASICS

Electricity provides us with comfort and conveniences that we often take for granted until something goes wrong. Fortunately for the do-it-yourselfer, electrical work is one of the easiest kinds of home improvement and repair. It's simple, neat, and logical; it doesn't require a shop full of specialized tools; and there's considerable standardization in home electrical systems and related materials. But before you embark on any electrical wiring project, it's important to understand a few things about electricity itself, electrical safety, and about your current wiring system.

This chapter provides a basic overview of how electricity energizes your home and how currents and circuits work. You'll learn how to work safely with electricity and how grounding protects your electrical system and guards against the possibility of electrical shock. We'll also help you assess your home's existing electrical capacity and calculate your electrical usage.

Read on as we define the basic elements of home electricity and then proceed to untangle the maze of wires inside your walls, floors, and ceilings.

WHAT IS ELECTRICITY?

Think of a pipe or a garden hose. When you turn on the water, it moves through the pipe and out the faucet or hose end. In a similar way, you can think of electricity as a current of very tiny particles (electrons) flowing inside a wire and through a light bulb or an appliance that's been switched on. Home wiring is fundamentally a matter of transporting this current in a safe, efficient manner.

DEFINING TERMS

Associated with this flowing current are some basic terms that electricians often work with.

VOLTS: Water inside a hose moves because it's under pressure from the water behind it. Likewise, electricity is also under pressure, and the force causing the current to flow is measured in volts. The utility company sets the household voltage level.

AMPERES: The amount of current that flows past a given point in one second is measured in amperes (amps). Amps are basically a function of wire size; the larger the wire, the higher the potential current-carrying capacity.

WATTS: The energy per second consumed by a light bulb or an appliance is expressed in watts. Household electrical usage is usually figured in kilowatt-hours (units of 1,000 watts multiplied by the time of usage in hours).

For the purposes of this book, the relationship between these three basic units is represented in this formula: volts × amps = watts. If you know two of these values, you can figure the third by multiplying or dividing. Some examples: A 20-amp circuit at 120 volts can deliver 2,400 watts; a microwave oven that uses 1,000 watts of 120-volt power consumes 8.3 amps; a 240-volt clothes dryer that pulls 5,600 watts of power requires at least a 23.3-amp circuit.

CONDUCTORS: The general term "conductor" applies to anything that permits, or conducts, the flow of electricity. Electricity flows in the path of least resistance, and certain materials allow energy to flow more freely than others. Copper, for example, is a good conductor; most wires are made of copper, although aluminum and copper-clad aluminum wires are also used.

RESISTANCE: This is the property of an electric circuit that restricts the flow of current. Electrical resistance or impedance is measured in ohms.

THE CIRCUIT LOOP

Now that we're thinking of electricity as a current flowing through conductors, let's look at a second basic concept: the continuous loop of a circuit.

In order to flow, electricity must have a continuous, closed path from start to finish—like a circle. The word "circuit" refers to the entire course an electric current travels, from the source of power, through an electrical device, and back to the source. So what may appear to be a hopeless tangle of wires running through the walls, floors, and ceilings of your home is actually a well-organized system composed of several circuits.

Each circuit can be traced from its beginning in the entrance panel (page 12) or subpanel through various receptacles, fixtures, or appliances and back to the panel. The current flows to the devices (called loads) through a "hot" wire and returns via a "neutral" wire—so-called because under normal conditions it's maintained at zero volts, or what is referred to as ground potential.

A BASIC CIRCUIT

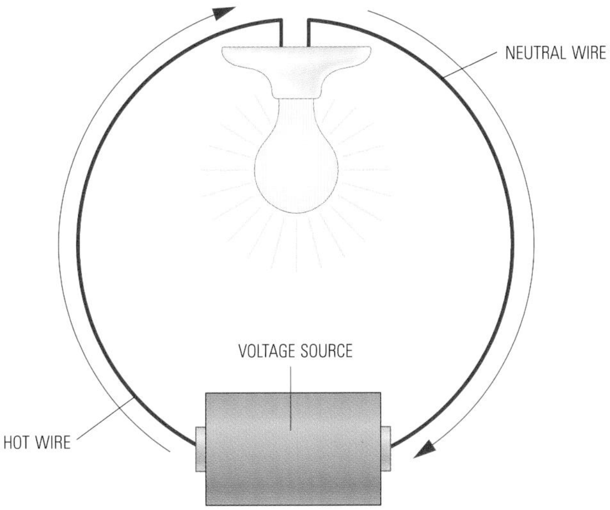

NEUTRAL WIRE

VOLTAGE SOURCE

HOT WIRE

DIRECT AND ALTERNATING CURRENT

DIRECT CURRENT

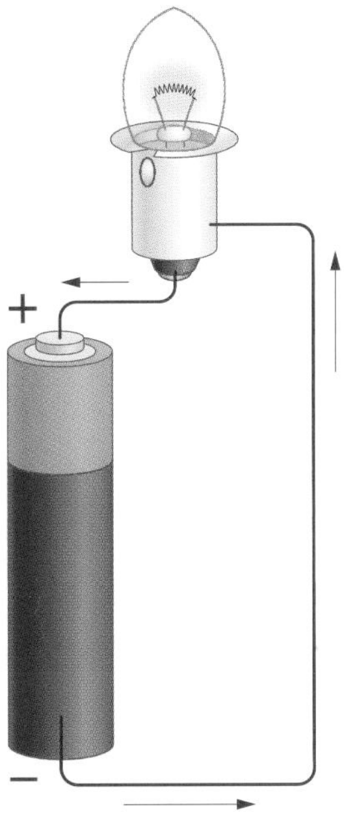

Originally, electrical power was formed by chemical reaction, and that's still the way that batteries work. This type of current, known as direct current (DC), flows from a negative pole, through an electrical device (such as a light bulb), and on to the positive pole.

However, direct current can't be transmitted over long distances without a debilitating drop in voltage. Utility companies now provide households with alternating (AC) current, which actually pulses—or reverses direction—120 times, or 60 cycles, per second (called 60 hertz power). AC power moves in waves, as shown below. Light bulbs actually flicker as power ebbs and flows, but the human eye can't detect it.

NOTE: An explanation is in order about the designation of the voltage supplied by the utility company. As mentioned on the facing page, voltage is electrical pressure. That pressure can fluctuate from roughly 115 volts to 125 volts, even within the same day, which is why you may see references elsewhere to household voltages other than 120. This book uses 120 as the voltage for each hot line from the utility company.

ALTERNATING CURRENT

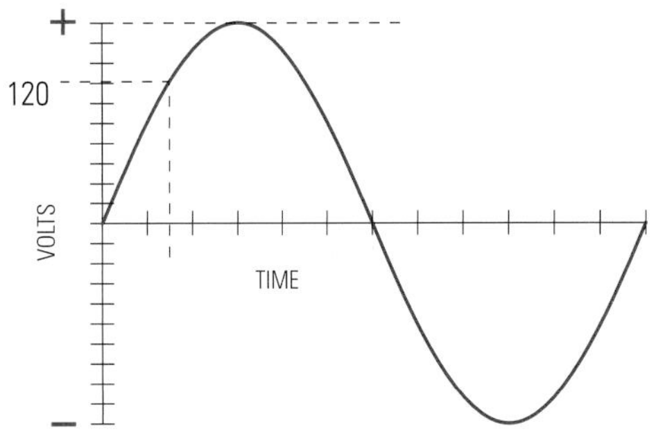

120

VOLTS

TIME

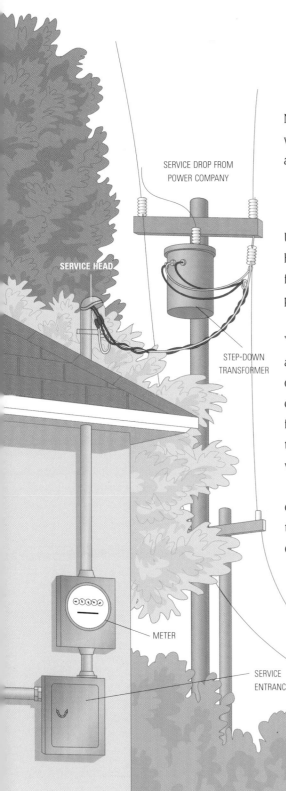

SERVICE DROP FROM
POWER COMPANY

SERVICE HEAD

STEP-DOWN
TRANSFORMER

METER

SERVICE
ENTRANCE PANEL

HOW ELECTRICITY
ENERGIZES YOUR HOME

Now let's see what actually happens in a residential electrical system and why. We'll trace the electrical path through your home step-by-step, starting at the point where the utility company supplies the home with electricity.

YOUR ELECTRICAL SERVICE

Utility companies distribute power to individual households through overhead wires or underground cables. The actual power may be generated via fossil fuels, water, nuclear energy, thermal activity, solar power, or even wind power.

As depicted below, AC electricity travels from the power plant through "step-up" transformers that boost voltage via huge magnetic coils and send it along high-voltage lines to substations, where it then moves through "step-down" transformers. From the substation, this reduced power moves along city streets until it nears your home, where yet another step-down transformer converts it to household voltage. The wires that connect this last transformer to your home (called a service drop) enter via an overhead service head or through buried conduit (pipe).

Today, most homes have three-wire service. That is, the utility company connects three lines to your home's service entrance panel: two hot conductors (wires) each supplying electricity at about 120 volts, and one neutral conductor.

Three-wire service provides both 120-volt and 240-volt capability. One hot conductor and the neutral combine to provide for 120-volt needs, such as light fixtures or wall receptacles. Both hot conductors combine with

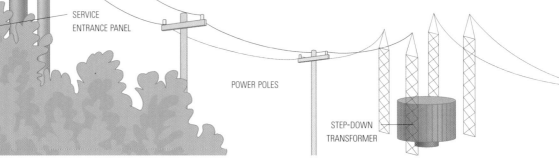

SUBSTATION

POWER POLES

STEP-DOWN
TRANSFORMER

HOW TO READ YOUR METER

Learning to read your electric meter can help you keep close track of your energy consumption, check your electricity bill, or simply satisfy your curiosity about that silent, sleepless counter.

Most electric meters have four or five dials with numbers and pointers. (Newer installations have five.) A quick look at these dials shows that their numbering alternates between clockwise and counterclockwise.

To take a reading of your meter, jot down the numbers indicated by the pointers, starting with the left dial. When the pointer is between two numbers, always read the smaller number. When the pointer appears to be directly on a number, check the next dial to the right. If the pointer of that dial is on zero or has passed zero, record the number indicated by the pointer of the first dial. If the pointer of the second dial has not yet reached zero, write down the number preceding the one indicated on the first dial.

In the example below, the pointer of the first (left-hand) dial is between 0 and 1, so the number to record is 0; on the second dial, the pointer is between 4 and 5, so write down the number 4. The pointer of the third dial is almost directly at 2, so look at the pointer of the fourth dial. It has passed 9 but not quite reached 0. For the third dial, then, 1 is the number to record; for the fourth dial the number is 9. And on the last dial, since the pointer is between 7 and 8, record the number 7. The reading is therefore 04197 kilowatt-hours.

If you want to figure out the number of kilowatt-hours consumed during a certain period of time, subtract the meter reading at the start of the period from the reading at the end. You can use this to check your utility bills.

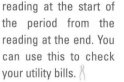

---

the neutral to provide 120/240 volts for large appliances, such as a range or a clothes dryer. The selling feature of 240-volt power is that it's twice as powerful and twice as efficient as 120 volts. In other words, it not only allows you to run higher-wattage appliances, but at half the amps. (Remember, watts divided by volts equals amps.)

Many older homes have just two-wire service, with one hot conductor at 120 volts and a neutral conductor. As a result, the system may not be able to handle the higher-voltage requirements of an electric range or dryer.

THE METER

Once electricity arrives at your doorstep, it passes through a meter—owned, installed, and serviced by the utility company—before it enters the service panel. The meter measures the electrical energy consumed in kilowatt-hours (the rate of energy consumption in kilowatts multiplied by the time of usage in hours).

To read and interpret your meter, see "How to read your meter," above.

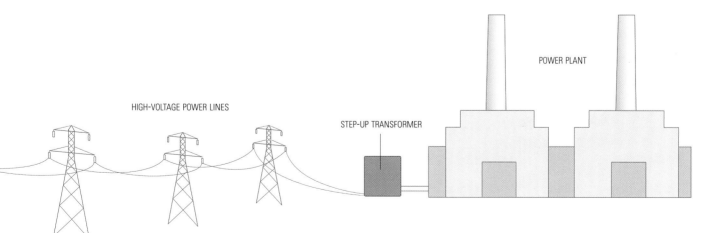

POWER PLANT

HIGH-VOLTAGE POWER LINES

STEP-UP TRANSFORMER

THE SERVICE ENTRANCE PANEL

The control center for a home electrical system is the service panel, sometimes referred to as the fuse box or panel box. This cabinet or box usually houses the main disconnect (the main fuses or main circuit breaker), which shuts off power to the entire electrical system and, in many cases, the fuses or circuit breakers that protect the individual circuits in the home.

Electricity runs from the utility company lines, through the meter, and into the service panel. As mentioned earlier, the service drop typically contains three conductors. Two hot conductors go to the main disconnect. The neutral conductor goes directly to a device called the neutral bus bar, which in turn connects to the grounding electrode conductor. This continuous conductor connects the neutral bus bar to the metal water supply pipe entering your home and to a metal ground rod driven into the earth. This safety feature provides excess current with an uninterrupted metal pathway into the ground. For more on grounding, see pages 16–19.

Though the ultimate capabilities are usually the same, the exact location and type of service equipment vary from home to home. The service panel might be on the outside of a home, below the

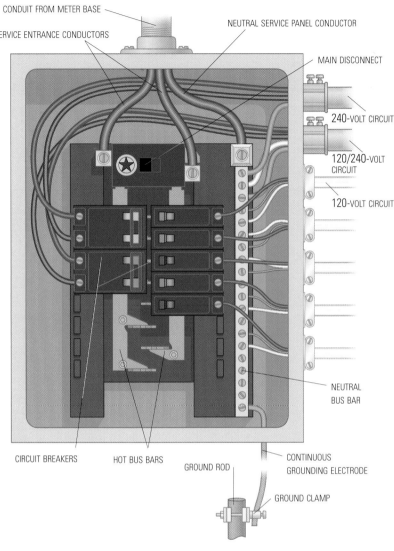

BREAKER-TYPE PANEL

CONDUIT FROM METER BASE

HOT SERVICE ENTRANCE CONDUCTORS

NEUTRAL SERVICE PANEL CONDUCTOR

MAIN DISCONNECT

240-VOLT CIRCUIT

120/240-VOLT CIRCUIT

120-VOLT CIRCUIT

NEUTRAL BUS BAR

CIRCUIT BREAKERS

HOT BUS BARS

GROUND ROD

CONTINUOUS GROUNDING ELECTRODE

GROUND CLAMP

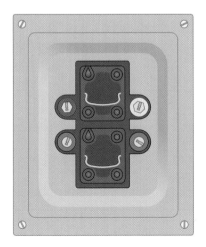

FUSE-TYPE PANEL

meter, or on an inside wall, often directly behind the meter. It might have a single main disconnect, or it could have as many as six switches controlling disconnection. Also, the service entrance panel may or may not contain overcurrent protection devices for individual circuits. Variations also occur in the type of overcurrent protection devices. Most systems use circuit breakers; older models may use fuses.

Because of these differences, don't be concerned if your service panel doesn't look like the drawings on the facing page. The principles of safety and protection are the same regardless of the location and type of service equipment.

THE DISTRIBUTION CENTER

After passing through the main disconnect, each hot conductor connects to one of two hot bus bars in the distribution center, where energy is divided to branch circuits. Note that the distribution center may be either part of the service entrance panel or a separate subpanel located elsewhere in the house (for more details, see pages 124–125). Regional electrical codes dictate placement; fire codes and weather are contributing factors.

The hot bus bars accept the amount of current permitted by the main fuses or circuit breaker and allow you to divide that current into smaller units for the branch circuits.

SAFEGUARDS IN THE ELECTRICAL SYSTEM

Fuses and circuit breakers, collectively referred to as overcurrent protection devices, guard electrical systems from damage by too much current.

Whenever wiring is forced to carry more current than it can safely handle—whether because of a sudden surge from the utility company, use of too many appliances on one circuit, or a problem within your system—fuses will blow or circuit breakers will trip (activate), disconnecting the supply of electricity.

A fuse or circuit breaker is inserted into each circuit at the service entrance panel (or in some cases at a subpanel). For adequate protection, the amperage rating of a fuse or breaker must be the same as that of the circuit conductor it protects. For example, a circuit using #12 copper conductors has an ampacity (current-carrying capacity) of 20 amperes; the fuse or circuit breaker, therefore, must also be rated for 20 amperes. Never replace any fuse or circuit breaker with one of higher amperage.

A fuse contains a short strip of an alloy with a low melting point. When installed in a socket or fuse holder, the metal strip becomes a link in the circuit. If the amperage flowing in the circuit becomes greater than the rating of the fuse, the metal strip will melt, opening the circuit and stopping the flow of electricity. When that happens, the fuse is ruined and must be replaced.

FUSES

A circuit breaker serves as both a switch and a fuse. As a switch, it allows you to open a circuit (by turning the switch to "off") whenever you want to work on the wiring. As a fuse, it provides automatic overcurrent protection.

When a circuit breaker is installed in a service entrance panel or subpanel, a bimetallic strip becomes a link in the circuit. Heat from excessive current will bend the metal strip, causing a release to trip and break the circuit. (The toggle goes to "off" or an intermediate position when this happens.) Unlike fuses that work on the self-destruct principle, circuit breakers can be reset (turned back on) once they've tripped.

For specifics about choosing and using fuses and breakers, see page 172.

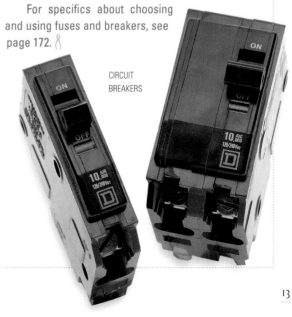

CIRCUIT BREAKERS

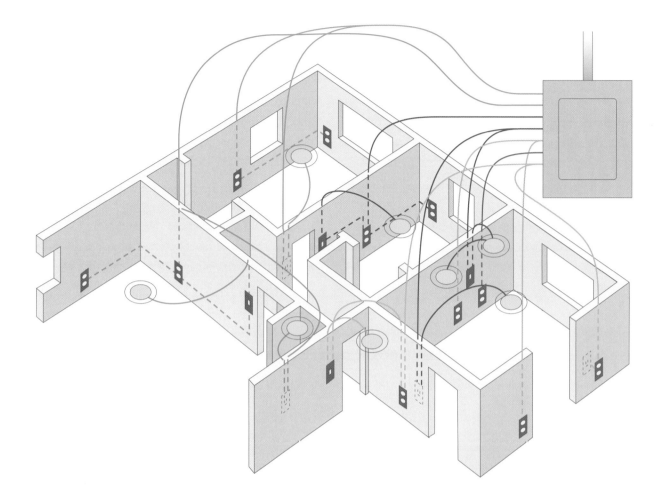

BRANCH CIRCUITS

The drawing above shows distribution of electricity through a typical service panel to the branch circuits of a house. Branch circuits feed power to receptacles, switches, fixtures, and appliances in different areas of the house. Each one attaches to one or both hot bus bars in the distribution center by means of a branch circuit overcurrent protection device, otherwise known as a fuse or circuit breaker.

A 120-volt circuit consists of one hot conductor and one neutral conductor. The hot conductor originates at a breaker or fuse connected to one of the hot bus bars. A 240-volt circuit requires both hot bus conductors, so it originates at a breaker or fuse connected to both hot bus bars.

All neutral conductors for branch circuits originate at a neutral bus bar in the distribution center. They are all in direct contact with the earth through the grounding electrode conductor at the main service entrance panel, as shown on page 12. In order that ground potential (zero volts) be maintained at all times, a neutral conductor must never be interrupted by an overcurrent protection device.

CIRCUITRY 101

As discussed on page 9, a circuit is a continuous closed path along which electricity flows from the source of power, through a device, and back to the source. The hot wire brings electricity to a device, and the neutral wire returns electricity to the service panel. The individual fixtures or receptacles on a circuit are connected by either parallel or series wiring. Switches may or may not be added along the way.

In real life, light fixtures, receptacles, and switches are mounted in housing boxes, which also contain and protect all wiring connections. Numerous routing options exist. When wiring a switch circuit, for example, the cable may run through the switch box first and on to the light, or it may run through the light first, with a separate "switch loop" running to the switch. Additional wires may also pass through one or both boxes, unswitched, on their way to other devices.

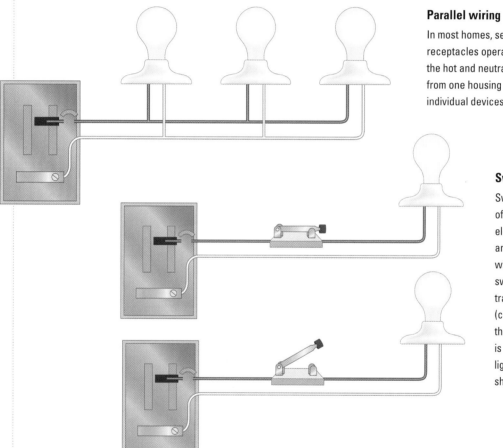

Parallel wiring

In most homes, several light fixtures or receptacles operate on the same circuit with the hot and neutral wires running together from one housing box to another; wires to individual devices branch off from them.

Switch wiring

Switches turn things on and off by controlling the flow of electric current. Switches are installed only on hot wires. The simple knife-blade switch shown top left illustrates how a switch closes (completes) a circuit, turning the light on. When the switch is open, it disconnects the light from the hot bus bar, as shown bottom left.

Series wiring

This type of circuit passes the hot wire through a series of devices before joining the neutral wire that returns to the source. Series wiring is rarely used for home light circuits because when one light bulb fails, all the lights go out in the circuit. A string of old-style Christmas tree lights is an example of series wiring.

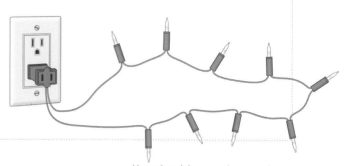

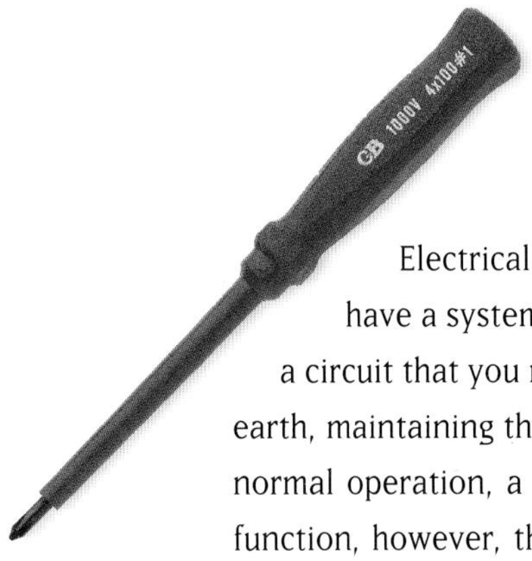

GROUNDING

Electrical codes now require that all 120- and 240-volt circuits have a system of grounding. Grounding assures that all metal parts of a circuit that you might come in contact with are connected directly to the earth, maintaining them at zero voltage. This is a preventive measure. During normal operation, a grounding system does nothing; in the event of a malfunction, however, the grounding protects you and your home from electric shock or fire.

To see why grounding is necessary, turn back to the drawing on page 9, which shows a circuit during normal conditions. Now let's take that same circuit and add a metal ceiling fixture. If the hot wire accidentally became dislodged from the fixture terminal and came into contact with the light fixture's metal canopy, which is highly conductive, the fixture would become electri-

WHAT CAUSES SHOCKS?

The discussion of circuits on page 9 describes how current flows in a continuous closed path from the source, through a device that uses the power, and back to the source. But electricity need not flow in wires to make the return trip to the source. It can return through any conducting body—including a person—that contacts the earth directly or touches a conductive object or material that in turn enters the earth. And if you accidentally become a link in an electrically live circuit, as shown here, you'll get a shock.

The key word is "link." To get an electric shock, you must be touching a live wire or device at the same time you're touching a grounded object or another live wire. This may sound like a rather unlikely situation, but consider that whenever you're touching any metal plumbing fixture, standing on the ground or on a damp concrete floor or patio, or partially immersed in water, you're in contact with a grounded object. In other words, you're satisfying one of the two requirements for getting a shock.

There may be two requirements for getting a shock, but there's only one requirement for not getting one: Always make sure that the circuit you intend to work on is dead.

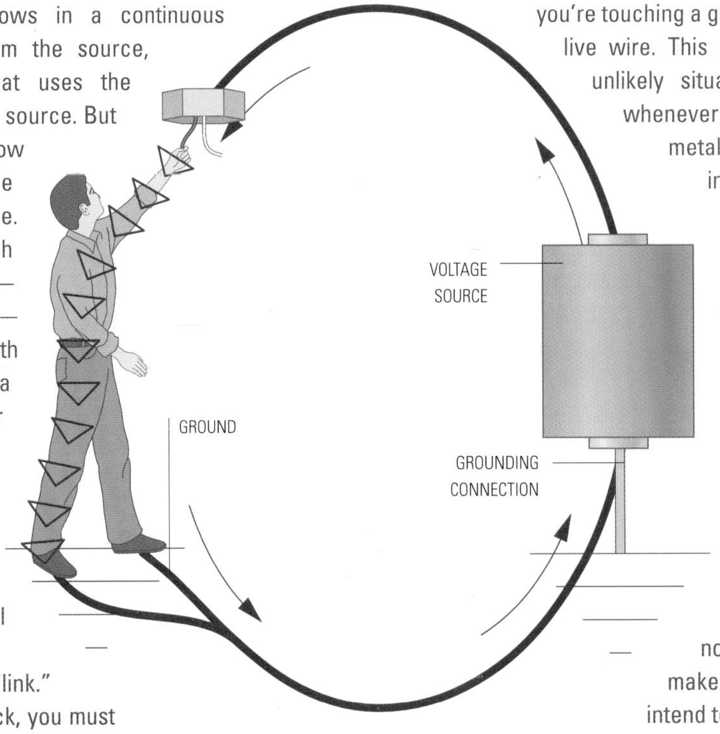

VOLTAGE SOURCE

GROUND

GROUNDING CONNECTION

cally charged, or "hot." If you were to touch the fixture under those conditions, a current leakage, or "ground fault," could occur in which you would provide the path to ground for the electric current, and you would get a shock.

The same result could occur in any number of places where electricity and conductive materials are together, such as in power tools and appliances with metal housings, in metal housing boxes, and in metal faceplates.

In our example, shock could have been prevented if the circuit had a grounding system. A grounding wire connecting the neutral bus bar in the service entrance panel to the metal housing of the light fixture would provide an auxiliary electrical path to ground. This grounding wire would carry the fault current back to the distribution center, where the fuse or circuit breaker protecting the circuit would open, shutting off all current flow.

GROUNDING LOGISTICS

In a typical house circuit, the wiring method dictates how grounding is done. When a home is correctly wired with armored cable, metal conduit, or flexible metal conduit, the metal enclosure can itself serve as the grounding path. But most modern construction uses nonmetallic sheathed cable (type NM), so a separate grounding wire must be run with the circuit wires. Running a separate grounding wire isn't as complicated as it may sound because NM cable contains a grounding wire (see page 28).

In any of these systems, the end result is the same: an auxiliary path for fault current is provided leading to the neutral bus bar in the service entrance panel, which is tied to ground via the grounding electrode conductor.

In the drawing at right, the bare grounding wire of the NM cable provides the grounding continuity. The final grounding connection to the receptacle is made through a short piece of wire called a jumper that is bonded to the metal box with either a grounding screw or a grounding clip. If a nonmetallic box were used instead, the grounding wire would be connected directly to the receptacle because that kind of box needs no grounding. (For a closer look at receptacle wiring, see pages 92–97.)

GROUNDING WITH NM CABLE

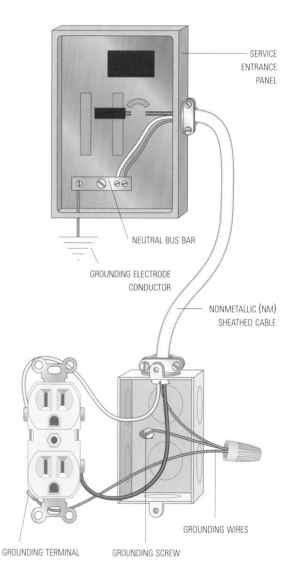

SERVICE ENTRANCE PANEL

NEUTRAL BUS BAR

GROUNDING ELECTRODE CONDUCTOR

NONMETALLIC (NM) SHEATHED CABLE

GROUNDING WIRES

GROUNDING TERMINAL

GROUNDING SCREW

ENTER THE GFCI

The ground fault circuit interrupter (GFCI or GFI) also protects against electric shock. Whenever the amounts of incoming and outgoing current are unequal, indicating current leakage, the GFCI opens the circuit instantly, cutting off the power. GFCIs are built to trip in 1/40th of a second in the event of a ground fault of 0.005 ampere.

There are two types of GFCIs, both shown below. The GFCI breaker is installed in the service panel; it monitors the amount of current going to and coming from an entire circuit. A GFCI receptacle monitors the flow of electricity to that receptacle, as well as to all devices installed in the circuit from that point onward (called "downstream").

The electrical code now requires that receptacles in bathrooms, kitchens, garages, and outdoor locations (in other words, any potentially damp location where the risk of shock is greatest) be protected by a GFCI. You can use either type to serve these areas.

GFCI BREAKER

GFCI RECEPTACLE

Electricity is something we use freely with just a flick of a switch. Electricity is also something to be treated with caution and respect. While these two statements seem to express conflicting viewpoints, together they give a good foundation for working safely with electricity. Once you understand and respect the potential hazards, electrical wiring is quite safe to do.

SHUTTING OFF POWER

The most important rule for all do-it-yourself electricians is never to work on any electrically "live" circuit, fixture, or appliance.

Before starting any work, disconnect (or "kill") the circuit at its source in the service panel. If the circuits are protected by fuses, removing the appropriate fuse will disconnect the circuit from incoming service. If the circuits are protected by circuit breakers, disconnect the circuit by switching its breaker to the "off" position. For detailed instructions, see page 172.

To make sure you disconnect the correct circuit, turn on a light fixture, a plug-in lamp, or an appliance that's connected to the circuit before you remove the fuse or turn off the circuit breaker. The device will go out when you remove the correct fuse or turn off the correct breaker. If you have any doubt about which fuse or breaker protects which circuit, shut off all current coming into your home at the main disconnect, as detailed on page 170.

When you're shutting off power to a circuit at the service panel, spend another moment to prevent a possible disaster. As a safety measure, tape a note on the panel explaining what you're doing so that no one will come along and replace the fuse or reset the circuit breaker while you're working on the wiring. Then, either put the fuse in your pocket, tape the circuit breaker in the "off" position, or lock the service panel.

One more step before starting to work is to double-check that the circuit is actually dead by using a neon tester, as described on page 50. If the light bulb on the neon tester doesn't glow, the circuit is dead. If it does, return to the service panel and locate the correct fuse or circuit breaker.

Finally, when working on a portable electric appliance, such as a lamp, always unplug it first. Just turning off the switch is not enough.

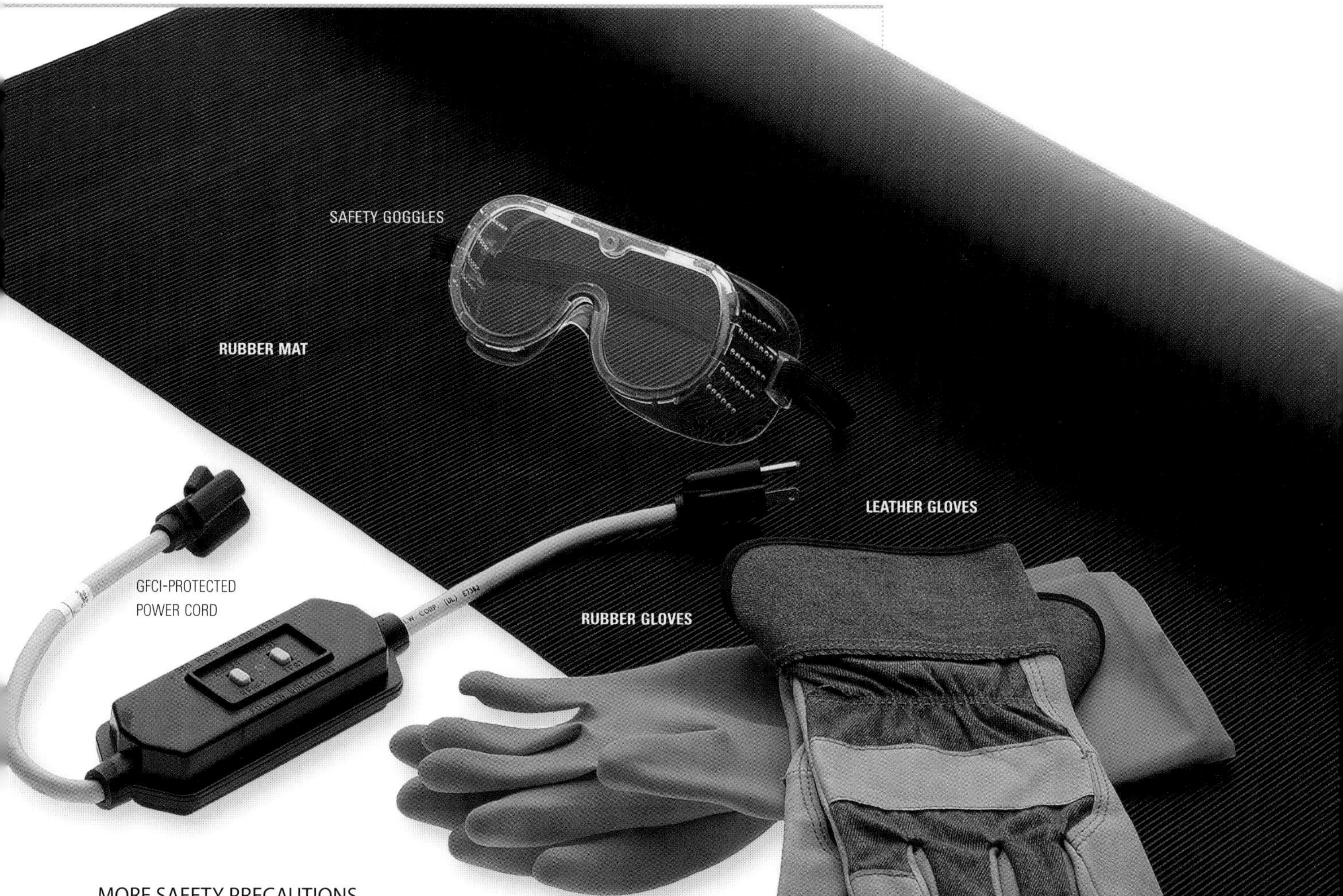

SAFETY GOGGLES

RUBBER MAT

LEATHER GLOVES

GFCI-PROTECTED
POWER CORD

RUBBER GLOVES

MORE SAFETY PRECAUTIONS

With the electricity turned off, electrical work can be performed safely. Still, it's a good idea to keep a few additional precautions in mind.

√ Remember that water and electricity don't mix. Never work on wiring, fixtures, switches, or appliances in damp or wet conditions. Lay down dry boards or a rubber mat to stand on if the floor or ground is wet, and wear rubber boots.

√ Equip yourself with proper safety gear before starting to work. Wear safety glasses when using power tools or hammers and in cramped quarters. Double-insulated, grounded power tools and hand tools with insulated handles are a must. (For details, see Chapter Three, "Tools of the Trade.") Plug power tools into a GFCI-protected receptacle or use an extension cord equipped with its own built-in GFCI. Leather gloves will protect your hands; rubber gloves can provide an extra barrier of insulation against electrical shock.

√ Study how your particular home is wired before you modify or work on the electrical system. The procedures described in this book are based on the assumption that the existing wiring was done correctly.

EVALUATING YOUR SYSTEM

"What do I have to work with?" That's the first question you should ask yourself when considering any repairs, alterations, or additions to your present electrical system. Once you know what you have, you can start planning additions or changes as required.

SERVICE RATINGS

The first step in evaluating your system is to determine what type of electrical service you have. Looking through the glass window of your meter, you'll see several numbers printed on the faceplate. The designation "120V" indicates two-wire service; "240V" indicates three-wire service with both 120-volt and 240-volt capabilities.

Any electrical system is also rated for the maximum amount of current (measured in amperes) it can carry. This rating, determined by the size of the service entrance equipment, is called the service rating. Keeping you within the bounds of your service rating is the job of the main fuses or circuit breaker.

Service ratings have increased through the years to accommodate greater electrical demands and higher safety standards. Today, the minimum service rating of most new homes is 100 amps. Depending to a large extent on the age of your home, your service rating could be as low as 30 amps or as high as 400 amps. In between the two extremes are the following common service ratings: 60, 100, 125, 150, and 200 amps.

The best way to find out your service rating is to look at the main disconnect, if you have one. The service rating will usually be stamped on the main fuses or circuit breaker.

If your system doesn't have a main disconnect, call the utility company or your local building inspection department rather than trying to figure out the service rating yourself. Someone from either of those two offices should be able to advise you.

KNOW YOUR CIRCUIT STRUCTURE

Once you've established your service rating, you should map out the lamps, light fixtures, switches, and appliances on each of the circuits. The illustration on the opposite page shows how. If the circuits aren't identified on the service panel or if the labeling is out of date, take the time to identify them properly so that when you're working on your wiring, you'll be able to kill power to the correct circuit.

Here are some tips to remember when charting branch circuits:

✓ Starting with the 120-volt circuits, turn off or remove circuit breaker or fuse number 1. (If it's not labeled, just choose one to start with.) Using a small table lamp, a night-light, or a neon tester, go through the house and check all switches and receptacles; on your map, label those that are now dead with the circuit number 1. Turn the circuit back on or replace the fuse. Repeat with each circuit.

✓ Make sure to test both halves of duplex receptacles.

✓ Don't forget to test the switches on any garbage disposal units or dishwashers.

✓ Once the 120-volt circuits are charted, go on to the 240-volt circuits. These circuits—identified in your service panel by a double circuit breaker or a pull-out fuse block with cartridge fuses—go to individual high-wattage appliances such as electric ranges, clothes dryers, water heaters, heating systems, or central air conditioners. Trace the 240-volt circuits by disengaging one overcurrent protection device at a time and finding out which appliance doesn't work.

CIRCUIT MAPPING

Using numbers and electrical symbols, you can make a good working drawing of your electrical system. Such a drawing or map can save you a lot of time, whether you plan to wire a new home, alter existing wiring, or troubleshoot a problem. This circuit map is of a typical two-bedroom house. Note that the dashed lines indicate which switch controls which fixture; they do not show wire routes. ✂

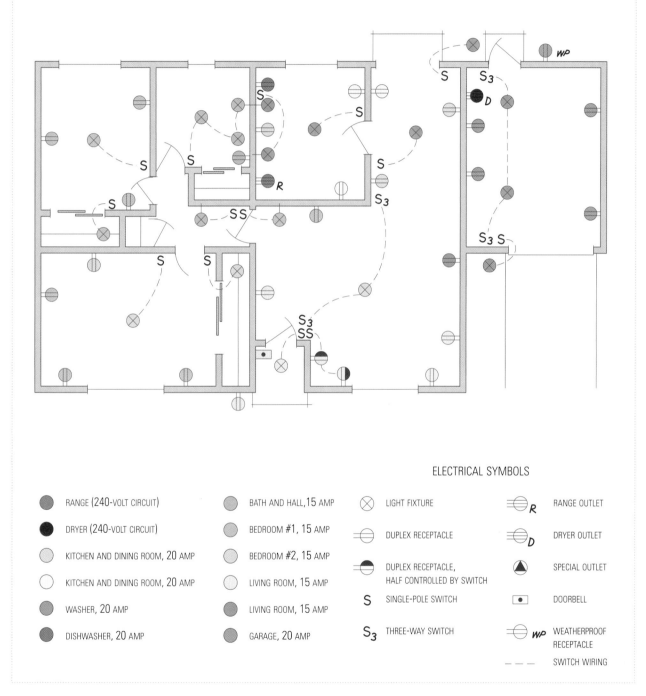

ELECTRICAL SYMBOLS

●	RANGE (240-VOLT CIRCUIT)	●	BATH AND HALL, 15 AMP	⊗ LIGHT FIXTURE	⊖R RANGE OUTLET
●	DRYER (240-VOLT CIRCUIT)	●	BEDROOM #1, 15 AMP	⊖ DUPLEX RECEPTACLE	⊖D DRYER OUTLET
○	KITCHEN AND DINING ROOM, 20 AMP	●	BEDROOM #2, 15 AMP	⊖ DUPLEX RECEPTACLE, HALF CONTROLLED BY SWITCH	▲ SPECIAL OUTLET
○	KITCHEN AND DINING ROOM, 20 AMP	○	LIVING ROOM, 15 AMP	S SINGLE-POLE SWITCH	▪ DOORBELL
●	WASHER, 20 AMP	●	LIVING ROOM, 15 AMP	S₃ THREE-WAY SWITCH	⊖WP WEATHERPROOF RECEPTACLE
●	DISHWASHER, 20 AMP	●	GARAGE, 20 AMP		- - - SWITCH WIRING

CALCULATING ELECTRICAL USAGE

After mapping out your home's wiring circuits, the next step is to determine your present usage, or electrical load. This would be a time-consuming task if you had to go around the house and add up all the wattages of the lights and appliances; however, the National Electrical Code has established certain values that represent typical electrical usage.

Three watts per square foot of existing living space and space for future use is used to figure electrical load for general-purpose circuits (general lighting and receptacles). A nominal value of 1,500 watts is used for each 20-amp small-appliance circuit (circuits that power receptacles in the kitchen, dining room, family room, breakfast room, and pantry) and for a laundry circuit.

By applying these values to your own home and using the actual nameplate values affixed to major appliances, you can use one of several formulas to calculate your electrical load.

100 AMPS OR MORE: One formula for homes with 120/240-volt service and a rating of 100 amps or more is presented as a worksheet below.

To understand how the formula works, consider the example of a house with 1,800 square feet (based on outside dimensions) of finished living space and space adaptable for future use. The house has the usual two small-appliance circuits (3,000 watts), a laundry circuit (1,500 watts), a hot water heater (5,500 watts), a clothes dryer (5,600 watts), a dishwasher (1,500 watts), a garbage disposal (600 watts), a range (15,000 watts), and a central air conditioner (5,000 watts).

The first step is to multiply 1,800 square feet by 3 watts per square foot. The total is 5,400 watts for lighting and general-purpose circuits. Add 3,000 watts for the two small-appliance circuits and 1,500 watts for the laundry circuit for a total of 9,900 watts. Next, add the values of all the major appliances, except the air conditioner, for a total of 38,100 watts.

HOW TO DETERMINE YOUR ELECTRICAL LOAD

A quick way to estimate your load *(120/240-volt service of 100 amps or more):*

_____ sq. ft. of living area (outside dimensions)
× 3 watts per sq. ft. =   _____ watts

_____ 20-amp small appliance circuits
× 1,500 watts =   _____ watts

Laundry circuit (1,500 watts)   _____ watts

Appliance nameplate values (if values are given in amps, multiply by volts to get watts)

water heater	_____ watts
dryer	_____ watts
dishwasher	_____ watts
garbage disposal	_____ watts
range	_____ watts
other	_____ watts

Total of all entries above =   _____ **watts**

Take 40% of the amount over 10,000 watts.
Subtract 10,000 watts from total.   −10,000 watts
Difference =   _____ watts
0.40 × difference =   _____ watts

Find subtotal by adding 10,000 to amount computed above.   +10,000 watts
Subtotal =   _____ watts

Air conditioner or heater(s) (whichever has the largest value).   _____ watts

Add the last two lines.
YOUR ESTIMATED LOAD =   _____ **watts**

Convert load to current by dividing by 240 volts.
Estimated load in watts ÷ 240 volts = _____ **amps**

TYPICAL WATTAGES AT A GLANCE

Air conditioner, central	5,000	Furnace, fuel-fired	800	Refrigerator, standard	720
Air conditioner, room	800–1,600	Garbage disposal	300–900	Roaster	1,425
Blender	350–1,000	Hair dryer, hand-held	260–1,500	Sander, portable	540
Broiler	1,000–1,500	Heater, built-in		Saw, circular	1,200
Can opener	100–216	(baseboard)	1,600	Sewing machine	75–150
Coffee grinder	85–132	Heater, space	1,000–1,500	Shaver	12
Coffeemaker	850–1,625	Heating pad	75	Soldering iron	150
Computer	125–200	Heat lamp	250	Steam iron	1,100
Computer, printer for	125–200	Lamps, fluorescent		Stereo, equipment	
Computer monitor	300	(per bulb)	15–75	compact disc player	12–15
Corn popper	600	Lamps, incandescent		receiver	420
Dishwasher	1,080–1,800	(per bulb)	25–200	turntable	12
Drill, portable	360	Lamps, halogen	20–50	turntable-receiver	50–75
Dryer, clothes	5,600–9,000	Microwave oven	975–1,575	Sunlamp	300
Fan, exhaust		Mixer, portable	150	Telephone	
(for range)	176	Mixer, stand	225	answering machine	10–12
Fan, ceiling	150	Projector,		Television, color	300
Fan, portable	100	movie or slide	350–500	Toaster	800–1,600
Fax machine	125–200	Radio	100	Trash compactor	1,250
Food processor	200	Range	8,000–15,000	Vacuum cleaner	250–800
Freezer, frostless	1,056	Range, cooktop	4,000–8,000	VCR	17–23
Freezer, standard	720	Range, oven	4,000–8,000	Washer, clothes	840
Frying pan	1,250–1,465	Refrigerator, frostless	960–1,200	Water heater	4,000–6,000

The next step is to figure 40 percent of the amount over 10,000 watts (0.40 × 28,100 = 11,240 watts). Adding the 10,000 watts to the 11,240 watts gives a subtotal of 21,240 watts. Then add the 5,000 watts of the air conditioner for a grand total of 26,240 watts. This is your estimated load in watts.

To figure the current needed to carry that load, divide 26,240 watts by 240 volts. The total comes to 109.33 amps; therefore, of the standard service ratings (60, 100, 125, 150, and 200), the rating for the sample house should be 125 amps or higher.

Now you can try it yourself: Enter the values appropriate to your home on the worksheet, then compare the total load in amps with your present service rating. If the two values are close together, your present service cannot handle the addition of many new loads.

LESS THAN 100 AMPS: If your service rating is less than 100 amps, you can't use the formula given on the work-

sheet to calculate your load. You can, however, use a different formula that incorporates the same NEC values for typical electrical usage. Therefore, the general-purpose circuits, small-appliance circuits, and laundry circuits are computed exactly as they are in the first three entries of the table.

Once you've figured the general-purpose circuit load (3 watts × number of square feet of living area), add 1,500 watts for each 20-amp small-appliance circuit and laundry circuit. Using this total, add 100 percent of the first 3,000 watts and 35 percent of the balance over 3,000 watts [3,000 + 0.35 (total − 3,000)].

Add to this value the nameplate ratings of all major appliances (space heater, garbage disposal, dishwasher, etc.). This gives you your estimated load in watts. You can find the current by dividing the total wattage by your voltage—120 volts for two-wire service or 240 volts for three-wire service.

CHANGING PRESENT WIRING

To get more out of your existing electrical system, you can do one of three things: extend an existing circuit, add a new circuit, or install a subpanel. Remember: The number of receptacles, circuits, or subpanels is not important. What is important is the total house load; it must not exceed the total service rating for the house (pages 22–23).

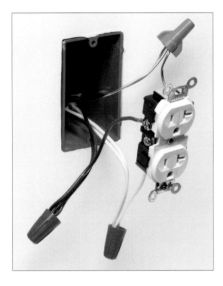

EXTENDING A CIRCUIT: Perhaps the easiest way to add to a wiring system is to extend an existing circuit. This would be useful, for example, if you find yourself depending on extension cords. Extension cords are for temporary use only; the cord wires and jackets are not made for long-term durability and are dangerous when they break down.

One of the key requirements for tapping into an existing circuit is the presence of both a hot and a neutral wire that are in direct connection with the power source at the service panel. In general, this means that any accessible switch, receptacle, or light fixture can be used.

Two exceptions are a switch box that is wired with two hot wires only, as in the case of a switch loop, and a switch-controlled light fixture at the end of a circuit. For details on selecting a power source and extending a circuit, see pages 62–69.

ADDING A NEW CIRCUIT: This is often the answer when an existing circuit can't handle a new load or when a new appliance requires its own circuit. Before adding a new circuit, though, calculate the total house load, including the new load, to make sure it will still be within your service rating. Note that all new 120-volt branch circuits must have a grounding wire and must comply with present code requirements (consult "Room-by-Room Requirements" on page 58).

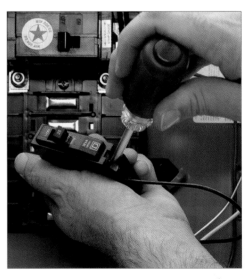

Don't think that just because your distribution center is full of fuses or circuit breakers you can't add any new circuits. If your panel uses breakers, one option is to replace one 120-volt breaker with a 120-volt, two-circuit breaker especially designed to fit in the space of one breaker.

ADDING A SUBPANEL: Another option to consider, whether you have fuses or circuit breakers, is adding a subpanel. To do this, remove two branch circuits from your distribution center to make room for a two-pole breaker for subfeeds; then route the subfeeds to the new subpanel. (For details, see pages 124–125.) There is no limit to the number of subpanels you can have, as long as your load doesn't exceed your service rating. By placing subpanels at areas of high usage, such as the kitchen and the workshop, you can route your branch circuits from the subpanels rather than routing all the circuit runs from the service entrance panel. Since this method means shorter, more direct circuit runs, it saves both time and material costs.

NEW SERVICE CONSIDERATIONS

If your current wiring system can't accommodate your proposed additions, you have one more option: upgrading the service entrance equipment.

You can figure the service rating you'll need the same way the load calculations are done on pages 22–23. If you're uncertain of the wattages of some of the appliances you plan to have, refer to "Typical Wattages at a Glance," page 23.

Loads of less than 10,000 watts, with no more than five two-wire circuits, can have a service rating lower than 100 amps but no less than 60 amps, according to the NEC. You might find this size service in a cabin or small vacation home. For all practical purposes, however, the minimum size is 100-amp, three-wire service that can deliver 24,000 watts.

Higher service ratings are also available, of course, depending on your electrical load. For example, the next larger standard ratings are 125, 150, and 200 amps. Don't cut any corners when estimating your new service rating. In fact, you should leave an extra margin of service for the future. It's much easier and cheaper to install larger service entrance equipment the first time than it is to increase your service a short time later.

The type of service equipment you need will depend both on its location and on how you plan to run your circuits. If your service entrance is centrally located, for example, you will probably want to run all branch circuits directly from it. On the other hand, if your service entrance panel is in an out-of-the-way spot, it may be preferable to have a smaller service entrance panel and use subpanels, fed by a set of subfeeds from the main panel, elsewhere in your home and garage.

NUTS AND BOLTS

A quick trip to an electrical supply store is all it takes to rattle most Saturday electricians—there's an incredible range of materials, tools, and gadgets to choose from. In this chapter, we'll discuss just those materials you're most likely to use in wiring projects inside your home. On the following pages, you'll first find a gallery of wires, cables, and conduit. Then we tour your basic options in housing boxes, receptacles, switches, and light fixtures and bulbs.

Use this chapter as a shopper's guide. When you go to buy materials, make sure that all products you choose bear the stamp or label of an electrical materials testing laboratory and that they comply with regulations in your local code.

When it's time to actually run cable or conduit, you'll find step-by-step instructions in Chapter Five, "Rough Wiring," beginning on page 56. For help installing receptacles, switches, or light fixtures, turn to Chapter Six, "Finish Wiring," starting on page 88. If it's telephone wire and hardware you're after, turn to Chapter Seven, "Telephone Systems" (page 126). Interested in other low-voltage cables and components? See Chapter Eight, "Low Voltage, High Tech" (page 138). And for a closer look at outdoor wiring materials, see Chapter Nine, "The Great Outdoors" (page 156).

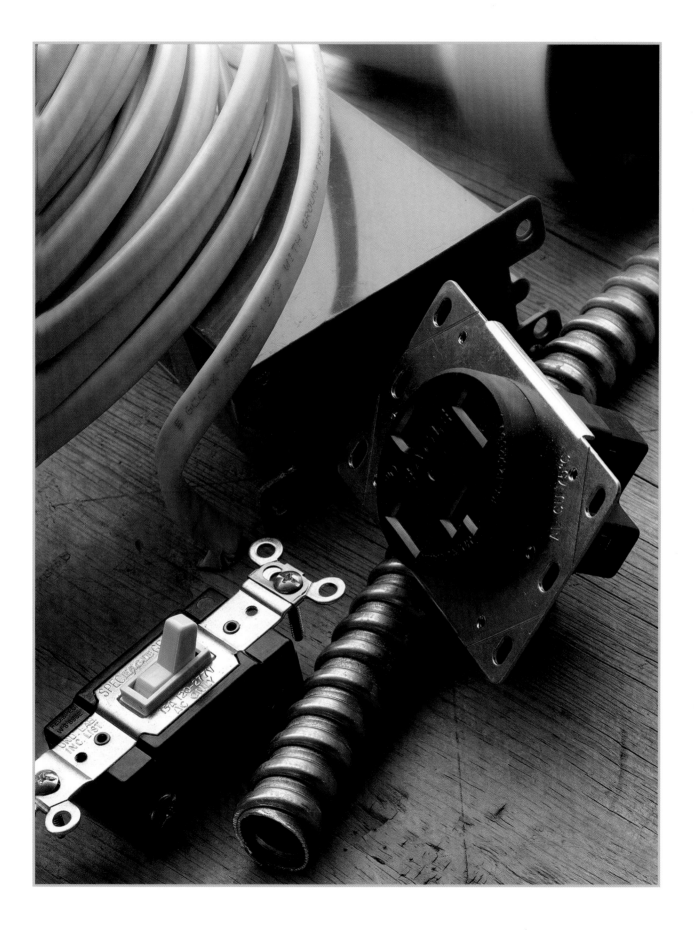

SINGLE CONDUCTOR WIRES

Solid-core wire

Stranded wire

MULTICONDUCTOR CABLES

Type NM (nonmetallic sheathed) cable "12-2"

For interior circuits; routed behind walls, ceilings, floors.

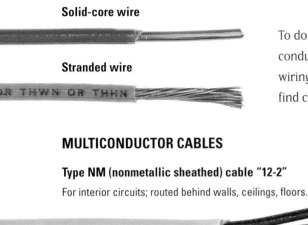

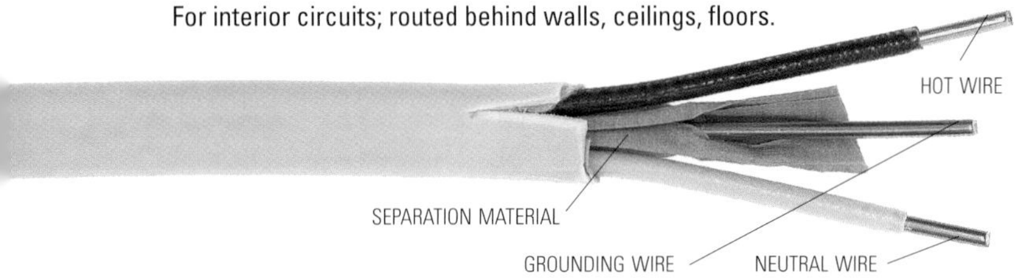

HOT WIRE

SEPARATION MATERIAL

GROUNDING WIRE   NEUTRAL WIRE

Type NM (nonmetallic sheathed) cable "14-3"

For interior circuits; contains two hot wires.

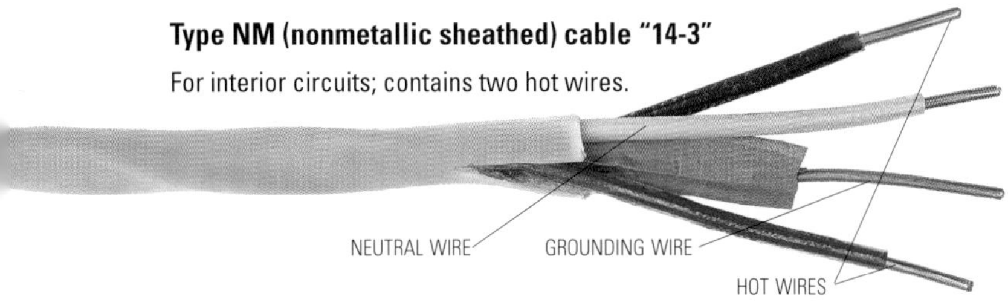

NEUTRAL WIRE   GROUNDING WIRE

HOT WIRES

Large appliance cable

For dedicated 120/140-volt circuits;
stranded wires are bendable—but barely.

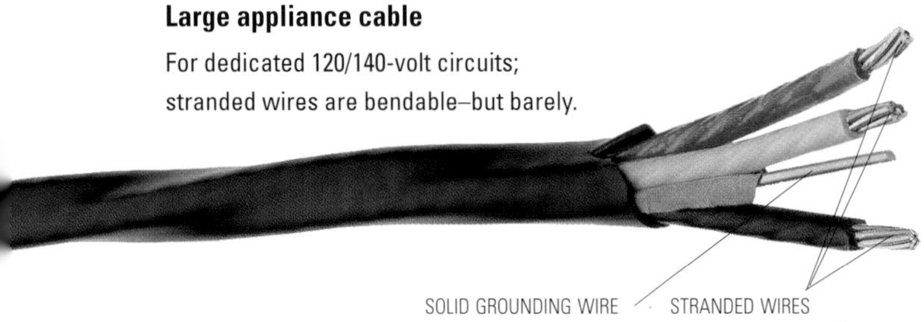

SOLID GROUNDING WIRE   STRANDED WIRES

Type MC armored cable

For interior circuits only.

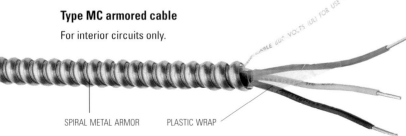

SPIRAL METAL ARMOR   PLASTIC WRAP

WIRES AND CABLES

To do electrical work in your home, you can use either a combination of single conductors (individual wires) or a multiconductor cable. Though wire sizes and wiring techniques were developed for single conductors, today most people find cable more convenient to use.

Two common single conductors are type THW and type THWN/THHN. Both are rated for either dry and wet locations and for temperatures up to 75°C (167°F). Typically, you run these individual wires inside protective metal or plastic conduit (see page 30). You can buy either solid-core or stranded wire; solid-core is stiffer, which makes it more difficult to snake through conduit, but it makes better connections. Wire is usually sold by the foot and in 50- to 500-foot spools.

Cable typically combines a neutral wire, one or two "hot" wires, and a grounding wire inside a plastic or metal covering. The individual conductors within a cable are usually insulated from one another by a color-coded thermoplastic material that doesn't carry current (we say "usually" because a grounding wire may be bare, particularly when it is contained within a cable). White or gray insulation indicates neutral wires, green is used for grounding wires, and all other colors (black, red, blue, etc.) are used to identify hot wires.

Several types of cable are shown at left. Type NM (nonmetallic sheathed cable) is the standard choice for most interior projects; it's sold by the foot or in boxes that house from 25 to 250 feet of coiled cable. The current version, called NM-B, is rated for dry locations only and temperatures to 60°C (140°F)—even though it houses 90° conductors. A beefier, black-sheathed version, sometimes called large appliance cable, has stranded wires to facilitate bending. Durable AC (armored cable) and its updated cousin, MC, are still used for some interior jobs but are expensive.

In addition to type of use, cable is identified by the number and size of the conductors it contains. For example, a cable with two #14 wires (one neutral and one hot) and a grounding wire is called two-wire cable or, more specifically, 14-2 with ground. The number 14 is an American Wire Gauge (AWG) designation that refers to the diameter of the metal conductor (not including the insulation). The larger the wire's diameter, the larger its current-carrying capacity, or ampacity, and the lower its gauge number. These numbers appear on the cable sheathing, as well as on the individual wires protected within the sheathing. (Table I, at left, lists the conductor currents permitted by the National Electrical Code. These restrictions apply when there are no more than three current-carrying conductors in a cable or enclosure.)

Although copper is the best and most commonly used metal for conductors, aluminum and copper-clad aluminum are also sometimes used. Because aluminum is not as efficient a conductor as copper, aluminum or copper-clad aluminum wire must be larger than a copper wire in order to conduct the same amount of electricity. If you're considering one of these wires, first check your local electrical codes.

TABLE I

ALLOWABLE AMPACITY OF INSULATED COPPER CONDUCTORS

WIRE SIZE	INSULATION TYPE	AMPACITY
14	TW, THW, THWN	15
12	TW, THW, THWN	20
10	TW, THW, THWN	30
8	TW	40
8	THW, THWN	50
6	TW	55
6	THW, THWN	65
4	THW,* THWN*	85
2	TW	95
2	THW,* THWN*	115
1	THW,* THWN*	130
2/0	THW,* THWN*	175

*EXCEPTION—THE FOLLOWING AMPACITIES APPLY WHEN USED AS SERVICE ENTRANCE CONDUCTORS AND SERVICE LATERALS AND FEEDERS THAT CARRY THE TOTAL LOAD TO DWELLING UNITS, 120/240-VOLT 3-WIRE SINGLE PHASE ONLY.

4	THW, THWN	100
2	THW, THWN	125
1	THW, THWN	150
2/0	THW, THWN	200

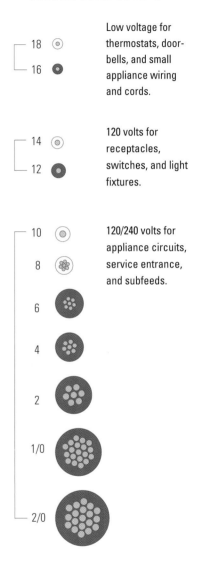

CROSS SECTIONS OF COPPER CONDUCTORS

18
16 — Low voltage for thermostats, doorbells, and small appliance wiring and cords.

14
12 — 120 volts for receptacles, switches, and light fixtures.

10
8
6
4
2
1/0
2/0 — 120/240 volts for appliance circuits, service entrance, and subfeeds.

CONDUIT

Pipelike conduit protects individual conductors from moisture and physical harm.

Thinwall metal conduit, called type EMT, is the standard choice for exposed interior locations—such as you might have in a garage or utility room. The thin metal may be bent with a conduit bender (page 44), but it's simpler to buy pieces with prebent angles. EMT comes in 10-foot lengths and in 1/2- to 2-inch diameters.

Flexible metal conduit, sometimes called Greenfield, is similar to MC (armored cable), but you supply the wires. Use it indoors where EMT would be too much trouble to route and for water heaters or other large appliances. Buy it by the foot or in 25- to 100-foot spools. It's available in 1/2- , 3/4-, and 1-inch sizes.

Rigid nonmetallic conduit, made from PVC plastic, is often allowed for interior installations. Schedule 40 plastic conduit comes in 10-foot lengths and requires PVC housing boxes—not the nonmetallic boxes used with cable. Note: This is not the same material as PVC plumbing pipe.

The size of conduit you need depends on the number and size of conductors it will be holding. For guidelines, see Table II, at left. If you're looking for a conduit to use outdoors, see Chapter Nine, "The Great Outdoors" (page 156).

Thinwall metal conduit, type EMT

The standard choice for exposed interior locations.

TABLE II

SIZE OF CONDUIT

WIRE SIZE THWN/THHN	NUMBER OF WIRES				
	2	3	4	5	6
14	1/2"	1/2"	1/2"	1/2"	1/2"
12	1/2"	1/2"	1/2"	1/2"	1/2"
10	1/2"	1/2"	1/2"	1/2"	3/4"
8	1/2"	3/4"	3/4"	1"	1"
THW	2	3	4	5	6
8	3/4"	3/4"	1"	1"	1 1/4"
6	3/4"	1"	1"	1 1/4"	1 1/4"
4	1"	1"	1 1/4"	1 1/4"	1 1/2"
2	1"	1 1/4"	1 1/4"	1 1/2"	2"
1/0	1 1/4"	1 1/2"	2"	2"	
2/0	1 1/2"	1 1/2"	2"	2"	
4/0	2"	2"			

Flexible metal conduit

Use it indoors where EMT would be too much trouble to route and for water heaters or other large appliances.

Rigid nonmetallic conduit

Made of PVC plastic, for interior and exterior installations.

HELPFUL HARDWARE

Some additional paraphernalia go hand-in-hand with your wire, cable, or conduit choices. These include wire nuts and compression sleeves for joining wires together; staples and straps for securing cable and conduit, respectively; grounding pigtails with grounding clips; protective metal plates; and electrical tape.

Wire nuts join and protect the stripped ends of spliced wires within housing boxes (for details, see page 54). They're sized to accommodate various wire sizes and combinations. Some jurisdictions require compression sleeves (see page 55) instead of wire nuts for grounding wires. If in doubt, contact your local building department.

Cable staples secure NM cable to the framing inside walls, floors, and ceilings. AC cable and metal and plastic conduit are secured with straps designed specifically for each of those materials.

Premade grounding pigtails combine a short length of copper wire and a grounding screw, useful for connecting devices such as receptacles to metal housing boxes. These green-coated, 6-inch pigtails are typically found in #14 and #12 sizes, suitable for use with 15- and 20-amp household circuits. You can, if you prefer, make your own pigtails from short lengths of green-colored or bare wire, and secure them with grounding screws or grounding clips (for details, see page 91).

Metal plates help guard NM cable that's run less than 1¼" from the front of wall framing. Electrical tape is useful for emergency splices and insulation repairs and for marking white wires that serve as second hot wires in a circuit (see page 101). Don't use tape for permanent wire connections—use a wire nut or compression sleeve instead.

Compression sleeves

Grounding pigtail

Wire nuts

Grounding clips

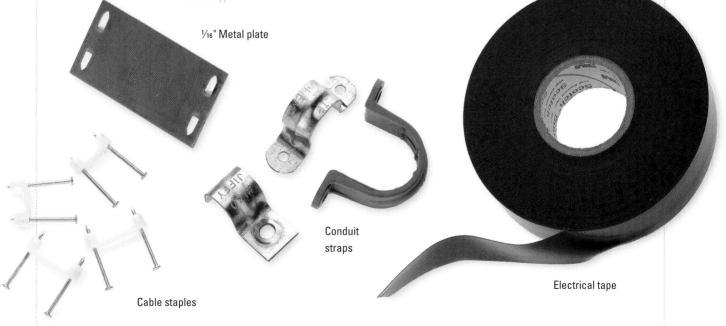

¹⁄₁₆" Metal plate

Conduit straps

Electrical tape

Cable staples

HOUSING BOXES

Boxes are essentially connection points, either for joining wires or for mounting devices such as receptacles, switches, and fixtures. Regardless of general trade terminology, many boxes are interchangeable in function. For example, with appropriate contents and covers, the same box could be used as an outlet (receptacle) box, a junction box, or a switch box.

The variety of sizes and shapes corresponds to differences in mounting methods, kind and number of devices attached to the box, and number of wires entering it. Rectangular boxes that hold only switches and receptacles are sometimes called switch boxes. So-called outlet boxes are square or octagonal and are used to hold receptacles, mount fixtures, or protect wire connections. A round or octagonal ceiling box might need to support a heavy fixture and often includes an adjustable or offset hanger bar. Each box has a certain volume in cubic inches that determines how many wires of a particular size may be brought into it. For help in choosing sizes, consult Table III, at left.

Housing boxes come in both metal and nonmetallic versions. Metal boxes are sturdier, but you must ground them. Nonmetallic (plastic) boxes cost less and don't require grounding. Unlike the old, breakable fiber boxes, most new plastic boxes are made of tough nylon and are fairly strong. Use plastic boxes with NM cable only; AC cable and metal conduit require metal boxes. Some electrical codes allow special PVC plastic boxes for exposed indoor and outdoor wiring with PVC conduit.

For mounting purposes, housing boxes fall into two main categories: new-work boxes and cut-in, or old-work, boxes. New-work boxes are for use in situations where there's no wall or ceiling covering to wrestle with, as during new construction; they're nailed directly to exposed studs or joists. If wall or ceiling materials are already in place, use cut-in boxes, which have brackets or spring ears designed expressly for remodeling work. To mount these boxes, you must cut into the existing wall or ceiling covering and then position them in spaces between studs or joists.

Outdoor wiring requires special, weather-tight boxes designed for wind, rain, or snow; for details, see page 158.

TABLE III

NUMBER OF CONDUCTORS* PER BOX

SIZE	NUMBER OF CONDUCTORS			
	#14	#12	#10	#8
Round or octagonal boxes				
4"x1¼"	6	5	5	4
4"x1½"	7	6	6	5
4"x2⅛"	10	9	8	7
Square boxes				
4"x1¼"	9	8	7	6
4"x1½"	10	9	8	7
4"x2⅛"	15	13	12	10
4¹¹⁄₁₆"x1¼"	12	11	10	8
4¹¹⁄₁₆"x1½"	14	13	11	9
Rectangular boxes				
3"x2"x2¼"	5	4	4	3
3"x2"x2½"	6	5	5	4
3"x2"x2¾"	7	6	5	4
3"x2"x3½"	9	8	7	6
4"x2⅛"x1½"	5	4	4	3
4"x2⅛"x1⅞"	6	5	5	4
4"x2⅛"x2⅛"	7	6	5	4

*COUNT ALL GROUNDING WIRES AS ONE CONDUCTOR.

COUNT EACH HICKEY, CABLE CLAMP, FIXTURE STUD, RECEPTACLE, AND SWITCH AS ONE CONDUCTOR.

COUNT EACH WIRE ENTERING AND LEAVING BOX WITHOUT SPLICE AS ONE CONDUCTOR.

PIGTAILS ARE NOT COUNTED AT ALL.

Nail-on boxes

These nonmetallic wall boxes are convenient for new construction. The 2-gang box below holds two devices.

Plain box

Adjustable ears allow this box to be mounted on wooden and plaster-and-lath walls. When a box is screwed directly on a wooden wall, the faceplate hides the ears.

Extender ring, adapter plate

These add-ons can customize a box to your requirements. The extender increases box depth to accommodate extra wires; adapter plates help you secure a receptacle, switch, or fixture to an oversize box or to one without mounting holes.

Junction box

When an outlet box contains only wire splices or cable connections—no devices—it's topped with a blank cover and referred to as a junction box.

Cut-in wall box with clamps

Available in both metal and plastic versions, this remodeling box has wing clamps for use in existing drywall or wood paneling.

EXTENDER RING

BLANK COVER

ADAPTER PLATE

Adjustable hanger bar

This ceiling box attaches to two joists to support a fixture; install it where you have access from above. The box slides along the bar, allowing you to fine-tune the fixture's placement.

Heavy-duty cut-in bar

The adjustable bar supports a box for ceiling fans and other large fixtures; use it where you don't have access from above.

Pancake box

As flat as, well, a pancake, this box attaches directly to a ceiling's hanger bar, a joist, or even a wood ceiling. It accommodates one two-wire cable.

Ceiling cut-in box

This nonmetallic box is used with lightweight fixtures.

RECEPTACLES

Code requires that all receptacles for 15- or 20-amp, 120-volt branch circuits (most of the circuits in your home) be of the three-prong, grounding type shown at right. The specific amperage and voltage a receptacle is suited for is stamped clearly on its front. Receptacles marked AL-CU may be used with either copper or aluminum wire; unmarked receptacles and those marked with a slash through the AL symbol can be used with copper wire only.

To eliminate the possibility of plugging a 120-volt appliance into a 240-volt receptacle, higher-voltage circuits use special receptacles, like the ones shown on the facing page, along with matching attachment plugs. You'll find both 240-volt and 120/240-volt models; the latter, often servicing a kitchen range or clothes dryer, combine both 240-volt power for the appliance's motor and 120-volt power for timers and other controls.

A note about quality: Receptacles are often labeled "residential," "contractor grade," "commercial," "spec," or "industrial." These terms are somewhat nebulous, but in general, residential or contractor grades are lower quality, while commercial, spec-grade, or industrial-duty versions are higher quality—and more expensive.

120-volt duplex receptacles

Grounded duplex receptacles consist of an upper and lower outlet, each with three slots. The larger (neutral) slot accepts the wide prong of a three-pronged plug; the smaller (hot) slot is for the narrow prong, and the U-shaped grounding slot is for the grounding prong. Both amperage and voltage are clearly stamped on the front. Many receptacles include push-in terminals in back, facilitating so-called "backwiring," explained on pages 52–53 (note that this wiring method is illegal in some areas). Duplex receptacles come in several colors.

GFCI receptacle

The ground fault circuit interrupter (GFCI, or sometimes GFI) is a device that protects you from electric shocks. A 120-volt GFCI receptacle takes the place of a standard duplex receptacle and monitors electrical current; whenever the amounts of incoming and outgoing current are not equal, such as during a ground fault or current leakage, the GFCI opens the circuit instantly, cutting off the electricity. GFCIs are required in kitchens, bathrooms, garages, and other exposed, damp areas where ground faults are most likely. Several designs and colors are available.

240-volt receptacles

This 3-pole receptacle has two hot slots and a third grounding slot; its configuration matches a specific plug and amperage (see box at right) and is not interchangeable with other plugs. The design prevents you from, for example, plugging a 30-amp table saw into a 20-amp circuit. Both surface-mounted and recessed (flush-mounted) models are available. Industrial-grade versions include a locking device that holds the plug in the slots—a safety measure for stationary power tools and other heavy equipment.

120/240-volt receptacles

These outlets provide both 240- and 120-volt power and have four poles: two hot, one neutral, and one grounding slot. As with the 240-volt receptacle, each slot pattern is designed for a specific plug and amperage; be sure you buy the right one. Both surface-mounted and recessed models are available.

RECEPTACLE SLOTS

Outlets are configured for specific amps and volts. Here's a sampling of popular patterns.

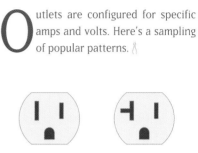

15-amp (120V)

20-amp (120V)

15-amp (240V)

20-amp (240V)

30-amp (120/240V)

50-amp (120/240V)

30-amp (240V)

50-amp (240V)

Switches

Like receptacles, switches are rated according to the specific amperage and voltage they're suited for. Switches marked AL-CU may be used with either copper or aluminum wire. Unmarked switches and those marked with a slash through the AL symbol can be used with copper wire only. Make sure the switch you're going to install has the same amperage and voltage ratings as the one you're replacing or that it is suitable for the circuit.

Besides the classic two-way toggle, you'll also find three-way and four-way switches, pilot switches, motion sensors, timer switches, and a wide range of dimmer designs. New offerings appear constantly. Unlike the lowly receptacle, switches are now available in a wide range of colors, finishes, and toggle designs, including night-light versions that glow in the dark.

Basic switches often come in several grades: the lowest grade is "residential" or "contractor"; more rugged models are called "heavy-duty," "commercial," or "spec." So-called designer switches and dimmers may be labeled for looks only, not their construction.

Note: Traditional switches did not have grounding terminals—the plastic toggles on them were considered shockproof. However, most of the models we show here do include grounding terminals for extra protection. Some local codes require grounded switches in new kitchens, in bathrooms, or where metal faceplates are used with plastic housing boxes.

Single-pole switches

Identified by two screw terminals and the words ON and OFF printed on the toggle, the classic single-pole switch (upper left) controls a light or receptacle from one location only. It comes in 15- and 20-amp versions. An updated version (upper right) includes a grounding screw. The standard two-way toggle type is most economical, but many other designs (like that at left) are available.

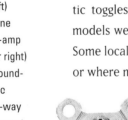

Three-way switch

Identified by three hot terminals and a plain toggle, three-way switches operate in pairs to control a light or receptacle from two locations.

Four-way switch

Identified by four hot terminals and no ON or OFF indicators on the toggle, a four-way switch is used only in combination with a pair of three-way switches to control a light or receptacle from more than two locations.

Pilot switch

This switch has a toggle that glows when the fixture or appliance is on but out of sight and mind. Popular uses for a pilot switch include basement lights, outdoor lights, and remote appliances such as attic fans.

Dimmer switches

These devices, sometimes called rheostats, allow you to get maximum brightness from a light or any gradation. Dimmers also help save energy. Numerous designs are available, some with presets and fade controls. All dimmers are rated for maximum wattage. (Note: Special dimmer switches are required for fluorescent lights.)

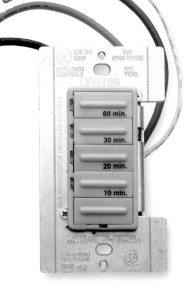

Timer switches

Standard timer switches allow you to set a light, bathroom heater, or other device to turn on and off at predetermined times each day. Programmable timer switches take things one step further, providing multiple daily settings for security lights, a fan, even the TV. Unlike most other switches, some timer switches require a neutral wire, as well as the hot wire.

Motion-sensor switch

Used for security, convenience, or energy savings, a motion-sensor switch turns on the light or lights when it detects movement in a room, then shuts it off after a predetermined interval. (A three-way model is shown.) Better designs allow you to adjust sensitivity and time interval and include a manual ON/OFF lever.

LIGHT FIXTURES

Design professionals divide lighting into three basic categories: task, accent, and ambient. When choosing a fixture, first consider which effect you want.

Task lighting is used to illuminate the area where a visual activity—such as reading, sewing, or preparing food—occurs. Individual fixtures that direct light onto a work surface are task lights.

Accent lighting is primarily decorative. Like task lighting it also consists largely of directional light, but it's used to focus attention on artwork, highlight architectural features, or set a mood.

Ambient, or general, lighting provides a soft level of light appropriate to such activities as watching television or entertaining. Ambient lighting may come from fixtures that provide a diffuse spread of illumination. A directional fixture aimed at a wall can also provide a soft wash of light.

When it comes to fixtures, you can choose from surface, recessed, and track designs. Fixtures may be either line voltage (120 volts) or low voltage; the latter type uses a transformer—either built-in or placed in a remote location—to "step down" 120-volt power to 12 or so volts. Traditional line-voltage installations are detailed on pages 104–111; for installing low-voltage fixtures, turn to pages 142–143.

Lighting pros often advise choosing the bulb first, then the fixture housing. Bulbs and tubes can be grouped into general categories according to the way they produce light. The chart opposite includes information on a number of different bulbs and tubes. Of course, these are only a few of the available options; visit a lighting showroom or home center for more.

Surface fixtures

Surface-mounted fixtures are either mounted directly to a housing box (in the case of wall sconces and incandescent and fluorescent ceiling fixtures) or suspended from the box by chains or a cord (like the pendant above). Some undercounter task lights plug into a nearby receptacle. Most surface fixtures come with their own mounting hardware, which is adaptable to any standard fixture box. Heavy fixtures, however, may require beefier attachments.

NEW-WORK DOWNLIGHT

Recessed downlights

Today, recessed downlights usually are prewired and grounded to their own housing boxes. These fixtures need several inches of clearance above the ceiling, so they're most easily installed below an unfinished attic or crawl space. Where space is tight, you can buy low-clearance fixtures. New-work units, used where you have access, are easy to install; cut-in, or remodeling models, are also available. Many downlights produce a lot of heat, so you must either remove insulation within 3 inches of the fixture or buy an "IC" fixture that's rated for direct contact with surrounding materials.

CUT-IN DOWNLIGHT

COMPARING LIGHT BULBS AND TUBES

BULB	DESCRIPTION	USES
INCANDESCENT		
A—Bulb	Familiar pear shape; frosted or clear.	Everyday household use.
T—Tubular	Tube-shaped, from 5" long. Frosted or clear.	Cabinets, decorative fixtures.
R—Reflector	White or silvered coating directs light out end of funnel-shaped bulb.	Directional fixtures; focuses light where needed.
ER—Ellipsoidal reflector	Shape and coating focus light 2" ahead of bulb, then light spreads out.	Recessed downlights and track fixtures.
Low-voltage strip	Like Christmas tree lights; in strips or tracks, or encased in flexible, waterproof plastic.	Task lighting and decoration.
FLUORESCENT		
Tube	Tube-shaped, 5" to 96" long. Needs special fixture and ballast.	Shadowless work light; also indirect lighting.
PL—compact tube	U-shaped with base; 5¼" to 7½" long.	In recessed downlights; some PL tubes include ballasts to replace A-bulbs.
Circline	Circular, 6" to 16" long; may replace A-bulbs or require special fixtures.	In compact circline fixtures.
QUARTZ HALOGEN		
Tube-shaped	Tube-shaped; non-directional; protected by glass cover due to high temperatures.	In specialized task lamps, torchères, and pendants.
Low-voltage MR-16—(mini-reflector)	Tiny (2"-diameter) projector bulb; gives small circle of light from a distance.	Low-voltage track fixtures, mono-spots, and recessed downlights.
Low-voltage PAR	Similar to auto headlight; tiny filament, shape and coating give precise direction.	To project a controlled spread of light a long distance.

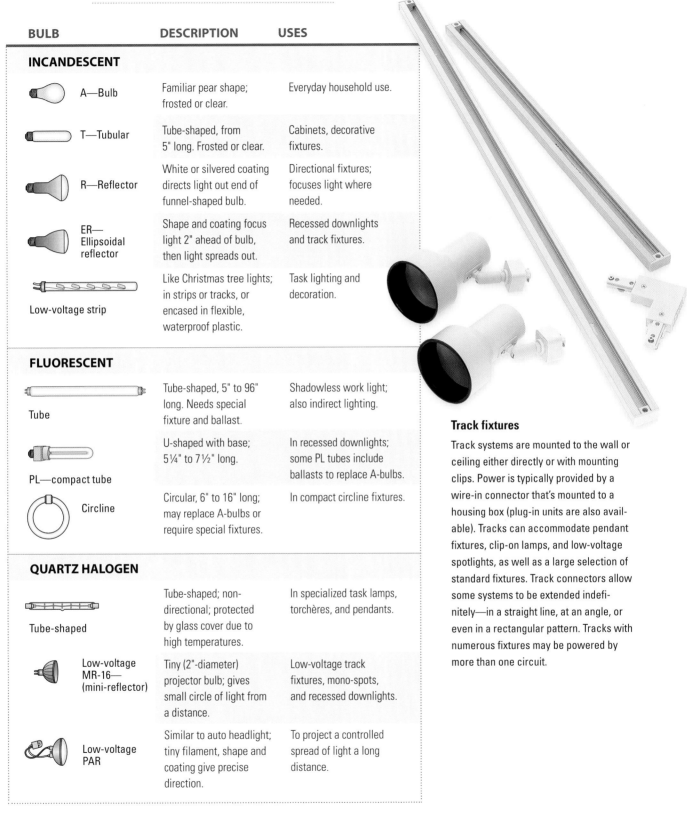

Track fixtures

Track systems are mounted to the wall or ceiling either directly or with mounting clips. Power is typically provided by a wire-in connector that's mounted to a housing box (plug-in units are also available). Tracks can accommodate pendant fixtures, clip-on lamps, and low-voltage spotlights, as well as a large selection of standard fixtures. Track connectors allow some systems to be extended indefinitely—in a straight line, at an angle, or even in a rectangular pattern. Tracks with numerous fixtures may be powered by more than one circuit.

TOOLS OF THE TRADE

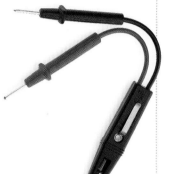

Knowing the right tool for the job is the first step toward becoming a skilled electrician. Fortunately, wiring is not tool-intensive. Still, a good pair or two of pliers and some other basics make all the difference. As in other building trades, the standard advice applies: Buy the best tools you can afford.

Testing devices are mandatory safety and diagnostic tools. Always use a neon tester to confirm that power to the circuit is off before beginning any electrical work. The continuity tester, multi-tester, and circuit analyzer are also invaluable aids for assessing existing wiring conditions, troubleshooting and making repairs, or for checking your work once it's complete.

A few general remodeling tools could also be in order. Some might already be in your homeowner's kit. When it comes to acquiring these tools, the rule of thumb is to buy the basics, then rent the more expensive power tools as you need them; if you need them again, consider purchasing your own.

Some simple safety gear goes hand-in-hand with tool use; for pointers, see page 19. Finally, an electrician's tool pouch helps keep your tools in one place and has handy pouches for your measuring tape, hammer, and electrical tape, as well as for an arsenal of pliers, screwdrivers, and testing tools.

AN ELECTRICIAN'S TOOL KIT

You can handle virtually any home wiring task with the electrical tools shown here. Many of these items, such as lineman's pliers, diagonal cutters, and wire strippers, make it easier and safer to prepare wire ends and to make sound wire connections at lamp sockets, switches, receptacles, and other electrical devices. The multipurpose tool, as its name suggests, handles several basic tasks.

You'll find some additional tools on page 44. The humble screwdriver is indispensable for mounting housing boxes, devices, and faceplates, as well as for making many electrical repairs. A fish tape is a crucial addition to your tool kit if you're planning to route wire behind existing walls, ceilings, and flooring. A conduit bender is tricky to use for beginners but is the traditional tool for working with exposed metal conduit.

Lineman's pliers

These are the electrician's basic tool. Use the serrated jaws to hold or twist bare wires and the cutters to snip through wire and cable. Look for either an 8" or 9" model with some heft to it (the bigger the pliers, the more force they can apply). For added safety, buy pliers with insulated handles.

Long-nose pliers

The long, thin snout is much better than lineman's pliers for bending bare wire ends into hook shapes to attach to screw terminals; the blades also cut through wire, although it takes some work. Buy long-nose pliers that comfortably fit your hand—some versions are too small.

Diagonal cutters

Popularly known as dikes, these specialty cutters are used for snipping #6 and smaller wires. They make closer, cleaner cuts than other pliers, but you could probably make do without them.

Wire strippers

Wire strippers remove the thermoplastic insulation from individual wire ends without damaging the wire. Stripper options range from simple two-piece scissors to complex multi-action, self-clamping types. This is one specialty tool that's definitely worth having.

Multipurpose tool

It cuts wires, strips insulation from wires of various gauges, and attaches crimp connectors to wire ends (but no, it won't dice vegetables). However, the multipurpose tool doesn't do any of these tasks quite as well as the specific tools designed for them. This tool comes in many designs and configurations; function and quality vary widely.

Cable ripper

This simple, low-cost tool slices through the outer insulation on flat, two-wire NM cable. The ripper won't work on bigger, round cable, however; use a pocket knife or utility knife to score that kind of sheathing.

Fuse puller

This esoteric item makes it easy to remove and replace cartridge fuses. To reduce the risk of electrical shock, choose a fuse puller made of plastic or another nonconductive material.

SUPER-INSULATED HAND TOOLS

Many electrical pliers, cutters, and screwdrivers have rubber or plastic handles, which may offer some protection from shock if the tool happens to come in contact with a live wire. Still, for the highest degree of safety, search out some insulated hand tools made specifically for electrical work. You can distinguish them by their orange color and the figure "1000" marked on the handle. These tools are designed to absorb a shock of up to 1,000 volts.

The 1000-series screwdrivers and nutdrivers feature orange insulated handles and shafts. Pliers, cutters, and strippers have orange insulated handles with flaring ridges on top—they're designed to keep your hand from slipping up the handles and into trouble.

Even when working with insulated tools, though, always turn the power off before going to work.

Conduit bender

This tool is a necessity for shaping EMT conduit. If you have a lot of bending to do, you may wish to purchase one. Otherwise, plan to rent a bender—or better yet, buy prebent angles.

Fish tape

Typically made from flattened spring steel wire, this device allows you to route wires or cable behind existing walls, floors, and ceilings. Fish tapes commonly come in 25' and 50' lengths, coiled inside a case that resembles an oversize fly-fishing reel. Nonconductive fiberglass models are also available.

Standard screwdrivers

Slotted tip widths of ⅛", ⁹⁄₁₆", ¼", and ⁵⁄₁₆" fit most screw heads found on electrical devices, including screw terminals and grounding screws within housing boxes. If you don't want a lot of screwdrivers around, look for a model that takes interchangeable tips. Insulated handles are a must for safety; better yet, buy "1000"-series screwdrivers (see page 43), which are designed specifically for electrical work.

STANDARD
SCREWDRIVER

OFFSET
SCREWDRIVER

PHILLIPS
SCREWDRIVER

Phillips screwdrivers

A basic screwdriver collection includes several Phillips-head versions—at least a #0 and #1. (Many screw heads on boxes and devices are slotted, but some now have combination patterns that work with Phillips drivers. Light fixtures and appliances often have Phillips-head screws.) Again, insulated handles are a must.

Offset screwdrivers

These small hand tools with driver tips at right angles to their shafts can save the day in tight quarters—when you need one, you really need one. Offset drivers come in both standard and Phillips versions or may feature one of each.

Power screwdriver

This battery-operated hand tool eliminates the drudgery of driving screws by hand. It's great for mounting boxes, switches, and cover plates, but it goes too fast for connecting wires to terminals—you'll end up stripping the screws. Look for a model with reversible gears that takes interchangeable tips. Quality tools are more powerful, hold a charge longer, and recharge faster than cheap ones.

TESTING DEVICES

Several basic diagnostic tools can help in electrical work. The complete kit includes a neon tester, a continuity tester, a multitester, and one or more analyzers.

The inexpensive but critical neon tester is used to confirm that power to a circuit is turned off before you touch any exposed wire ends (for details, see page 50). If the circuit is live, the bulb in the neon tester will light up. By carefully testing bare wires inside a housing box, you can also determine which one is the hot wire.

A battery-powered continuity tester sends a low-voltage current through a circuit to determine whether the electrical path is undamaged. One type contains a battery and light; another uses a battery and a buzzer or bell. You can use either kind of continuity tester to tell whether a circuit is open or broken or whether a short circuit exists. Before you use a continuity tester, make very sure the power is off: at the service panel or subpanel, either turn off the appropriate breaker or pull the fuse (page 172).

The multitester, also known as a voltage or VOM meter, is the professional's diagnostic tool of choice. In addition to determining continuity, it can measure voltage, including low-voltage current and resistance in ohms. Some models have a clamp-on ammeter that detects current passing through a closed cable or appliance cord. The multitester comes in both analog and digital versions; the latter is considered more accurate. Some meters require you to set the approximate voltage range before testing; others switch automatically.

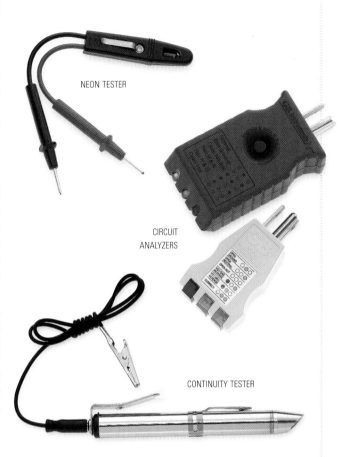

NEON TESTER

CIRCUIT ANALYZERS

CONTINUITY TESTER

MULTITESTER

Plug-in circuit analyzers come in several forms. The most basic model plugs into a receptacle; three diagnostic lights indicate whether there is power to the receptacle, whether it is grounded properly, and whether the wiring is correct. Larger, expensive digital circuit analyzers can check all the way back to the service panel to detect voltage drops and tiny current leaks.

HELPFUL REMODELING TOOLS

If you're planning to run new cable or to add receptacles, light fixtures, or other devices where there were none before, you may need a few extra weapons.

Some of these tools you're likely to have already. For example, you might need a measuring tape, hammer, handsaw, chisel, pry bar, utility knife, and small torpedo level. A hacksaw is good for cutting AC cable and both plastic and metal conduit. If you're working in a basement or attic, you might want a utility light and a flashlight or headlamp. You may also need a ladder; if so, remember that fiberglass and wood are nonconductive—unlike aluminum.

At right, we detail some carpenter's tools that can make cutting, drilling, and other cable-routing tasks much easier. The hand tools generally are inexpensive to buy; some of the power tools can be rented. Double-insulated, grounded power tools are a necessity when working near potentially live wires; always plug them into a GFCI-protected receptacle or use an extension cord fitted with its own GFCI. Cordless power tools are even safer to use.

³⁄₈" Reversible drill

For most drilling, the ³⁄₈" drill offers the best compromise between power and speed; it also handles a wide range of bits and accessories. A variable-speed drill allows you to suit the speed to the job—very handy when starting holes, drilling metals, or driving screws. Cordless drills are much more powerful and recharge more quickly than models available just a few years ago; if insulated, they also offer extra protection around potentially live wires.

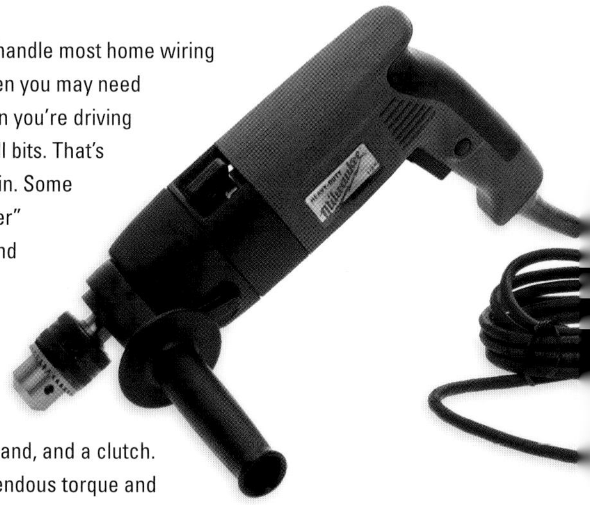

¹⁄₂" Drill

Although the ³⁄₈" drill will handle most home wiring tasks, there are times when you may need more power, such as when you're driving long or large-diameter drill bits. That's where the ¹⁄₂" drill comes in. Some models double as "hammer" drills, allowing you to pound holes through masonry. If you're considering one, be sure it's a variable-speed model equipped with a pistol grip, a right-angle grip for your other hand, and a clutch. These drills develop tremendous torque and can twist your wrist and arm in a flash if something goes wrong. Learn how to use them properly.

Right-angle drill

Most drills work in a straight line, but in tight quarters you may not be able to get a drill body, your hand, and your line of sight into the space you need to drill in. That's where a right-angle drill shines. Be careful, though: like the ¹⁄₂" drill, these powerful tools require an experienced hand and extra caution. Right-angle drills now come in smaller, cordless versions, as shown at left.

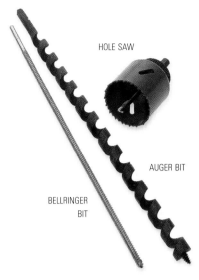

HOLE SAW

AUGER BIT

BELLRINGER
BIT

Drill bits

A collection of drill bits is shown here. Twist bits make small holes in wood and metal; spade bits are great for drilling access holes for NM cable in wood. A hole saw makes even bigger holes—up to 2½" with a ⅜" drill. Need to drill deeper than a standard bit will go? So-called bellringer bits are extra-long twist bits; you can also buy several lengths of extension bits. Auger bits bore more aggressively, but may require a beefier ½" drill. Screwdriver bits, available in both standard and Phillips sizes, turn a variable-speed drill into a power screwdriver. Nutdrivers turn your drill into a power wrench.

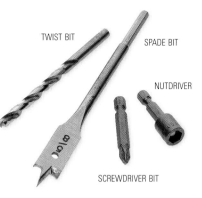

TWIST BIT

SPADE BIT

NUTDRIVER

SCREWDRIVER BIT

Electronic stud finder

When remodeling, you may be fishing cable through walls and ceilings where you can't really see what's going on. How do you find those hidden wall studs and ceiling joists in order to maneuver around them? The easiest, most efficient way is with a battery-powered stud finder, which lights up or beeps when it encounters framing members behind wallboard or plaster.

Drywall or "jab" saw

A low-tech, hand-tool version of the jigsaw below, a drywall saw is great for cutting box holes and access notches in gypsum wallboard—new or old—without making an undue mess. The jab saw (shown at right) uses the same blades as a reciprocating saw (below left), enabling you to make controlled cuts in wood or metal.

Jigsaw

This portable power tool, sometimes called a saber saw, cuts wood, metal, drywall, and even plaster when fitted with the right blade for the job. However, unlike the case with some other saws, you can't control the depth of cut, so be sure the blade's entire travel is free of obstructions before you go to work.

Reciprocating saw

The number one power tool for "roughing-in" or demolition work, the reciprocating saw can handle (with the right blade) old wood studs and joists, lath and plaster, steel pipe, and even nails. Most reciprocating saws have two speeds; use the lower speed for fine work and for cutting metal, the high speed for making rough cuts in wood. Some models feature variable-speed triggers for more precise control. Saw blades are flexible, which helps when you're making tricky cuts, but they can snap if you're not careful. Have extras on hand.

WIRING KNOW-HOW

To wire receptacles, switches, light fixtures, and appliances properly, you need to know some basic techniques, including stripping, securing, and splicing wire. These are described in easy-to-follow instructions over the next few pages.

The first thing you need to know is how to strip wire. Non-metallic sheathed cable, the type of cable used most commonly for interior wiring projects, consists of insulated and bare wires bundled together and wrapped in an outer sheath of thermoplastic insulation. Before connecting a cable to a device or joining it to another cable, you'll need to cut open and remove the outer sheath, cut away all paper or other separation materials inside the sheath and between the bundled wires, and strip the insulation from the ends of the individual conductors.

Once the wires are stripped, you can then join them to receptacles and the like by forming loops in the wire ends and attaching them securely to a device's connection terminals, or join wires together with solderless, mechanical wire nuts or compression sleeves.

When it's time to actually install that receptacle, switch, light fixture, or appliance, you'll find step-by-step instructions in Chapter Six, "Finish Wiring," beginning on page 88.

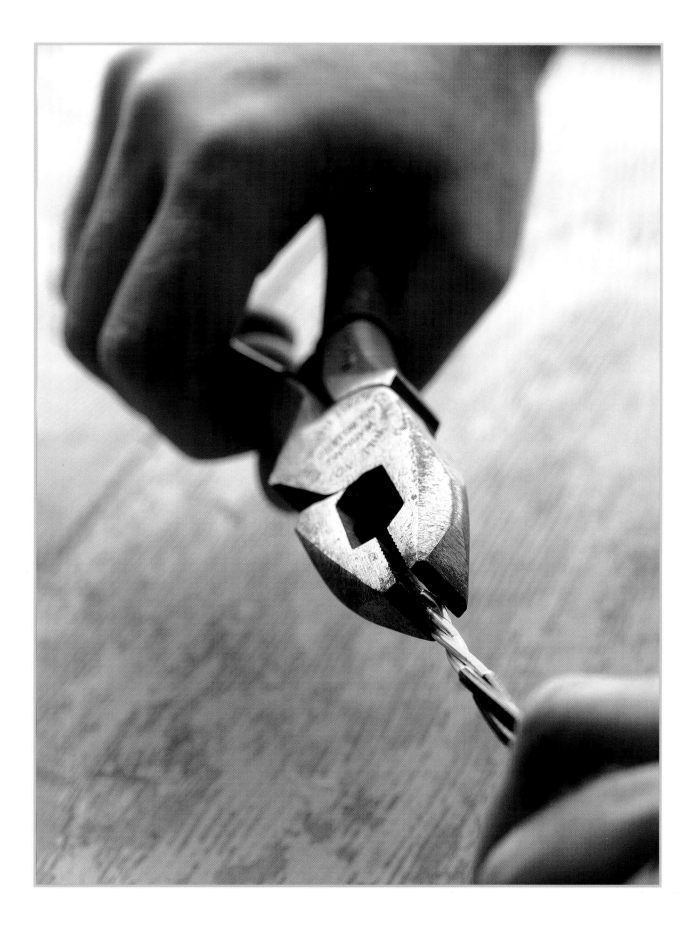

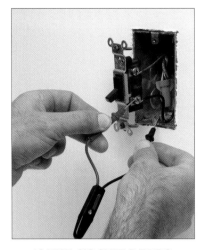

IS THE CIRCUIT DEAD?

Whenever you're working with wire, make it an iron-clad rule to check first that power to the area you're working on is turned off at the service entrance panel or subpanel. To learn how to remove a fuse or shut off a circuit breaker, see page 172.

Before you touch bare wire ends, use a neon tester, as shown above, to confirm that the circuit is dead. Touch one tester probe to a hot wire or terminal and the other to a neutral wire or terminal, the grounding conductor, or the grounded metal box. The tester will light up if the circuit is live.

Be careful: If by some chance you didn't turn off the right circuit or if there's a short in the system, the wires may still be hot. Make sure to hold the tester probes by their insulation—not their metal ends—or else you may get a shock or cause a short circuit.

If a lamp or appliance doesn't work, that doesn't necessarily mean the circuit is dead; the appliance itself could be faulty. Insert the probes of the neon tester into the slots of a receptacle, as shown at right; if the tester lights up, the circuit is still hot. ⚒

CUTTING AND STRIPPING WIRES

Wire is cut to length at the rough-wiring stage; splitting and stripping are done when wiring devices. Each step requires a different tool.

To cut wires or cable to length, simply use lineman's pliers or diagonal cutters.

To open up flat cable, such as two-wire NM (with or without ground), use a cable ripper or knife to score the sheath lengthwise. If you're working with round, three-wire cable—such as when wiring three-way switches—use a pocket knife or utility knife so you can follow the curve of the twisted wires without cutting into their insulation.

Don't cut cable while it rests on your knee or thigh. Use a flat board or wall surface. Also, don't cut toward your body—always work away from it.

Once you've exposed the wires and cut off the outer sheath and any paper or other separation materials, you're ready to strip the insulation off the ends of the wires. You can easily strip small solid-core wires from sizes #18 to #10 using wire strippers or the graduated wire stripper jaws on a multi-purpose tool. To strip larger wires—from #8 to #2/0—use a pocket knife to take off the insulation as if you were sharpening a pencil, again cutting away from your body. The length of wire you'll need to strip varies depending on the job. For some guidelines, see pages 52–55.

Be careful not to nick the wire when you're stripping off its insulation. A nicked wire will break easily when bent to form a loop for a connection to a screw terminal. If you do nick a wire, snip off the damaged wire end and begin again.

HOW TO RIP CABLE

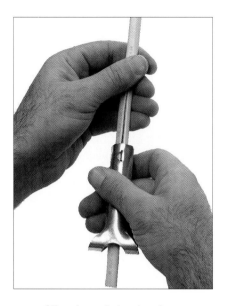

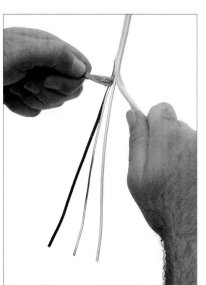

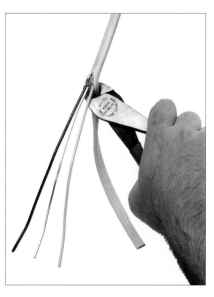

1 Slice through the sheath

To cut flat cable, first slide a cable ripper up the cable. Press the handles of the cable ripper together and pull toward the end of the cable. This action will score the outer sheath.

2 Expose the wires

Bend the cable back to crack the score and then peel open the outer sheath of insulation. Pull the outer sheath and all separation materials away from the cable end, exposing the wires.

3 Cut off the sheath and separation materials

Using a pair of diagonal-cutting pliers or utility scissors, cut off the opened sheath and paper or other separation materials, leaving just the insulated wires.

HOW TO STRIP WIRE

1 Grip the wire

Using wire strippers, first insert the wire into the matching slot, or set the adjustment screw for the gauge of wire. Holding the wire firmly in one hand with your thumb extended toward the end of the wire, position the strippers on the wire at an angle with your other hand and press the handles together.

2 Slide off the insulation

Next, rock the strippers back and forth until the insulation is severed and can be pulled off the wire in one quick motion. Once you get the hang of it, wire stripping is easy.

JOINING WIRES TO TERMINALS

Many switches and receptacles come with two sets of connection points where wires join them: screw terminals and backwired terminals. Screw terminals are tried-and-true connection points. To make these hookups, you need to strip insulation off the wire ends (see page 51), then use long-nose pliers to bend the ends of the wires into hooks. The only other tool you need is a standard screwdriver. Screw terminals can accommodate only one wire; if you need to join several wires at a single screw terminal, use a pigtail splice (see page 55).

To backwire a device, you make the wire-to-terminal connection by poking each wire into its appropriate hole on the back of the device. Typically, a jaw inside the hole allows the wire to enter but prevents it from being withdrawn unless you release the tension by inserting a small screwdriver blade into a special slot next to the hole. With other designs, you'll need to tighten down the adjacent screw terminal.

Note: Only some receptacles and switches have backwired terminals, and backwiring is suitable for copper and copper-clad aluminum wires only—not aluminum wires. Many professionals and some codes discourage the use of backwiring, at least for 20-amp receptacles. The wire attachments just don't seem as secure as they are at screw terminals.

WORKING WITH STRANDED WIRE

Stranded wire (page 28) is commonly found in lamp cord; it's also sold in larger sizes for circuit wiring, typically routed inside conduit. Working with stranded wire calls for some different tricks.

To make a wire connection using stranded wire, begin by stripping about ¾" of insulation from the wire end. Never use a utility knife to remove the insulation; you risk cutting into some of the stranded wires. Instead, use wire strippers. Once the insulation is removed, inspect the strands. If a wire end is damaged, snip off the end and begin again.

Using your thumb and forefinger, twist together the exposed strands in each wire tightly in a clockwise direction. To attach the wire to a screw terminal, shape the twisted strands into a loop and hook it around a screw terminal in a clockwise direction. Tighten the screw, making sure that no stray wires are exposed.

JOINING WIRES TO SCREW TERMINALS

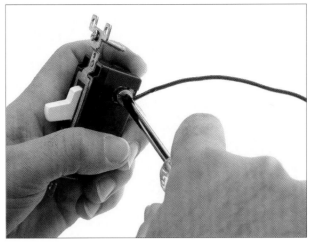

1 Form a hook

To make wire-to-screw-terminal connections, first strip about ½" to ¾" of insulation off the wire end. Then, using long-nose pliers, form a two-third to three-quarter loop in the bare wire: starting near the insulation, make progressive right-angle bends, moving the pliers toward the wire end, until a loop is formed.

2 Secure a terminal connection

Hook the wire clockwise around the screw terminal. As you tighten the screw, the loop on the wire will close. If you hook the wire backward (counterclockwise), tightening the screw will tend to open the loop.

BACKWIRING A DEVICE

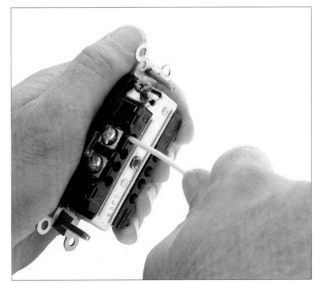

1 Use the strip gauge

When backwiring, first use the molded strip gauge on the back of the device to measure the amount of insulation to be stripped.

2 Make the connections

Poke the stripped wires into their appropriate holes, then check to make sure they're secure. Finally, be sure to tighten down any unused screw terminals; this will help prevent any loose metal from ending up in the box.

SPLICING WIRES

Wires are joined—or spliced—with wire nuts or compression sleeves.

Wire nuts come in about four sizes to accommodate various wire combinations. Each manufacturer has its own color code to distinguish the various sizes. For example, one brand uses a red wire nut to splice four #12 wires or five #14 wires. Once you know how many wires of what size you'll be splicing, check the wire nut packaging to make sure you get the proper size.

Some jurisdictions require the use of compression sleeves for grounding wires because they provide a more permanent bond than wire nuts. You can use the special jaws on a wire stripper or multipurpose tool to attach these connectors; a special two- or four-jawed crimping tool serves the same purpose. Make sure that you use enough pressure to shape the metal into tight contact with the wires. A special two-compartment connector is required for splicing aluminum wire to copper wire.

Never use electrician's tape in place of a wire nut or compression sleeve. Tape is useful for emergency repairs, but it's not a substitute for a good mechanical splice.

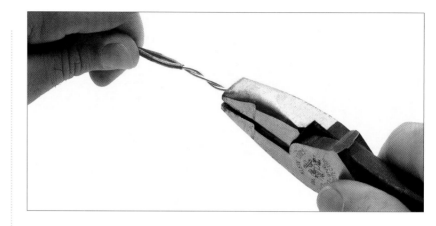

1 Strip wire ends, twist them together
First, strip off about 1" of insulation from the ends of the wires you're going to join. Twist the stripped ends together clockwise at least one and one-half turns.

2 Trim ends
Next, snip ⅜" to ½" off the twisted wires so the ends are even.

3 Screw on the wire nut
While holding the wires with your free hand, screw the wire nut on clockwise until it is tight and no bare wire is exposed. Test the splice by tugging on the wires; if any come loose, redo the splice so it's secure.

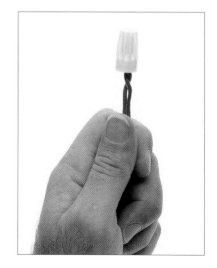

HOW TO PUT ON A COMPRESSION SLEEVE

First, twist the wire ends clockwise at least one and one-half turns. Snip ⅜" to ½" off the twisted ends so that they are even. Then slip a compression sleeve onto the wire ends, and crimp the sleeve using a multipurpose tool. If code requires, put on an insulating cap.

MAKING A PIGTAIL SPLICE

This connection is nothing more than several wires spliced together, with one of the wires (the pigtail) connecting to a terminal on an electrical device such as a switch or a receptacle (shown below at left). A pigtail may also run to the grounding screw on a metal housing box (shown below at right). The pigtail wire, usually 6 inches long, must match the gauge of the other wires in the splice. A wire nut or a compression sleeve is used to secure the splice.

ROUGH WIRING

This chapter illustrates specific techniques for installing concealed wiring in wood-frame homes where wall, ceiling, and floor coverings are already in place. It also offers advice for routing cable in new homes before the walls, ceilings, and floors are installed. Both types of work are called roughing-in or rough wiring. Finish work—the final installation of receptacles, switches, light fixtures, and appliances, as well as the final hookup to the power source—is the subject of Chapter Six, "Finish Wiring," which begins on page 88.

Before starting any job, read through this chapter to get a feel for the project ahead. Also study the specific wiring diagrams for receptacles, switches, light fixtures, and appliances in Chapter Six. Then check with your local building department about getting an electrical permit. Once you've finished the job, request an inspection. Obtaining a permit and a follow-up inspection add up to a solid guarantee that the work will be performed properly. It's also an inexpensive way to get expert advice from a pro—your electrical inspector.

Nonmetallic sheathed cable (type NM) is used in most residential wiring and is what we will be using throughout most of this chapter. If you're planning to install exposed conduit, you'll find installation pointers on pages 82–87.

PLANNING NEW WIRING ROUTES

Planning is crucial when extending a present circuit or adding a new one. The time you spend at this stage can save both time and money when you do the actual wiring.

ROOM-BY-ROOM REQUIREMENTS

Start your planning by reviewing the following National Electrical Code branch circuit requirements. Remember that these are minimum requirements; more circuits can—and, in many cases, should—be added.

KITCHEN AND RELATED AREAS: The parts of a home with the most restrictions are the kitchen, pantry, dining room, family room, and breakfast room because of the high amp-pull of the appliances in these rooms and the greater potential for shock. The receptacles in each of these areas must be served by at least two 20-amp, small-appliance circuits and protected by GFCIs (see page 18). Light fixtures and other outlets must be on a separate circuit or circuits.

The receptacles also should be evenly distributed between the small-appliance circuits. That is, if eight receptacles are required to serve the kitchen, four receptacles should be on one circuit and four should be on the other.

Dishwashers and garbage disposal units must have their own separate 20-amp circuits. An electric range or a wall oven-cooktop combination should be supplied by an individual 50-amp, 120/240-volt major-appliance circuit.

BATHROOM: The bath area now requires its own 20-amp receptacle circuit for small appliances. The receptacles must be protected by GFCIs, and light fixtures must be on another circuit. A ventilation

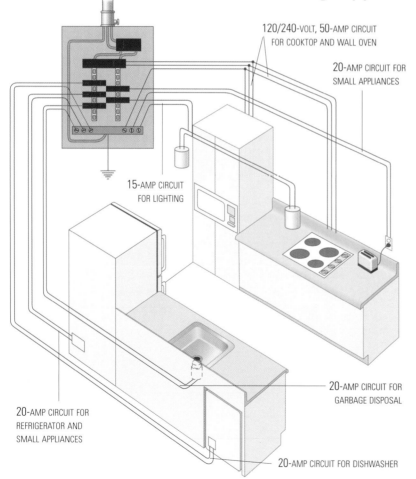

120/240-VOLT, 50-AMP CIRCUIT
FOR COOKTOP AND WALL OVEN

20-AMP CIRCUIT FOR
SMALL APPLIANCES

15-AMP CIRCUIT
FOR LIGHTING

20-AMP CIRCUIT FOR
REFRIGERATOR AND
SMALL APPLIANCES

20-AMP CIRCUIT FOR
GARBAGE DISPOSAL

20-AMP CIRCUIT FOR DISHWASHER

fan may require its own 20-amp circuit; a whirlpool bath may require a dedicated 120- or 120/240-volt circuit, depending on its motor.

LAUNDRY AREA: Code requires a separate 20-amp circuit to supply the receptacle for a washing machine. If the laundry equipment includes an electric dryer, you'll need an individual 30-amp, 120/240-volt major-appliance circuit for it.

THE REST OF THE HOUSE: Circuits for the living room, bedrooms, and utility areas can all be 15-amp general purpose circuits. These circuits supply power to light fixtures, switches, and receptacles. (Note: Major-appliance circuits, such as those needed for a water heater or a central heating system, generally require their own dedicated 240-volt circuits.)

You can find out how many 15-amp general purpose circuits you should have by dividing 500 square feet into the total square footage of your home. If your home is 1,500 square feet (based on outside measurements), you should allow at least three 15-amp circuits. If you have 1,600 square feet, allow at least four. (For any amount over a round number, you should go up to the next number of circuits.)

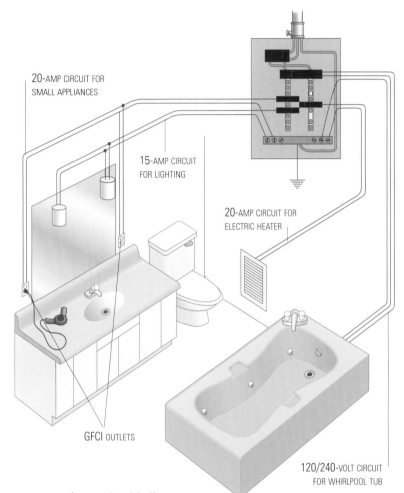

20-AMP CIRCUIT FOR SMALL APPLIANCES

15-AMP CIRCUIT FOR LIGHTING

20-AMP CIRCUIT FOR ELECTRIC HEATER

GFCI OUTLETS

120/240-VOLT CIRCUIT FOR WHIRLPOOL TUB

CHARTING YOUR COURSE

The first step in planning a wiring improvement is to draw a diagram showing the location of each proposed switch, receptacle, light fixture, and appliance. Refer to the symbols shown on page 21 to make this task easier.

Give some thought to possible power sources for your new wiring. You'll have to choose between adding new circuits to your distribution center and tapping into existing circuits at receptacle, fixture, switch, or junction boxes. To determine whether existing circuits can carry an additional load, you must first evaluate your present wiring (see pages 20–23).

Also be sure to review the National Electrical Code requirements for receptacles and light fixtures outlined on page 73.

ACCESS FOR CABLE

The next step is to study possible access routes for running cable from the power source to the locations for new devices. But to do that, you'll first need to bone up on some basic house anatomy.

Wood-frame homes are not all built the same way, but most have 2×4 stud walls, 2×8 (or larger) floor joists, and 2×6 (or larger) ceiling joists. These wooden structural members are normally spaced 16 inches apart from center to center. In some new homes, however, the spacing is 24 inches, and in some roughly built older homes, it's somewhat random. The illustration on the facing page shows the skeleton of a typical wood-frame house.

In new construction, all rough wiring is done before wall, ceiling, and floor coverings are added. Extending a circuit in a finished house is a different story; you have to find ways to route cable behind existing walls, above ceilings, and under floors.

The best route is one that is direct and accessible, but accessibility is generally more important than directness. The savings in time and effort from avoiding extensive cutting and patching of walls, ceilings, and floors nearly always offsets the added material costs for an indirect cable run.

WHERE YOU HAVE ACCESS: In some parts of your home, installing cable and boxes might be quite easy. These are areas such as attic floors and unfinished basement ceilings where wall, ceiling, or floor coverings are attached to only one side of the framing. You simply work from the uncovered side, drilling holes and threading cable through studs or joists. You can also "fish" cable through finished walls from these locations (page 65).

When working in an attic, don't put any weight on the floor area between the joists. Step only on the joists or on planks laid across them, and be sure to walk gently so you don't crack the ceiling surface of the room below.

WHERE ACCESS IS LIMITED: Getting cables into walls, floors, or ceilings that have coverings on both sides involves cutting through the coverings, installing cable, and patching up the holes. The amount and difficulty of cutting and patching depend only partly on where the cable goes; surface material is also a factor.

Gypsum wallboard, the most common wall and ceiling covering, is relatively easy to cut away and replace. But some other materials—such as ceramic tile, certain types of wood flooring, and plaster—are more difficult to cut and patch and should be left alone when possible.

WOOD-FRAME ANATOMY

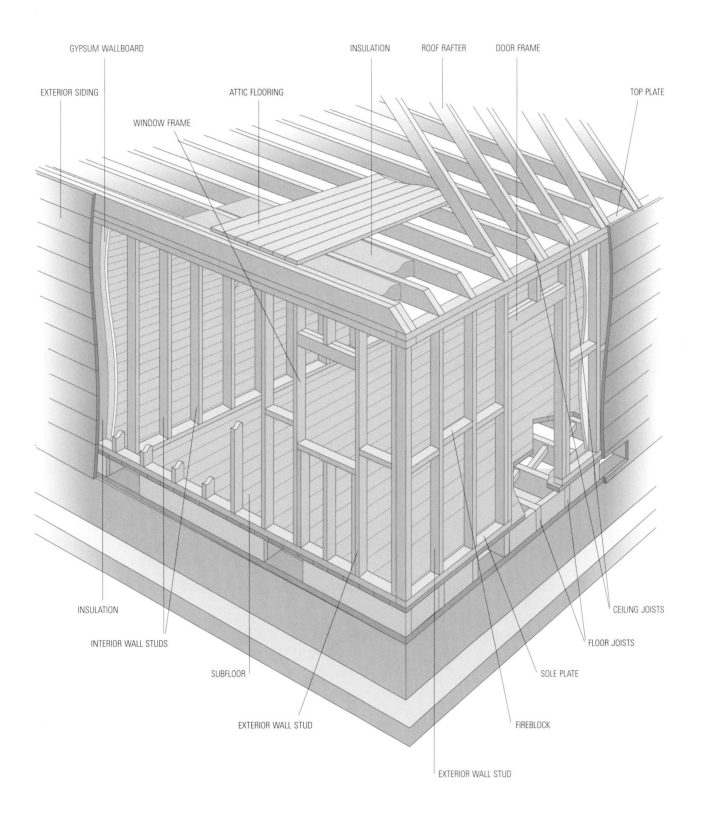

GYPSUM WALLBOARD

INSULATION

ROOF RAFTER

DOOR FRAME

EXTERIOR SIDING

ATTIC FLOORING

TOP PLATE

WINDOW FRAME

INSULATION

INTERIOR WALL STUDS

SUBFLOOR

EXTERIOR WALL STUD

CEILING JOISTS

FLOOR JOISTS

SOLE PLATE

FIREBLOCK

EXTERIOR WALL STUD

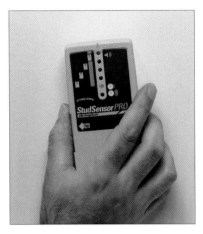

WHAT'S THE BEST WAY TO LOCATE FRAMING MEMBERS?

Hunting for hidden wall studs can involve a lot of guesswork. Sometimes you can measure to find them on 16- or 24-inch centers, but not always. You can knock on the wall with your knuckles, listening for a solid rap that suggests something is behind the wall covering, but knocks often sound alike all over the wall.

An electronic stud finder, shown above, is a very effective tool for locating wall studs. To use one, move it slowly along the wall in a horizontal direction. When it passes over a stud, it will light up or beep. To find surrounding studs, first measure out 16 or 24 inches, then use the stud finder to make sure they're there.

A stud finder can help you find hidden ceiling joists, too. Like studs, these members are usually, but not always, spaced 16 or 24 inches apart.

OLD WORK: EXTENDING A CIRCUIT

Your remodeling plans may call for adding a new receptacle, switch, or light fixture to an existing circuit. In this section we explain techniques for extending a circuit with nonmetallic sheathed cable (type NM) where wall, ceiling, and floor coverings are already in place.

The first step is to determine where to tap into the existing circuit. Then you cut the hole for the new device, run cable from the power source to the new box location, and mount the new box. Be sure you use wire for the extension that's the same size as the existing circuit wires (assuming the existing wires are the correct size).

SELECTING A POWER SOURCE

You can tap a circuit at any accessible receptacle, switch, fixture, or junction box. The only exceptions are switch boxes that don't have a neutral wire and switch-controlled fixtures at the end of a circuit (see pages 100 and 104).

Before deciding where to tap the circuit, consider how you'll route wire to the new switch, receptacle, or fixture. Look for the easiest paths behind walls, above ceilings, and under floors.

The box tapped must be large enough to accommodate the new wires (see page 32) and must have a knockout hole through which you can thread the new cable. If the source is accessible, but the box isn't right, get a new box.

PREPARING FOR A NEW BOX

Old-work, or "cut-in," housing boxes for remodeling mount easily where wall or ceiling materials are already in place. Most boxes are designed to be mounted in gypsum wallboard. If your wall is plaster or wood, choose the so-called plain box (see page 33).

If you're putting a new box in a room that already has boxes, try to place it at the same distance from the floor as the old ones. Otherwise, place a new receptacle box 12 to 18 inches off the floor and a switch box 48 inches high. Mount a fixture box wherever you want the light.

SELECTING A BOX LOCATION: Boxes are mounted in open spaces between studs. To position a box in a wall or ceiling, you'll need to locate the underlying studs and joists, as well as any obstructions, such as pipes or wires. Be sure to shut off power to all circuits that might be wired behind the wall or ceiling before you drill any holes.

The simplest way to locate studs and joists is with an electronic stud finder (see the facing page). Once you've found what seems to be a suitable area, drill a small test hole where you want the box. Then bend a 9-inch length of stiff wire to a 90-degree angle at its midpoint, push one end of the wire through the hole, and rotate it. If it bumps into something, move over a few inches and try again until you find an unobstructed space.

When locating a box on a lath-and-plaster wall, use a cold chisel to chip away enough plaster around the test hole to expose a full width of lath. The box should be centered on the lath.

CUTTING THE HOLE: Some housing boxes come with hole-cutting templates. If yours doesn't, trace the box's outline on the wall or ceiling, omitting any protruding brackets. Then proceed as shown below. Try to be as precise as possible; an oversized hole will require patching and may not leave enough wall or ceiling surface for anchoring the box.

CUTTING BOX HOLES IN PLASTER

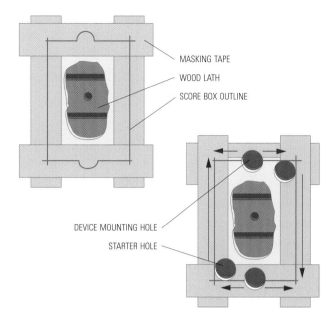

When working with plaster and wood lath, first use a cold chisel to chip away enough plaster to expose one width of lath. Tape around the perimeter of the hole as shown at top left, then score the box's outline several times with a utility knife. Drill starter holes as shown at bottom right, then cut slowly in the direction of the arrows.

CUTTING HOLES IN GYPSUM WALLBOARD

1 Draw the outline
If your box comes with a paper template, use it to mark the exact hole shape on wall or ceiling. Otherwise, trace the box's outline directly, as shown, omitting any protruding wings or brackets.

2 Make the cut
For a tidy cut in wallboard, use a drywall saw or a jab saw. You can often start the cut by simply rapping on the saw handle; or drill starter holes as shown and saw along the outlines.

ROUTING CABLE
WHERE THERE'S ACCESS

After cutting the hole but before mounting the box, you must run cable from the power source to the new box location. Access from an unfinished basement, an unfloored attic, or an adjacent garage or utility space can make your work much easier.

Where you have access from a basement, a crawl space, or an attic, plan to run cable along joists or beams, or through holes drilled in them (see pages 76–79). From these areas you can "fish" cable through walls that are covered on both sides.

After cutting the box hole, drill a small, discreet guide hole up through the ceiling or down through the floor to mark the location. Then, from the basement or attic, drill a ¾-inch hole into the wall frame next to your guide hole, as shown below right.

Now you'll need some "fishing" gear. Run fish tape (see page 44) or wire in through the box hole and down (or up) through the drilled hole. Attach the cable to the tape or wire and draw it back through the box hole (see "Fishing Tips" on the facing page).

For distances of more than 1 to 2 feet, which are tricky to negotiate, you'll need a partner and possibly two fish tapes. To make sure your path is clear, have your helper hold a flashlight in the box hole while you peer through the drilled hole. If you can't see the light beam, a fire block or some other obstruction is in the way. Either drill through the block or cut away the wall covering and notch the block.

FISHING A SHORT RUN FROM BELOW

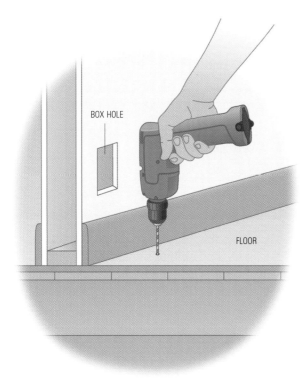

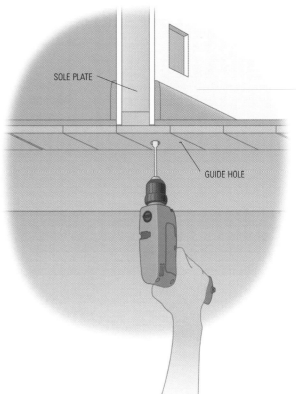

1 Drill a guide hole
After making a hole for your box in an open space between studs, drill a small guide hole down through the floor to mark the center point of the box.

2 Drill the cable hole
Next, drill a larger hole up through the sole plate from below, using the guide hole for reference. Run a wire or fish tape in through the box hole and down through the drilled hole. Attach cable and draw it up into the box hole.

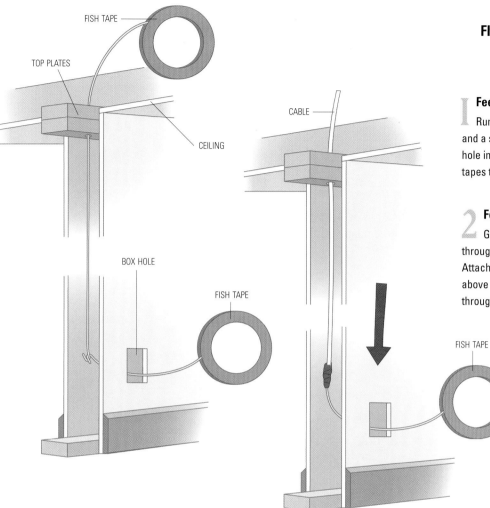

FISH TAPE

TOP PLATES

CEILING

CABLE

BOX HOLE

FISH TAPE

FISH TAPE

FISH TAPE

FISHING A LONG RUN FROM ABOVE

1 Feed two fish tapes

Run one tape in through the box hole and a second fish tape down through a hole in the top plates. Then hook the two tapes together inside the wall.

2 Feed the cable

Gently tug the hooked tapes up through the wall; detach the first tape. Attach cable to the second tape from above and, pulling slowly, work it down through the box hole as shown.

FISHING TIPS

To help you route cable through covered walls and ceilings, you're going to need some fishing gear. For short distances, you can use a straightened coat hanger or a piece of #12 wire with one end bent into a hook. But the best tool, especially for longer runs, is a fish tape (shown on page 44), which comes on a 25- or 50-foot reel. For long cable runs, you may need a pair of fish tapes.

To attach cable to a fish tape, first strip off several inches of sheathing. Then bend the wire ends around the hook on the fish tape (above left) and wrap the connection with electrical tape (above right), making the splice as small in diameter as you can.

WORKING WITH MOLDING

When routing cable behind window or door molding, keep these points in mind:

✓ Molding may split, so be sure you can buy replacement pieces before you begin.

✓ Before removing molding, use a utility knife or a putty knife to break the paint bond between the molding and the wall or ceiling covering.

✓ Use a 4" (or wider) putty knife or chisel to pry molding from the wall. Take your time, gently prying up the molding without cracking it.

✓ Cable installed less than 1¼" from a finished surface must be protected by ¹⁄₁₆" metal plates mounted to framing members.

✓ When nailing molding back up, position the nails above and below the channel in the wall so you don't nail through the cable.

ROUTING CABLE WITHOUT ACCESS

Getting cable into walls, ceilings, or floors that have coverings on both sides requires some special tricks. You'll probably need to cut away some of the surfaces. Wallboard is relatively easy to cut away and replace (for repair techniques, see page 87). But some other materials, such as ceramic tile and certain types of plaster, are more difficult to patch and should be left alone when possible.

The following pages show several ways to route cable. Where cable passes through wood less than 1¼ inches from a finished surface, you'll need to install ¹⁄₁₆-inch metal plates on the framing members to protect the cable from being damaged when wall or ceiling coverings are nailed in place (see page 77).

When routing cable across a ceiling, try to run the cable parallel with the ceiling joists. Whenever you run cable across a joist, you have to drill through or notch it.

ROUTING CABLE BEHIND A BASEBOARD

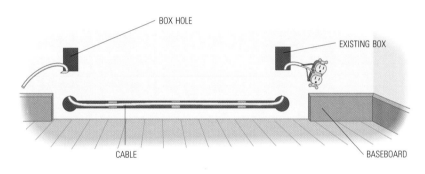

First, remove the baseboard between box locations. Then cut away the wallboard as shown and route cable along notched studs. Cover the cable with protective metal plates.

ROUTING CABLE ALONG A WALL

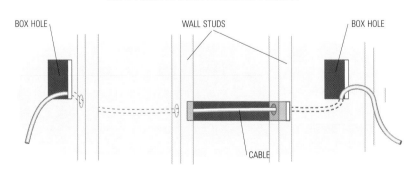

Cut the box hole or holes, then neatly cut a straight, narrow strip of wall covering to expose studs, as shown. Drill through the center of each stud, then run cable through holes.

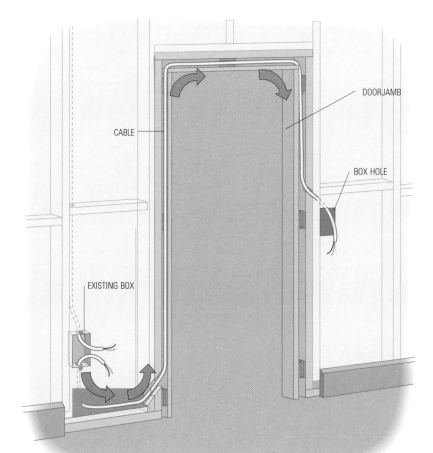

CABLE

DOORJAMB

BOX HOLE

EXISTING BOX

RUNNING CABLE AROUND A DOORWAY

First remove the door casing and base-board, as required. Then run cable between the doorjamb and rough framing, notching spacer blocks or shims wher-ever necessary. Note: If you're also adding or replacing a door, install it before wiring—otherwise, new hardware or fas-teners could damage the cable.

INSTALLING BACK-TO-BACK DEVICES

When cutting a new box hole opposite an existing device, offset the new hole a few inches from the first. Then pull the existing device temporarily from its box and route cable through a knockout hole in that box directly to the new box hole.

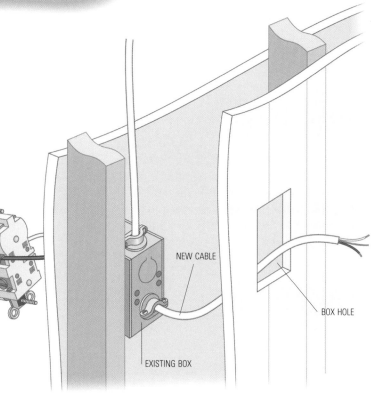

NEW CABLE

BOX HOLE

EXISTING BOX

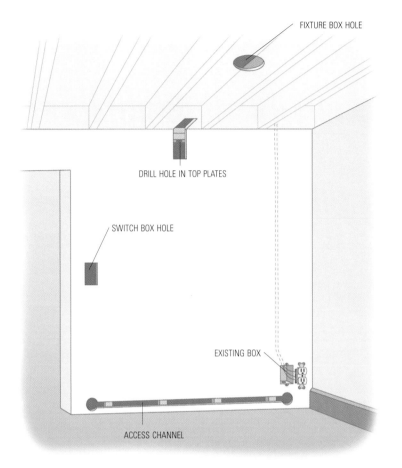

FIXTURE BOX HOLE

DRILL HOLE IN TOP PLATES

SWITCH BOX HOLE

EXISTING BOX

ACCESS CHANNEL

ROUTING CABLE FOR A LIGHT AND SWITCH

1 Cut the access holes

Mark the fixture box location between two ceiling joists and cut its hole. Cut a hole for the switch box, and make a hole where the wall meets the ceiling. Drill a hole in the top plates as shown. Then cut an access channel along the baseboard between the switch box location and the existing power source (for details, see page 66).

2 Route cable through the wall

Run one cable between the power source and the switch box hole. Then fish a second cable from the switch hole to the access hole, first doubling back along the baseboard, as shown.

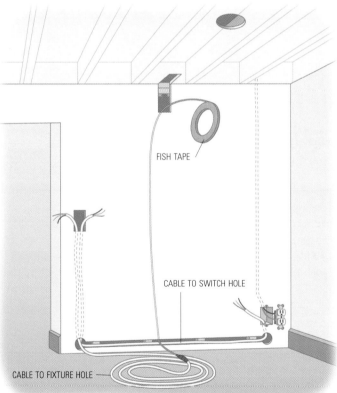

FISH TAPE

CABLE TO SWITCH HOLE

CABLE TO FIXTURE HOLE

CABLE

FISH TAPE

3 Extend cable to the fixture box hole

Fish from the fixture box hole to the access hole via the drilled hole in the top plates. Attach the second cable, then pull it through the access hole and top plates and out the fixture box hole.

SURFACE WIRING

Where routing wire through walls and cutting into walls, ceilings, and floors is too difficult, surface wiring may be the answer. Surface wiring systems are safe and neat, usually consisting of protective channels (shown at right) or strips that allow you to mount wiring and boxes on practically any floor, wall, or ceiling material. Cable is fished through the channels.

Surface wiring materials differ by manufacturer. Consult your electrical supplies dealer for more information about the various systems available.

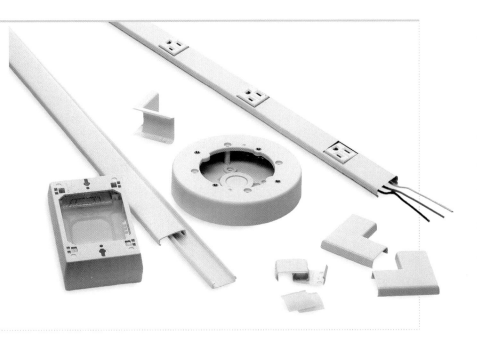

MOUNTING THE NEW BOX

When you've cut the hole and routed the cable, most of the messy work is over. The only remaining jobs are mounting the box, making the wiring connections, and doing any patch-up work.

Before mounting the box, insert the cable through a knockout hole. To remove a knockout, punch it with the end of a pair of lineman's pliers or with a screwdriver, then twist it off with the pliers' jaws, as shown on page 81.

Cable must be secured to a metal box either with built-in cable clamps or with separate metal cable connectors (see pages 80–81). NM cable doesn't need to be clamped to a nonmetallic box if it's stapled with electrical staples to a stud or joist within 8 inches of the box; however, if you can't staple it, you'll have to choose a box with built-in clamps. Always leave 6 to 8 inches of cable extending into the box for connections.

How you mount the new box will depend on its type. Several old-work boxes used for remodeling are shown here. If you've chosen a box designed for new construction, see pages 74–75.

For a detailed look at wall-patching strategies, see page 87.

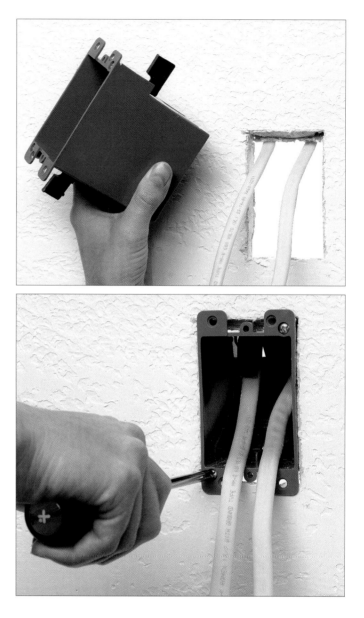

Cut-in wall box with wing clamps

This box combines front flanges with twin wings (shown at top) that fix it in place. First fold the wings flat and slip the box into the hole. Then drive home both screws at the front of the box, as shown above; as you tighten, each wing pivots and snugs against the back side of the wall.

Plain box

Check the box for proper fit in the hole. If necessary, adjust the ears so the front edge of the box is flush with the finished wall surface. When mounting a plain box on lath walls, mark screw placements on the lath, drill pilot holes for the screws, then screw the box to the lath. On wooden walls, just screw the ears to the wall surface as shown at left; the faceplate will hide the ears and screws.

Cut-in ceiling box with metal spring ears

Once this box is mounted, it can't be removed, so first try out the fit without the metal spring ears, and have the cable in place before you actually install it. To lock the box into place, tighten the screw at the back of the box, pushing the teeth into the back side of the ceiling.

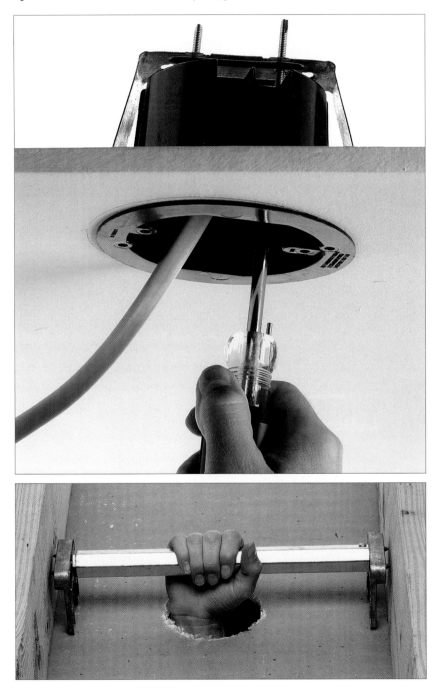

FINE-TUNING BOX FIT

What if, despite your best efforts, your cut-in box doesn't really fit the previously-cut box hole? If the hole is too small, no problem—just get out your saw again. If the hole's so big that the wings or clamps won't hold it to the wall, try gluing a thin wood scrap or shim to the inside of the wall—just enough to catch the box's mounting hardware. No luck? You'll have to add a replacement patch (see page 87)—then try again.

Heavy-duty cut-in bar

Slip this sturdy bar, designed for ceiling fans, end-first through a fixture box hole and align it between two joists. As you rotate the center bar, it lengthens, driving the barbed end brackets into the wood. Then install a matching fixture box with a special mounting strap that's tightened from inside the box.

NEW WORK: ADDING A CIRCUIT

Adding a new circuit to your service entrance panel or subpanel is often the solution when an existing circuit can't handle a new load. Before you add a circuit, though, you must calculate your total house load, including the new load, to make sure you'll still be within your service rating. For help, see pages 22–23.

The techniques covered in this section apply to new construction, where house framing is exposed. For situations where wall, ceiling, and floor coverings are in place, see pages 62–71. When you're ready to hook up your new devices, turn to Chapter Six, "Finish Wiring," beginning on page 88.

GETTING STARTED

Before you begin, you'll need to know the right type and size of branch circuit for your project. We'll help you sort that out below. In addition, keep in mind that some rooms have very specific rules for the number and distribution of circuits and electrical devices. For guidelines, see "Room-by-Room Requirements" on pages 58–59.

CIRCUIT TYPES: Branch circuits fall into three basic categories: 120 volt, 120/240 volt, and 240 volt.

Most circuits in your home are 120-volt circuits, either 15-amp, general-purpose or 20-amp, small-appliance versions. These require the basic hot, neutral, and grounding wires.

Some major appliances, such as clothes dryers and ranges, require the input of both 120 and 240 volts. These circuits require two hot wires (one from each hot bus bar), along with the neutral wire and, in most cases, a grounding wire.

Electric water heaters and central air conditioners are examples of appliances that require a straight 240-volt circuit. This kind of circuit consists of two hot wires and a grounding wire. The complete loop is formed by the two hot wires; thus, no neutral is needed.

WIRE SIZES: Here's how to choose the proper conductor size for your new branch circuit.

✓ **Standard 120-volt branch circuits:** For 15-amp, general-purpose circuits, #14 copper wire is the rule, although electricians often run #12 because it's less likely to get overloaded. Choose #12 wire for 20-amp, small-appliance circuits.

✓ **Major appliance circuits:** When planning for a major appliance, check the appliance installation information and your local electrical code for guidelines. Following are some typical circuit and conductor sizes:

Dishwasher: 20-amp, 120-volt, #12 copper wire

Garbage disposal: 20-amp, 120-volt, #12 copper wire

Electric dryer: 30-amp, 120/240-volt, #10 copper wire

Range or oven-cooktop combination: 50-amp, 120/240-volt, #6 copper wire

Water heater: 125 percent of nameplate amp rating, 240-volt

For matching wire size to any amp load, see page 29.

REQUIRED RECEPTACLES AND LIGHT FIXTURES

Some specific planning guidelines apply when determining type and number of receptacles and light fixtures. Remember that these are minimum requirements; more devices can—and in many cases, should—be added.

RECEPTACLES: For most areas of a house, the required number of receptacles depends on the size of the room. Any wall space that is 2 feet or more in width must have a receptacle. Receptacles must be no more than 12 feet apart and no more than 6 feet from each door or archway. This spacing allows a lamp or an appliance with a 6-foot cord to be used near any wall without an extension cord.

A receptacle located behind a stationary appliance, such as a refrigerator, does not qualify as one of those required every 12 feet. All those receptacles have to be accessible.

Every basement must have at least one receptacle; so must every hallway over 10 feet long.

GFCIs: In the kitchen and eating areas, every counter space wider than 12 inches should have a receptacle. At least one receptacle is also required near the water basin in a bathroom, on the outside of the house, and in the garage. All these areas require special protection, however, because of the possibility that you might contact a grounded metal plumbing fixture or a concrete floor at the same time you're using a defective electrical appliance. For this reason, all these receptacles must be protected by GFCIs.

The National Electrical Code permits the installation of GFCI protection in either of two ways. You can use a receptacle with a GFCI built into it, or you can install a GFCI in the service panel in place of the circuit breaker protecting that particular circuit.

LIGHT FIXTURES: Light fixtures fall into two groups—those that must be controlled by a wall switch, and those that may have any kind of turn-on arrangement.

The National Electrical Code states that every room, hallway, stairway, attached garage, and outdoor entrance must have at least one light fixture controlled by a wall switch. However, in most rooms other than kitchens and bathrooms, the wall switch may control one or more receptacles—into which lamps can be plugged—instead of a ceiling or wall-mounted light.

Hallways and stairs with more than six steps require 3-way switches at both ends. It's now illegal to have a bare-bulb fixture inside a closet. The globe of any surface-mounted, incandescent fixture used must be at least 12 inches away from shelves or storables; recessed fixtures and fluorescent tubes need only 6 inches of clearance.

In the "any kind of switching" category, the code requires one light fixture in utility rooms, attics, basements, and underfloor spaces used for storage or containing equipment that may require servicing.

MOUNTING NEW BOXES

First, you'll need to decide what boxes you need and where you want them. Put your plans on paper; on page 21 you'll find instructions for drawing a circuit map of your house.

Before buying boxes, make sure they have the right mounting holes for the devices you plan to install (you can, if necessary, use an adapter plate, shown on page 33). Also be sure the boxes have suitably placed knockout holes for routing cable in and out. Boxes may have built-in clamps for securing cable, or you may have to purchase separate cable connectors.

Keep receptacles a uniform 12 to 18 inches above the floor. Where wall coverings aren't yet in place, locate either the top or bottom of a switch box 48 inches from the floor; that way, if you'll be installing 48-inch-wide gypsum wallboard horizontally, you'll have to cut into just one piece instead of two. Be sure to avoid placing a switch box on the hinge side of a door opening. Remember that every box must be accessible.

Whether a new-work box is metal or nonmetallic, it should be straightforward to mount, using either an external nail or flange, an internal screw, or a hanger bar. Several standard installations are shown at right. If you want to hang a box between two studs or joists but don't have a hanger bar, you can nail a 2x4 between the members and attach the box directly to the wood.

The boxes should be installed flush with the finished wall or ceiling. If the covering is not yet in place, tack or hold a scrap of your finish material to the stud or joist next to your box and use it to align the box's front edge.

Screw-on handy box
The back or side of this box can be attached directly to the framing—or in this case, a scrap block mounted between wall studs.

Ceiling box with flange
Simply nail the flange to the side of an exposed ceiling joist, aligning its front so that it will be flush with the finished ceiling material. Some boxes have "spiked" flanges, which allow you to anchor the boxes first with a tap of the hammer before driving the nails home.

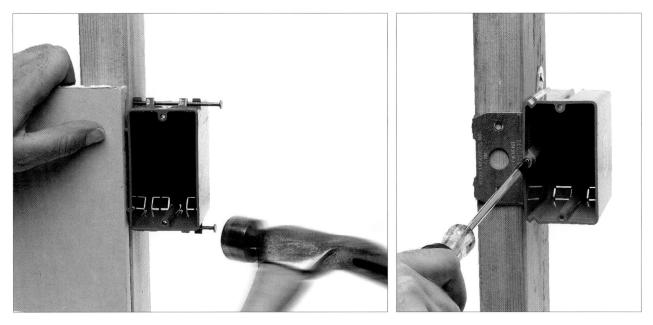

Nail-on wall boxes

These nonmetallic boxes are simple to install: simply butt them against a wall stud and nail them home. Some versions are side-mounted with integral nails; others are front-mounted (the thin mounting flange is covered by the wall material). Note that in the photo above left, a small wallboard scrap helps align the side-mounting box with the finished wall material; the flange on the front-mounting model shown above right adjusts to align the box.

Adjustable hanger bar

This ceiling box spans two joists. The two-piece bar can be narrowed or expanded to fit various joist spacings. The box also slides along the bar, allowing you to fine-tune the fixture's placement.

Pancake box

Simply screw this ceiling box to a joist or an exposed beam. Position the box so it will hide the hole drilled for the cable. Don't make wire or cable splices in this type of box—it's big enough to accommodate only two conductors and a grounding wire.

ROUTING CABLE: NEW CONSTRUCTION

In new construction, all rough wiring is completed before wall, ceiling, and floor coverings go in place. The following techniques will show you how it's done. If your access route passes through finished walls, ceilings, or floors, see pages 62–69.

Nonmetallic sheathed cable (type NM) is used for most new work. To make your work easier, plan to run cable along the surface of structural members (studs, joists, rafters, etc.) whenever possible. Where you must route it at an angle to the members, you'll have to drill holes and run the cable through the members (see photos at left).

DRILLING HOLES: Use the smallest drill bit that's practical when boring through joists or studs—typically $3/4$ inch. To avoid weakening the wood members excessively, drill through the center of the board. If the hole is less than $1\frac{1}{4}$ inches from the edge of the board, you must tack a $1/16$-inch metal plate over the edge, as shown on the facing page.

WORKING WITH CABLE: Make a rough sketch of your cable route, including critical dimensions such as the height of boxes from the floor and the distance between boxes. Total all the dimensions. Then, for box-to-box runs, add at least 4 feet (2 feet for each box) for mistakes, box connections, and unforeseen obstacles. When cable goes to a box from either a service entrance panel or a subpanel, add at least 6 feet (4 for the panel and 2 for the box).

Try not to kink or twist NM cable during installation. If you're having trouble, try pulling cable from the box and straightening it before you run it.

At top, a cordless right-angle drill bores a string of $3/4$-inch holes through a run of new wall studs. Whenever possible, drill through the centers of framing members, well away from the edges.

Above, a run of 12-2 NM cable makes its way through the parallel holes toward a new receptacle box.

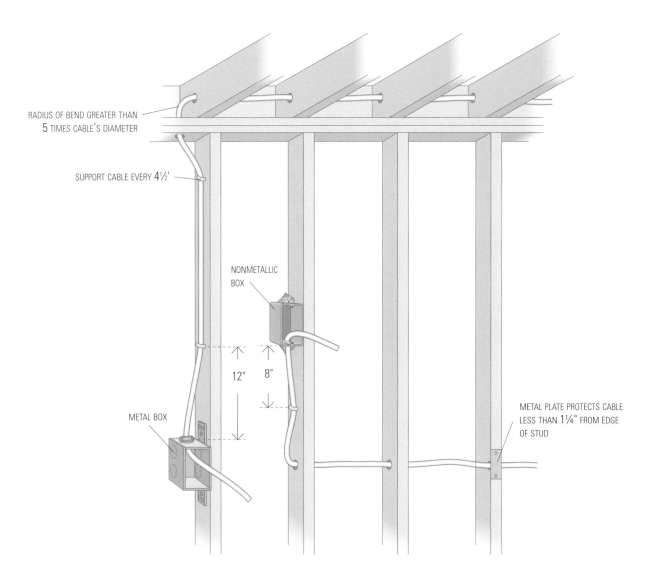

RADIUS OF BEND GREATER THAN
5 TIMES CABLE'S DIAMETER

SUPPORT CABLE EVERY 4½'

NONMETALLIC
BOX

12"   8"

METAL BOX

METAL PLATE PROTECTS CABLE
LESS THAN 1¼" FROM EDGE
OF STUD

WHAT'S THE BEST WAY TO SECURE CABLE?

In exposed (new) wiring, cable must be stapled or supported with straps every 4½ feet and within 12 inches of each metal box and 8 inches of each nonmetallic box. When using cable staples (left), be careful not to staple through or smash the cable. Staple the face of the cable, not the side. Use metal plates (right) to protect cable that's installed less than 1¼ inches from the front edge of a stud or other structural member.

Cable staples or supports aren't required when cable is fished behind walls, floors, or ceilings in concealed (old) work. However, the cable must be clamped to boxes using built-in cable clamps, metal cable connectors, or plastic cable connectors (if the box is nonmetallic). There is one exception: NM cable need not be clamped to a nonmetallic box if it's stapled within 8 inches of the box.

DOOR AND WINDOW ROUTING

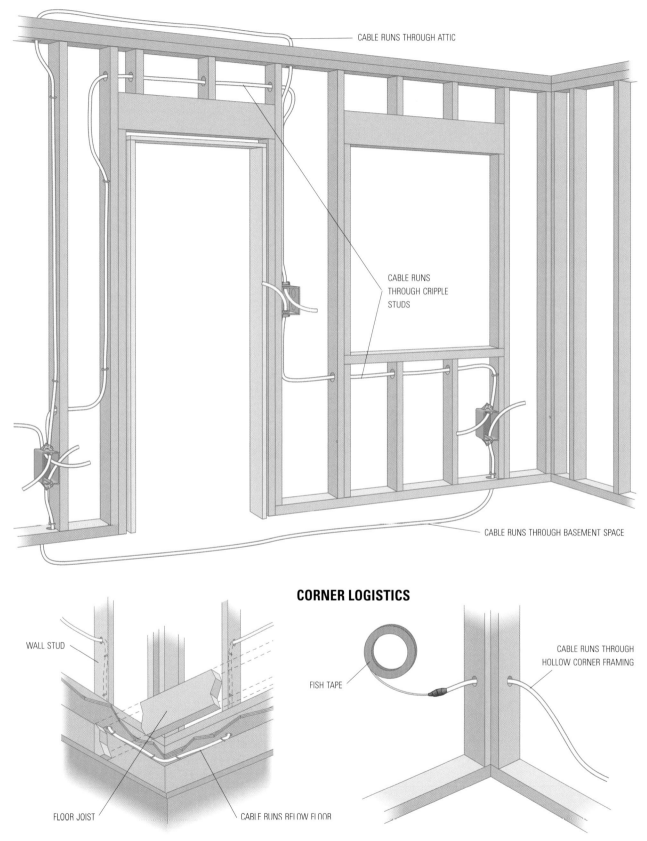

CABLE RUNS THROUGH ATTIC

CABLE RUNS
THROUGH CRIPPLE
STUDS

CABLE RUNS THROUGH BASEMENT SPACE

CORNER LOGISTICS

WALL STUD

FISH TAPE

CABLE RUNS THROUGH
HOLLOW CORNER FRAMING

FLOOR JOIST

CABLE RUNS BELOW FLOOR

CIRCUMNAVIGATING WINDOWS AND DOORS: Openings for windows and doors present obvious obstacles for continuous cable runs. Windows are usually simpler to bypass than doors, since most have stud framing below the sill through which you can run the cable. Doors and floor-to-ceiling windows are trickier. The best way to bypass these openings, when possible, is to route cable through the ceiling above or the floor below, as shown at the top of the facing page. If these avenues are closed, you'll need to take cable through the cripple studs above the header, or, as a last resort (for example, if there's a continuous header running to the ceiling), through the shim space just below the header.

CORNERS: An intersection where stud walls meet may also present a cable-routing challenge. Often the best strategy is to route cable above or below the area. If the corner is hollow, as shown on the bottom of the facing page, you can drill in from both sides, then feed the cable through, using one or a pair of wires or fish tapes (see page 65), as required.

ROUTING CABLE IN AN UNFINISHED BASEMENT: When run under the floor at an angle to floor joists, NM cable with two conductors smaller than #6 or three conductors smaller than #8 must be run through holes drilled in the joists, stapled to running boards nailed in place, or supported on the surface of structural members (see below). Larger cable may be fastened directly to the bottom edges of joists.

AN ATTIC OVERVIEW

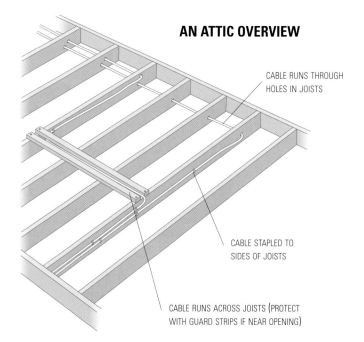

CABLE RUNS THROUGH HOLES IN JOISTS

CABLE STAPLED TO SIDES OF JOISTS

CABLE RUNS ACROSS JOISTS (PROTECT WITH GUARD STRIPS IF NEAR OPENING)

ROUTING CABLE IN AN ATTIC: Cable in an attic can run either atop joists or through holes drilled in joists; accessibility dictates how the cable will run. If a permanent staircase or ladder leads to the attic, cable running at an angle to structural members must be protected by guard strips, as shown above. In an attic reached through a crawl hole with no permanent stairs or ladder leading to it, the cable must be protected by guard strips only within 6 feet of the hole. Beyond that distance, cable can lie on top of the ceiling joists. Where cable runs parallel to joists, you can staple it to the joists' sides.

BASEMENT BASICS

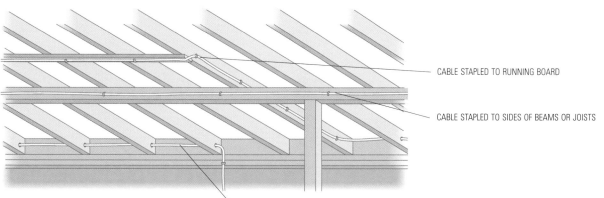

CABLE STAPLED TO RUNNING BOARD

CABLE STAPLED TO SIDES OF BEAMS OR JOISTS

CABLE RUNS THROUGH HOLES DRILLED IN JOISTS

USING BUILT-IN CLAMPS

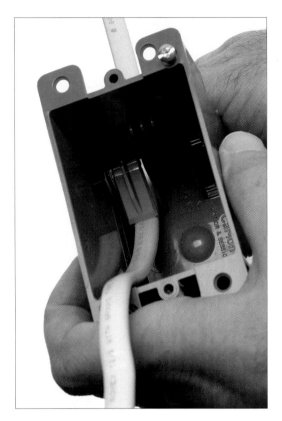

Some plastic boxes come with hinged knockouts instead of clamps. These "trap doors" open stubbornly (use a screwdriver tip) and work by friction. It's relatively easy to thread cable, once started, into the box; but it's very difficult to pull cable back out.

To connect cable to a box with a built-in clamp, feed the cable into the box through a knockout (you may first have to remove the clamp screw and clamp to reach a knockout located behind the clamp). Tighten the built-in clamp so that it holds the cable securely but does not bite into the sheathing.

CABLE CONNECTIONS

Now we're in the home stretch. If you're using a metal box, you must secure the cable to it, either with built-in cable clamps or a metal cable connector. If your box requires a cable connector, slip one onto the end of the cable and insert the cable through a knockout hole, leaving at least 6 to 8 inches of cable sticking into the box for wiring your new device. Fasten the connector to the box or tighten down on the clamp, as shown on the facing page.

Plastic boxes don't require clamping if the cable is secured within 8 inches of the box. In old work, where you're fishing cable behind walls, ceilings, or floors, you may not be able to support a cable within 8 inches of the box. In this case, you must secure the cable to the box. Some nonmetallic boxes are available with built-in cable clamps, as shown below. Some other models include hinged openings that grip cable reasonably well, as shown at left.

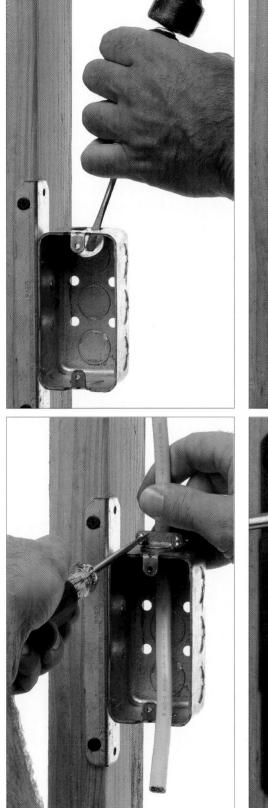

INSTALLING A METAL CABLE CONNECTOR

1 Open up a knockout
Using a hammer and screwdriver tip, sharply rap on the center of the round box knockout you wish to use.

2 Twist it off
Using a pair of lineman's pliers, push and pull the knockout disk until it separates from the box. It shouldn't take much work.

3 Secure the cable
Unscrew the locknut on the connector, then slip the connector over the cable end. Thread the cable through the knockout, allowing at least 6" to 8" of cable inside the box. Tighten the screws on the connector.

4 Secure the locknut
Slide the knurled locknut up the cable, then thread it by hand onto the connector. Use a screwdriver to tighten it securely.

ORKING WITH CONDUIT

Codes typically require that wires in exposed locations be enclosed in conduit. Below, we discuss techniques for installing thinwall metal conduit (type EMT) and flexible metal conduit (often called flex or Greenfield), as well as nonmetallic conduit (PVC). These types of conduit are good choices for interior projects. Other types, such as IMC and rigid steel, are used primarily outdoors. For details on these other conduit options, see Chapter Nine, "The Great Outdoors," beginning on page 156.

An important point to remember if you wire with conduit is that you must install the entire conduit system before pulling the individual conductors through it. Keep this in mind as you design your conduit system. Allow enough suitably placed fittings to ensure that the conductor pulls will be as direct as possible.

INSTALLING THINWALL METAL CONDUIT

Type EMT is a good choice for exposed wiring in laundry rooms, basements, and workshops. To determine what size conduit you need for the number of conductors you'll be using, refer to the chart on page 30. Remember that these are minimum requirements; it's easier to pull wires through a larger size.

To create a conduit system, you're going to have to cut, couple, and bend conduit to follow the cable route you've designed. Traditionally, EMT was bent with a conduit bender (page 44), which might still be the right choice if you have a lot of complex conduit work to do. Most homeowners, however, find it more practical to use prebent angles instead. A sampling of prebent angles and fittings is shown on the facing page.

You must use metal housing boxes with metal conduit. Screw the boxes to walls or ceilings through their backs, using panhead wood screws for wood framing and masonry screws or expanding anchors for concrete, brick, or block surfaces.

HOW TO CUT EMT

1 Cut conduit to length
Clamp EMT firmly in a vise, then cut it with a hacksaw. You'll get a cleaner cut if you support the cut end with your free hand during the last few saw strokes.

2 File the edges
Smooth and "de-burr" the inside of the conduit cut you just made, using a round metal-cutting file. This step removes sharp edges that could damage conductors.

CUTTING AND REAMING: A hacksaw or tubing cutter is all you need to cut EMT. But you must also clean out, or "ream," each cut to remove all burrs and sharp edges that could damage conductor insulation. Give a few quick turns around the inside of the cut with a round metal file.

ROUTING LOGISTICS: If your conduit run contains more than 360 degrees in total bends (such as four 90-degree bends or three 90-degree bends plus two 45-degree bends), you should plan to use a pull box somewhere along the line to help ease wires around the turns. This box is used only for pulling and connecting wires. The photo at right shows a square junction box with a single-device adapter plate used as a pull box. After the wires are pulled, a blank faceplate should be added. An alternative is to use corner elbows that break apart for pulling and then are sealed with cover plates. Always plan to install a pull box at a T intersection, where a conduit run splits in two.

EMT should be anchored with conduit straps within 3 feet of every box and at least every 10 feet elsewhere. Secure straps to wood framing with wood screws; on masonry walls, use masonry screws or expanding anchors.

MAKING CONNECTIONS: Use threadless setscrew couplings to join sections of EMT conduit. To install the coupling, simply slip the conduit inside the coupling's shoulder, then tighten the setscrew. Elbow fittings come with their own setscrew connectors.

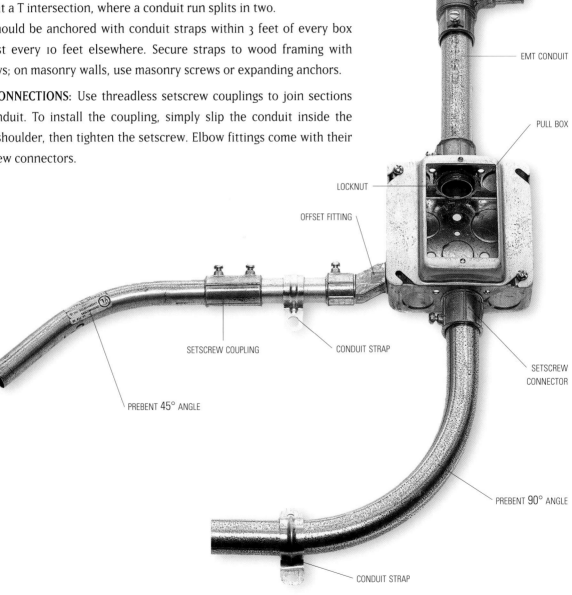

CORNER ELBOW

EMT CONDUIT

PULL BOX

LOCKNUT

OFFSET FITTING

SETSCREW COUPLING

CONDUIT STRAP

SETSCREW CONNECTOR

PREBENT 45° ANGLE

PREBENT 90° ANGLE

CONDUIT STRAP

JOINING CONDUIT TO BOXES: For indoor use, conduit joins a metal box through a knockout. You can't join conduit to a round box; use octagonal and square boxes instead. Be sure the boxes you get have knockouts large enough to accommodate the size conduit you're using.

If both the housing box and the conduit are mounted directly to the wall, you'll need to connect them with offset fittings. Secure the conduit to the offset fitting's integral setscrew connector, then join the fitting to the box with a locknut (see page 83).

GROUNDING EMT: Theoretically, a metal conduit system provides the grounding path back to the neutral bus bar in the service entrance panel. You aren't required to run a separate grounding wire with the conduit conductors. However, to maintain the grounding continuity, all couplings, connectors, fittings, and boxes must be metal and all connections must be tight. Because a faulty connection would interrupt the grounding path, many electricians play it safe and run a separate grounding wire with the other wires inside the conduit.

PULLING WIRES IN CONDUIT

Once you've installed your conduit and boxes, you need to pull the wires through. The following tips can help make this potentially vexing task as easy as possible.

If you're pulling a few #10, #12, or #14 wires, pull directly with a fish tape. Unreel the tape through the conduit until it's exposed at the other end. Strip several inches of insulation off the end of each wire and bend the ends tightly over the fish tape loop, as shown on page 65. Wrap the splice with electrical tape. Then pull the wires through the conduit by rewinding the fish tape. (If you have a long, complex route to follow, you can fish the wires in several stages, working toward a pull box or the removable cover plate of an elbow fitting.)

To avoid kinking or scraping insulation, have someone feed the wires in as you pull. In many instances it also helps to have your helper apply so-called "pulling lubricant" while feeding the wires into the conduit. Pulling lubricant is a special compound similar in consistency to waterless soap that makes conductors slide more freely yet is compatible with electrical insulation.

If you must do the pulling alone, precut all wires to the conduit length plus at least 3 feet. Lay the wires in a straight line from the end of the conduit so the pull will be as direct and easy as possible.

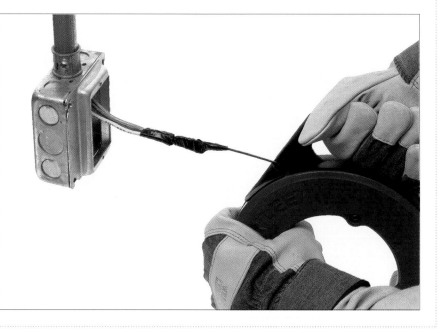

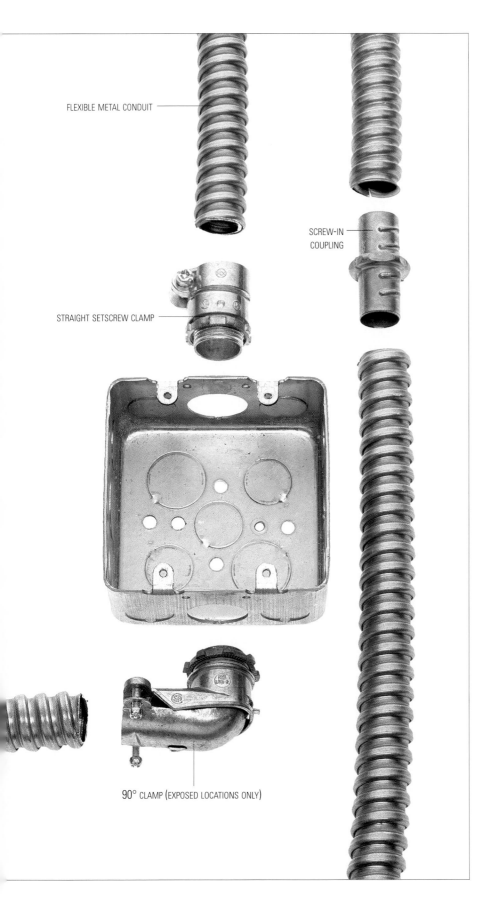

FLEXIBLE METAL CONDUIT

SCREW-IN COUPLING

STRAIGHT SETSCREW CLAMP

90° CLAMP (EXPOSED LOCATIONS ONLY)

INSTALLING FLEXIBLE METAL CONDUIT

This flexible conduit, often called "flex" or Greenfield, is a good choice where EMT might be too hard to bend and for wiring appliances such as water heaters or kitchen cooktops that might require moving for servicing. The photo at left shows several examples of flexible conduit connectors.

CUTTING: Cut flexible conduit with a hacksaw. You won't need to ream the ends if you use screw-in connectors and couplings.

BENDING AND SUPPORTING FLEXIBLE CONDUIT: Despite its flexibility, runs of flexible conduit between boxes and fittings must not bend more than the equivalent of four quarter turns. Flex must be supported with a conduit strap within 12 inches of every box or fitting and at intervals no longer than 4 1/2 feet.

GROUNDING FLEXIBLE CONDUIT: Because of code restrictions, most flexible conduit systems are grounded by running a separate grounding wire along with the circuit conductors.

INSTALLING RIGID NONMETALLIC CONDUIT

Several types of nonmetallic conduit are available, but Schedule 40 PVC is the one most homeowners use. It's rigid, flame-retardant, and heat- and sunlight-resistant. Though prohibited by some codes, this plastic conduit can be used in place of EMT in most areas; it's a bit cheaper than EMT and easier to cut and join. Note that PVC irrigation pipe is not the same thing as Schedule 40 PVC; look for the insignia of an electrical materials testing laboratory to make sure you're getting the right product.

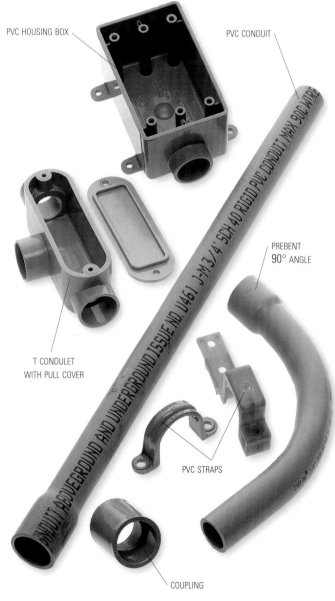

PVC HOUSING BOX

PVC CONDUIT

T CONDULET WITH PULL COVER

PREBENT 90° ANGLE

PVC STRAPS

COUPLING

You must use special PVC housing boxes with plastic conduit. (They're not the same as those used for NM cable.) Nonmetallic conduit does not constitute a grounded system, so you must run a separate grounding wire with the circuit conductors.

CUTTING AND TRIMMING: You can cut PVC conduit easily with a hacksaw or a handsaw. After cutting, trim the ends inside and out with a pocket knife to remove any rough edges that might damage conductor insulation.

JOINING PVC: PVC comes in 10-foot lengths, each with one coupling. Other fittings are available; for a sampling, see the photo at left. Glue conduit and fittings together with gray conduit cement (not the water pipe cement used with PVC irrigation pipe).

BENDING: It's much simpler to use prebent PVC angles, as shown at left. If necessary, though, bends in PVC can be made with a special infrared heater. Don't try to heat PVC with a torch; you'll just char the conduit.

Design your run so that no piece of conduit between two boxes or fittings bends more than the equivalent of four quarter turns.

SUPPORTING PVC: Supports for nonmetallic conduit should be placed within 4 feet of each box or fitting. In most instances, additional supports should be placed at least every 4 feet.

FINISHING UP

Once the boxes are mounted, some holes may need patching. If you've notched into walls or ceilings in the process of wiring, now is also the time to make them look like new again. Here are some tips for putting everything back together.

REPAIRING PLASTER: The National Electrical Code requires that you repair gaps or open spaces around the edges of housing boxes in plaster walls and ceilings.

Patching around a box is a simple matter. Use a wide-blade putty knife to apply commercial plaster compound. Try to match the texture of the surrounding wall.

For larger holes you'll have to nail on some backing (such as lath), clean and moisten the edges of the hole, and, in some cases, apply more than one coat.

REPAIRING GYPSUM WALLBOARD: For small repairs, simply use a wide-blade putty knife and some spackling compound.

To replace a larger section, you'll need to cut a new piece of wallboard to fill the hole. If there are no studs or joists underneath on which to nail the replacement piece, add some wooden blocks for support.

Attach replacement wallboard with drywall screws or nails, dimpling the surface slightly at the fastener heads as shown at top right. Use a wide-blade putty knife to spread joint compound across the dimples. With joint tape and compound, cover the edge joints around the replacement as shown.

Apply a second coat of compound to the nail heads and tape, feathering the edges of the first coat to produce a relatively smooth surface. Let dry, then sand the nail dimples and joints.

For a smooth wall, you may have to apply a third coat to both the joints and the nail heads and sand again. To duplicate a skip-trowel texture, apply a large amount of joint compound with a broad palette knife and draw the blade over the surface in one direction. A plaster texture can be created with the same tool by applying the compound in a semicircular motion. Duplicate a stipple finish with a paintbrush.

Let dry, then paint the surface.

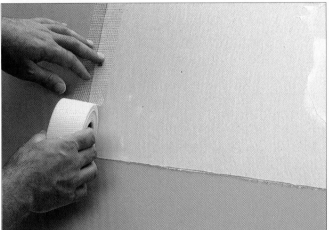

To repair wallboard, first screw a patch to wall studs or ceiling joists, driving fasteners slightly below the surface (top). Fill fastener holes with joint compound, then tape the joints (center). Finally, gently spread compound atop the tape (bottom).

FINISH WIRING

Now we're in the homestretch. If you've extended an existing circuit (pages 62–71) or added a new one (pages 72–81), it's time to finally hook up that receptacle, switch, light fixture, or appliance. In new construction, this so-called "finish work" is completed once new walls and ceilings are in place. Of course, to replace an existing device, you won't need to run cable or wield a paintbrush—simply turn to the appropriate section and follow the instruction details. Just be sure to shut off power to the circuit before beginning work.

You'll need some background info to complete this finish work. If you aren't sure what devices you need, see Chapter Two, "Nuts and Bolts," beginning on page 26. For a step-by-step course in basic wiring skills, see Chapter Four, "Wiring Know-How," beginning on page 48. Before doing any finish wiring, first check your local code to find out if there are any specific requirements in your area.

The very last step in this process is to make the connection to the power source—the existing circuit, service entrance panel, or sub-panel. We show you how on pages 120–125. However, if you're at all unsure of your abilities, it's best to leave this final job to a licensed electrician—you can still do all the work leading up to that point.

Fᴵʀꜱᴛ ᴛʜɪɴɢꜱ ꜰɪʀꜱᴛ

Installing receptacles, switches, and light fixtures is straightforward—assuming that you've planned carefully up to this point. Whether you're replacing a faulty switch or wiring a home from scratch, you'll first need an understanding of electrical concepts and how they play out in your own house. For a refresher course, see Chapter One, "An Introduction to the Basics."

The actual wiring is largely a matter of stripping cables or wires, connecting wires to screw terminals, and splicing wires together with wire nuts or compression sleeves. You'll find step-by-step details about each of these operations in Chapter Four, "Wiring Know-How," beginning on page 48. Also be sure to read "Getting Grounded," on the facing page.

The photos and drawings in this chapter are designed to be as clear and concise as possible. The wiring diagrams show typical arrangements for receptacles, switches, and light fixtures using nonmetallic sheathed cable with ground, metal boxes, and wire nuts for wire splices. The light fixtures are grounded to the boxes through the mounting screws. Many other combinations are possible, of course, but these drawings should guide you in planning your circuit arrangements.

We've shown metal housing boxes in the diagrams because they're a little trickier to wire than nonmetallic boxes. If you've chosen a plastic box (see pages 32–33), you can simply omit the grounding connection to the box itself.

The size wire nut you need depends on the number and size of the wires you'll be joining. We've shown wire nuts in various colors, but each manufacturer has its own color code to distinguish the various sizes. The packaging or bin labels will tell you what wires each wire nut color will take.

It's a very good idea to test your work once you've made the hookups. First walk through each circuit looking for problems. Think about what each wire is supposed to do, then verify that that's how you wired the circuit. For a closer look at basic testing procedures, see page 175.

COLOR CODING— AND ONE EXCEPTION

The wires illustrated on these pages are color-coded as follows:
- Hot wires: thick black or red
- Neutral wires: thick white
- Grounding wires: narrow copper-colored or green

Actual hot wires are usually black or red, but may also be any color other than white, gray, or green. Actual neutral wires are white or gray; grounding wires are bare copper or aluminum, green, or in rare cases, black.

Occasionally, the white wire in NM cable is used as a second hot wire—a switch loop (pages 100–101) is one example. In these cases the white wire should be taped or painted black near terminals and splices for easy identification.

GETTING GROUNDED

Your new device must be correctly grounded to the circuit grounding wire, which in turn runs back to the service entrance panel and on to the grounding electrode conductor. Grounding hookups vary depending on whether you're using metal or nonmetallic boxes, whether your device contains a grounding terminal or grounding wire, and whether the box is located in the middle of the circuit or at the end.

GROUNDING METAL BOXES: Metal boxes must be grounded. A separate grounding wire in NM cable provides the path for ground; a grounding screw or grounding clip bonds the box to the wire.

When you install an ungrounded switch or light fixture in the last box of a circuit run, attach the grounding wire of NM cable directly to the box. If the device has a grounding terminal, you'll have to add a grounding jumper from the terminal (see drawing top right). Twist all grounding wires and jumpers together and crimp with a wire nut or compression sleeve.

For a box that's not at the end of a circuit, you will have to make up one or more grounding jumpers (see right). For grounding jumpers, always use wire the same size as the circuit wires.

GROUNDING NONMETALLIC BOXES: Since nonmetallic boxes don't conduct electricity, they need not be grounded. Then what should be done with the grounding wire in NM cable when you use nonmetallic boxes?

A grounded receptacle or grounded switch in a nonmetallic box is no problem. If the box is at the end of the circuit, simply attach the grounding wire to the grounding terminal of the receptacle or switch. If the box is in the middle of a circuit run, the cable grounding wires are joined with a grounding jumper from the device.

If the device doesn't have a grounding terminal (as is the case with ungrounded switches and some older receptacles), bypass the device. If in the middle of a run, just join the cable grounding wires coming in and going out of the box. If your switch is at the end of the circuit, hold the grounding wire between the switch bracket and the box (see drawing upper right) with the mounting screw.

To ground a light fixture, choose a round fixture box with a metal grounding bar. If the fixture is at the end of the circuit, attach the cable grounding wire directly to the bar (see drawing at right). If the fixture is in the middle of a circuit, make up a grounding jumper to join the grounding bar to the cables' grounding wires. The light fixture will automatically be grounded when attached to the grounded box.

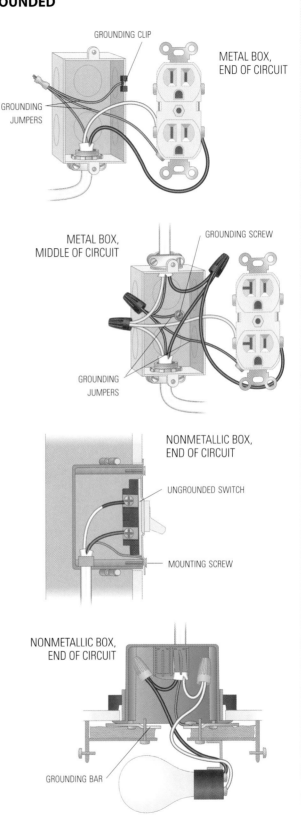

GROUNDING CLIP

METAL BOX, END OF CIRCUIT

GROUNDING JUMPERS

METAL BOX, MIDDLE OF CIRCUIT

GROUNDING SCREW

GROUNDING JUMPERS

NONMETALLIC BOX, END OF CIRCUIT

UNGROUNDED SWITCH

MOUNTING SCREW

NONMETALLIC BOX, END OF CIRCUIT

GROUNDING BAR

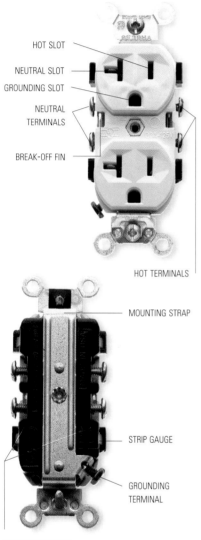

HOT SLOT
NEUTRAL SLOT
GROUNDING SLOT
NEUTRAL TERMINALS
BREAK-OFF FIN

HOT TERMINALS

MOUNTING STRAP

STRIP GAUGE

GROUNDING TERMINAL

BACKWIRING HOLES

RECEPTACLE WIRING

Receptacles are designed for either 120-volt, 120/240-volt, or straight 240-volt use. Remember that all receptacles are also rated for a specific amperage (for details, see pages 34–35).

CAUTION: Before wiring any receptacle, be sure to disconnect the circuit by removing the fuse or switching off the circuit breaker. For a 240-volt circuit, you may have to remove two fuses or trip a two-handled breaker (see pages 172–173).

INSTALLING 120-VOLT RECEPTACLES

Grounded 120-volt duplex receptacles, the kind most commonly used in homes, consist of an upper and a lower outlet with three slots each. Each outlet's large (neutral) slot accepts the wide prong of a three-prong plug; the small (hot) slot is for the narrow prong, and the U-shaped grounding slot is for the grounding prong. Receptacles for 20-amp, small-appliance circuits differ from 15-amp versions; be sure to buy what you need. Receptacles marked AL-CU may be used with either copper or aluminum wire. Unmarked receptacles and those marked with a slash through the AL symbol can be used with copper wire only.

As shown at left, grounded receptacles have three different colors of screw terminals. The brass-colored screws on one side of the receptacle are hot terminals; the white- or silver-colored screws on the opposite side are neutral terminals; and the green screw is the grounding terminal. Black (hot) circuit wires connect to brass-colored terminals; white (neutral) wires connect to silver terminals; and bare or green grounding wires connect to the green terminal. Wiring configurations are shown on pages 94–95.

If the receptacle is a backwired type, the black and white wires can be inserted into the holes located on the back of the receptacle (unless you have aluminum wiring, in which case you'd use the screw terminals for all wire connections). Black wires insert into the holes located on the same side of the receptacle as the brass-colored screws; white wires insert into the holes on the same side as the silver-colored screws. A molded plastic strip gauge on the back shows how much insulation to strip off the wire ends. The grounding wire must still be attached to the green screw terminal on the receptacle. Backwiring basics are discussed on page 53. Note: It's now illegal to backwire receptacles—at least 20-amp models—in some areas.

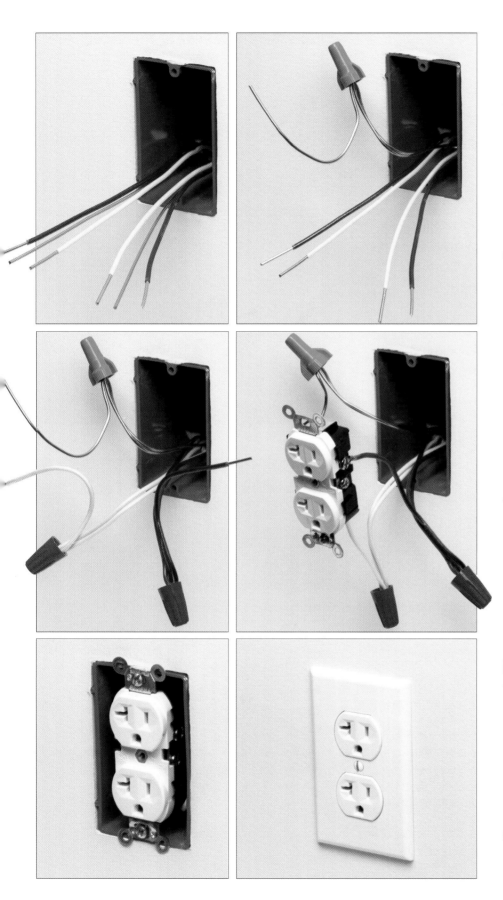

HOW TO WIRE A RECEPTACLE

1 Strip the wires
First remove the outer sheath of insulation and all separation materials from the cables inside the housing box; then strip insulation from the individual wire ends.

2 Connect grounding wires
Use a wire nut or compression sleeve to join the circuit's grounding wires with a grounding jumper from the receptacle. For a metal box, include a jumper from the box.

3 Connect hot and neutral wires
Join pairs of hot (black) and neutral (white) wires entering and leaving the box. Add a jumper from each splice.

4 Wire the receptacle
Attach the hot jumper to one brass screw terminal, and the neutral jumper to the silver terminal. Secure the grounding jumper to the green grounding screw. Tighten unused screw terminals.

5 Mount the receptacle
Carefully fold back the wires and screw the receptacle to the box. Adjust the screws in the mounting slots until the receptacle is straight. If it isn't flush, shim it out, using the break-off portions of the receptacle's plaster ears or washers sold for that purpose.

6 Attach the faceplate
Finally, screw the faceplate to the receptacle, as shown, using the screw included with the faceplate.

WIRING DIAGRAMS:
120-VOLT RECEPTACLES

The drawings at right show typical wiring configurations for receptacles in the middle or at the end of a circuit. Use them as a reference when you're planning a wiring route or installing a receptacle.

The usual arrangement is for several receptacles to be wired in parallel (see page 15) with all outlets always hot. In other cases, the power may need to be routed first through a fixture box and/or a switch box. A wall switch may also control a receptacle.

The drawings on these pages assume your housing boxes are metal; if they're not, you still have to ground each receptacle, but there's no need to also ground the boxes.

Whether you're using screw terminals or back-wiring holes to connect the circuit wires to the receptacle, always attach the grounding wire to the green grounding screw on the receptacle. Remember, you must be able to pull out and disconnect a receptacle without interrupting the grounding continuity of the circuit.

RECEPTACLE AT THE END OF THE CIRCUIT, ALWAYS HOT

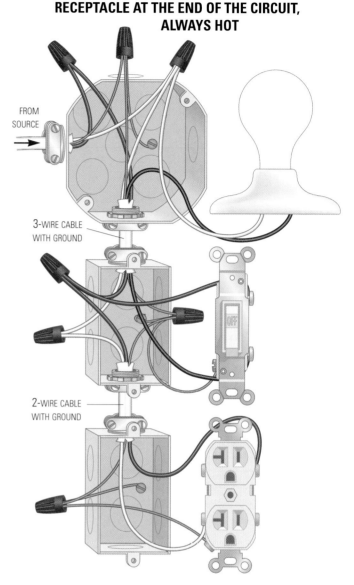

FROM SOURCE

3-WIRE CABLE WITH GROUND

2-WIRE CABLE WITH GROUND

SPLIT-CIRCUIT RECEPTACLES

Occasionally it may be appropriate to have the outlets of a duplex receptacle operate independently. For example, you might want one outlet to be controlled by a switch and the other one to be always hot. Or you may wish to wire the two outlets of a receptacle into different circuits. To make the outlets operate independently, use pliers to remove the break-off fin that connects them.

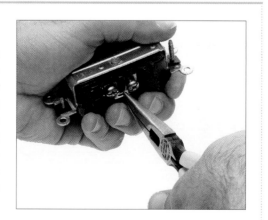

RECEPTACLES AT THE END OF THE CIRCUIT

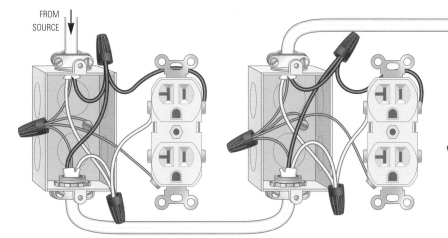

FROM SOURCE

SWITCH-CONTROLLED RECEPTACLE

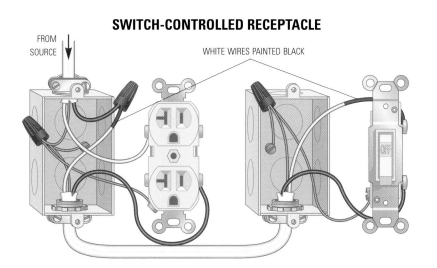

FROM SOURCE

WHITE WIRES PAINTED BLACK

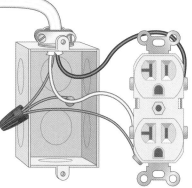

UNGROUNDED CIRCUIT?

If you want to add a receptacle to a circuit that doesn't have a grounding wire, you can either use a grounding type and run a separate grounding wire to an approved ground; install a GFCI; or, in some areas, use an old-style, nongrounding receptacle. See Chapter Ten, pages 184–185, for details.

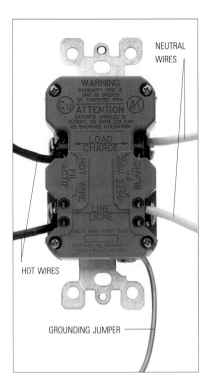

NEUTRAL WIRES

HOT WIRES

GROUNDING JUMPER

INSTALLING A RECEPTACLE-TYPE GFCI

A ground fault circuit interrupter, or GFCI, is an important safety device that is now required by code in kitchens, bathrooms, garages, and all outdoor locations.

A receptacle-type GFCI can be wired to protect a single location in the event of a current leak, or to protect multiple locations by also shutting down all devices on the circuit "downstream" of it. Wiring a GFCI is similar to wiring a standard receptacle except the terminals are labeled "line" and "load." To protect a single location, attach the incoming pair of black and white wires to the "hot" and "white" (neutral) terminals on the "line" end. For multiple-location wiring, the incoming wires are connected the same way, but the outgoing pair of black and white wires attach to the "load" end.

As an alternative to installing a GFCI receptacle, you could install a GFCI-type circuit breaker in the service entrance panel or subpanel in place of the standard circuit breaker protecting that particular circuit. For details, see page 18. In this case, you'd need only standard 120-volt receptacles, not receptacle-type GFCIs.

WHAT ABOUT GANGED DEVICES?

Modern homes often include multiple devices in one grouping, or "gang," for a variety of light fixtures, a fan, and/or a nearby small appliance. To install these side-by-side devices, you'll need a double-gang, triple-gang, or four-gang housing box. A triple-gang box is shown at right. Buy the deepest box you can get—all those wires can eat up a lot of box space.

Route multiple cables to the box as required, then connect the individual devices as you would any single switch or receptacle. A variety of faceplates is available for various combinations of ganged devices.

What if you run out of space in a box? You can effectively get two switches in the space of one with a double switch, or use a switch-receptacle combination. Both devices are shown. ✂

240-VOLT RECEPTACLES

To eliminate the possibility of plugging a 120-volt appliance into a 240-volt receptacle, higher-voltage circuits use special receptacles, as shown on page 35, and matching attachment plugs.

240-VOLT RECEPTACLE

WARNING

Although 240-volt is no more difficult to install than 120-volt wiring, the potential danger from shock or fire is far greater. If you're at all uncertain about your abilities, call in a professional to inspect your work and/or to make the final hookups.

Because a straight 240-volt circuit has two hot wires, a grounding wire, and no neutral wire, you'll need a two-pole, three-wire receptacle of the correct amperage.

Circuits rated for 120/240 volts have two hot wires and a neutral wire. When you're replacing an existing receptacle, some codes may permit you to ground the device connected to it through the neutral wire; in that case, you can use a three-pole, three-wire receptacle. However, in new construction, you must include a separate grounding wire and use a three-pole, four-wire receptacle. Two examples are shown here.

Many 240-volt receptacles feature push-in terminals, as shown at lower right. To connect wires to them, strip insulation from the ends of the wires, using the strip gauge on the receptacle's back as a guide; push the wires into the correct terminals and tighten the screws.

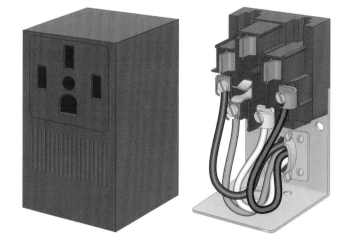

120/240-VOLT SURFACE-MOUNT RECEPTACLE

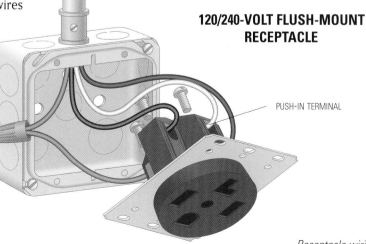

120/240-VOLT FLUSH-MOUNT RECEPTACLE

PUSH-IN TERMINAL

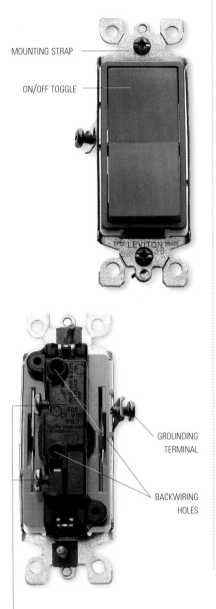

MOUNTING STRAP

ON/OFF TOGGLE

GROUNDING TERMINAL

BACKWIRING HOLES

HOT TERMINALS

SWITCH WIRING

Most switches in a home are of the single-pole type: an on-off toggle controls a light or receptacle from a single location. However, a whole range of specialty switches—dimmers, pilot switches, timers, and so forth—expand on the tried-and-true switching function. To control a light fixture or receptacle from two locations, you'll need a pair of three-way switches. To operate a device from three locations, two three-way switches work with a four-way switch. (For a discussion of switch options, see pages 36–37.) All these installations are detailed on the following pages.

INSTALLING SINGLE-POLE SWITCHES

Single-pole switches have two terminals of the same color (usually silver or brass) for wire connections and an obvious right side up. Some models also have terminals for backwiring (see page 53). All switches are wired into hot wires only; with a single-pole switch, it makes no difference which hot wire goes to which terminal. Most new designs are wired the same way as the standard single-pole switches. Switches marked AL-CU may be used with either copper or aluminum wire. Unmarked receptacles and those marked with a slash through the AL symbol can be used with copper wire only.

Traditional 120-volt switches had no grounding wires because their plastic toggles were considered shockproof. However, for extra safety, many switches now are available with grounding terminals. Installation is similar to that of a grounded receptacle (see "Getting Grounded," on page 91): join the incoming circuit grounding wires to a jumper connected to the green switch terminal, securing the wires with a wire nut or compression sleeve. If the housing box is metal, you'll also need to include a short grounding jumper to the box's grounding screw or grounding clip.

INSTALLING A SINGLE-POLE SWITCH

1 Strip wire ends
First remove the outer sheath of insulation and all separation materials from the cables inside the box; strip the insulation from the wire ends.

2 Splice neutral wires
Join the neutral (white) wires, if any, and cap with a wire nut.

3 Make the grounding connection
Join the grounding wires with a wire nut or compression sleeve. For a metal box, include a grounding jumper from the box.

4 Connect the hot wires
Connect the hot wires to the switch's screw terminals. It makes no difference which wire goes to which terminal. Secure the grounding jumper to the green grounding terminal.

5 Mount the switch
Fold the wires behind the switch and carefully push the switch into the box. Screw the switch to the box; align the switch vertically by adjusting the screws in the mounting slots. If it isn't flush with the wall, shim it out using the break-off portions of the switch's plaster ears or special washers sold for that purpose.

6 Attach the faceplate
Finally, screw the faceplate to the switch, as shown, using the screws included with the faceplate.

POWER ENTERS SWITCH BOX

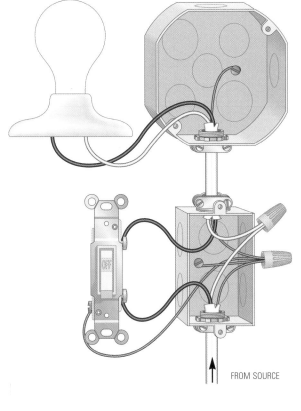

FROM SOURCE

WIRING DIAGRAMS: SINGLE-POLE SWITCHES

Because of cable-routing logistics, circuit wires may run from the service entrance panel or a subpanel to a switch in one of two ways: the wires can run through the switch box to the fixture that the switch controls, or they can run to the fixture box first, with a switch loop to the switch box. Three typical setups are shown here. The single-pole switches shown include grounding terminals. If your switch doesn't, just omit the grounding jumper between cable grounding wires and switch. For further details, see page 91.

POWER ENTERS FIXTURE BOX

SWITCH IN MIDDLE OF CIRCUIT

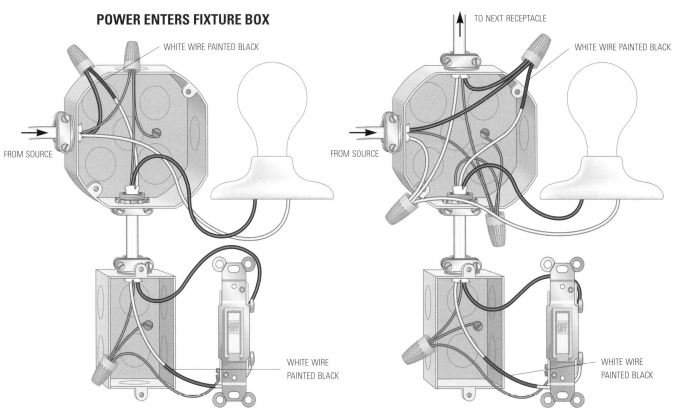

WHITE WIRE PAINTED BLACK

FROM SOURCE

WHITE WIRE PAINTED BLACK

TO NEXT RECEPTACLE

WHITE WIRE PAINTED BLACK

FROM SOURCE

WHITE WIRE PAINTED BLACK

SPECIALTY SWITCHES

Specialized switch types such as dimmers, timers, and motion sensors often have two hot-wire leads instead of terminals. Simply splice the switch's leads to the hot wires inside the box, using wire nuts. Some pilot switches and those with timers also require a neutral wire.

Several specialty switch hookups are detailed below.

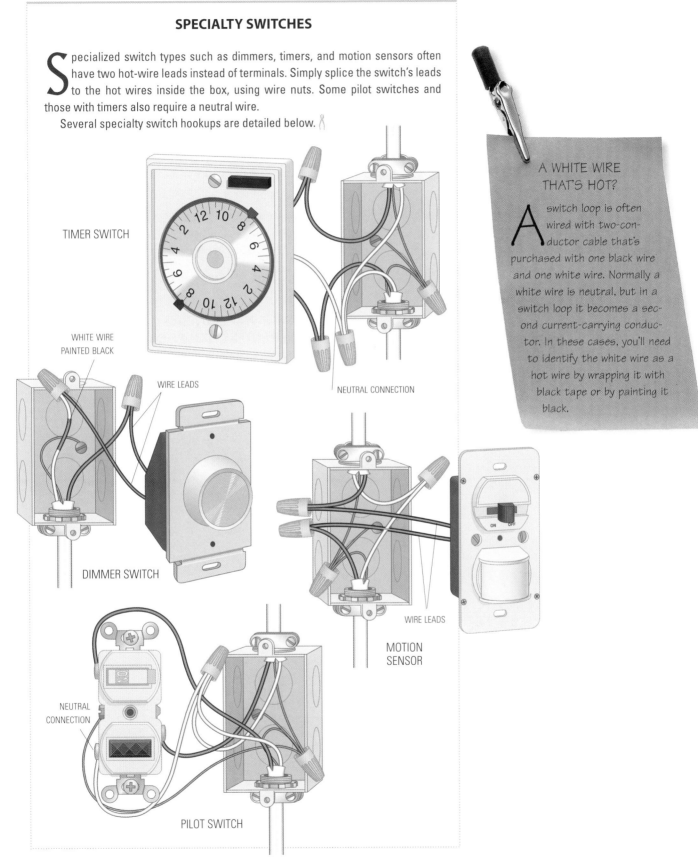

TIMER SWITCH

WHITE WIRE
PAINTED BLACK

WIRE LEADS

NEUTRAL CONNECTION

DIMMER SWITCH

WIRE LEADS

MOTION
SENSOR

NEUTRAL
CONNECTION

PILOT SWITCH

A WHITE WIRE THAT'S HOT?

A switch loop is often wired with two-conductor cable that's purchased with one black wire and one white wire. Normally a white wire is neutral, but in a switch loop it becomes a second current-carrying conductor. In these cases, you'll need to identify the white wire as a hot wire by wrapping it with black tape or by painting it black.

WIRING THREE-WAY SWITCHES

If you want to be able to turn a light on and off at two locations, such as at the top and bottom of a staircase or at either end of a hallway, consider installing a pair of three-way switches. They're called three-way switches because there are three possible positions: both up, both down, one up and one down.

Three-way switches have two terminals of the same color (brass or silver); these are sometimes called traveler terminals. A third terminal, of a darker color, is called a common terminal. Either end of a three-way switch can be the top. It's important to observe, though, which terminal is the common one; the exact placement may be different than it is on the models shown here.

To power a pair of three-way switches, circuit wires may run first through one switch box, through the fixture box, or through both switch boxes. To link the switches, first connect the hot wire from the service entrance panel or subpanel to the common terminal of one switch; then connect the hot wire from the fixture or receptacle to the common terminal of the other switch. Finally, run hot wires from the two remaining (traveler) terminals on one switch to the two remaining terminals on the other.

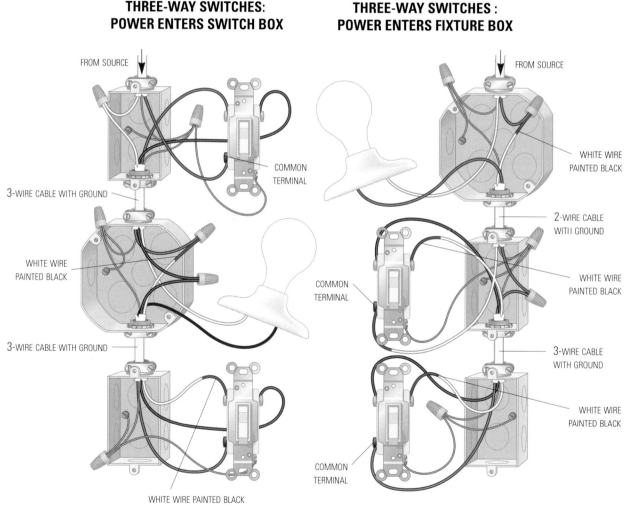

**THREE-WAY SWITCHES:
POWER ENTERS SWITCH BOX**

FROM SOURCE

COMMON TERMINAL

3-WIRE CABLE WITH GROUND

WHITE WIRE PAINTED BLACK

3-WIRE CABLE WITH GROUND

WHITE WIRE PAINTED BLACK

**THREE-WAY SWITCHES :
POWER ENTERS FIXTURE BOX**

FROM SOURCE

WHITE WIRE PAINTED BLACK

2-WIRE CABLE WITH GROUND

WHITE WIRE PAINTED BLACK

COMMON TERMINAL

3-WIRE CABLE WITH GROUND

WHITE WIRE PAINTED BLACK

COMMON TERMINAL

THREE-WAY SWITCHES: POWER GOES THROUGH SWITCHES TO FIXTURE

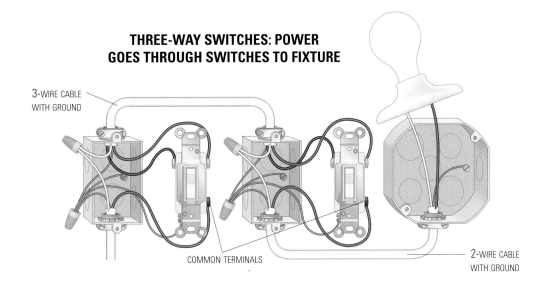

3-WIRE CABLE WITH GROUND

COMMON TERMINALS

2-WIRE CABLE WITH GROUND

WIRING FOUR-WAY SWITCHES

A four-way switch works in tandem with a pair of three-way switches to control a light from three locations, such as from three different entry/exit points in a room. The four-way switch is always placed in the middle of the wiring run, with the three-way switches on the ends. You can even add more four-way switches, as shown below, as long as the three-way switches remain on the ends.

Four-way switches have two pairs of screw terminals—usually one brass pair and one copper pair. The pairs are commonly found on opposite sides at top and bottom, as shown; however, some brands differ.

To install a four-way switch, connect one pair of wires to the traveler terminals on one of the three-way switches; then connect a second pair to the traveler terminals on the remaining three-way switch.

FOUR-WAY SWITCHES

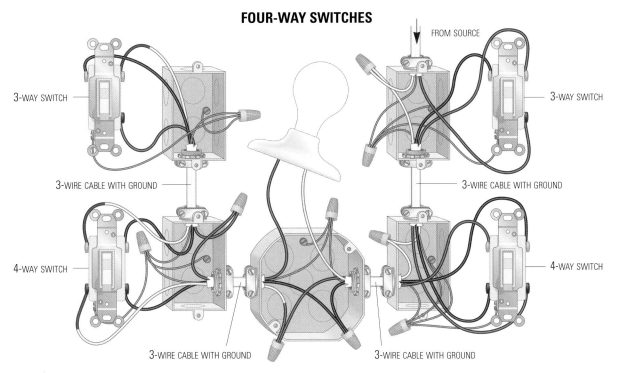

FROM SOURCE

3-WAY SWITCH

3-WAY SWITCH

3-WIRE CABLE WITH GROUND

3-WIRE CABLE WITH GROUND

4-WAY SWITCH

4-WAY SWITCH

3-WIRE CABLE WITH GROUND

3-WIRE CABLE WITH GROUND

INSTALLING LIGHT FIXTURES

If your plans call for new lighting, you can choose from surface-mounted, track, or recessed fixtures. On the following pages, we provide instructions for installing basic models of all three types. For more details on lighting options and bulb choices, see pages 38–39. Low-voltage light fixtures and accessories are discussed in Chapter Eight, "Low Voltage, High Tech," on pages 142–143.

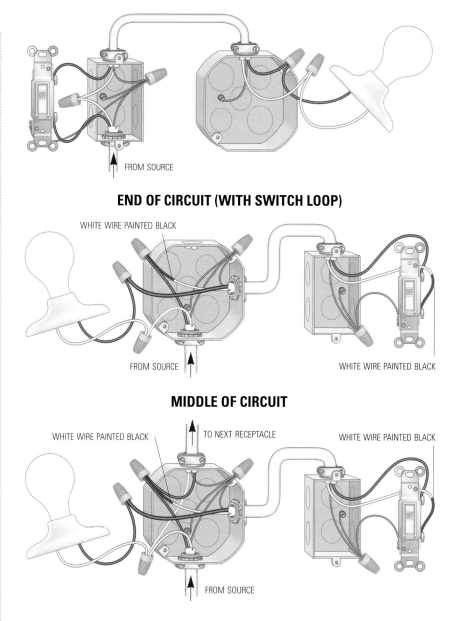

END OF CIRCUIT

FROM SOURCE

END OF CIRCUIT (WITH SWITCH LOOP)

WHITE WIRE PAINTED BLACK

FROM SOURCE

WHITE WIRE PAINTED BLACK

MIDDLE OF CIRCUIT

WHITE WIRE PAINTED BLACK

TO NEXT RECEPTACLE

WHITE WIRE PAINTED BLACK

FROM SOURCE

WIRING DIAGRAMS: LIGHT FIXTURES

Normally, one or two cables enter a fixture box. Power may run to the switch box first and then on to one or more light fixtures; or wires may be routed to the fixture box first, with a separate switch loop. Three common setups are shown above.

Note: A switch loop is wired with two-conductor cable that contains one black conductor and one white conductor. In some switch loops, the white wire may substitute as a second current-carrying wire; if this is the case, identify the white wire as a hot wire by wrapping it with black tape or by painting it black.

INSTALLING SURFACE-MOUNTED FIXTURES

Surface-mounted light fixtures are either mounted directly to a housing box or suspended from the box by chains or a cord.

The size and weight of the new fixture determine the mounting method. Small, lightweight ceiling and wall fixtures generally can be screwed directly to the fixture box's mounting ears. Heavier fixtures may need to be fastened to the box with a mounting bar, hickey, or stud (all three are shown below). Any fixture that weighs more than 50 pounds must be secured to a joist or beam, as well as to the box.

New fixtures usually come with their own mounting hardware; the hardware is adaptable to any standard fixture box.

GROUNDING METAL FIXTURES: All incandescent and fluorescent fixtures with exposed metal parts must be grounded. If you've chosen a metal box, the nipple or screws holding the fixture to the box will ground the fixture. If the box is at the end of the circuit, attach the grounding wire of the cable directly to the box's grounding screw or clip. If more than one cable enters the box, make a grounding jumper (pigtail), as shown on page 91.

A nonmetallic box doesn't need grounding, but you'll have to ground the fixture. Look for a box with a metal grounding bar (see page 91). If the fixture is at the end of the circuit, attach the cable grounding wire to the bar. If the fixture is in the middle of the circuit, make a grounding jumper to join the cable grounding wire to the bar.

A cord- or chain-hung fixture also needs a grounding wire run from the light bulb socket to the box. Most new fixtures are prewired with a grounding wire.

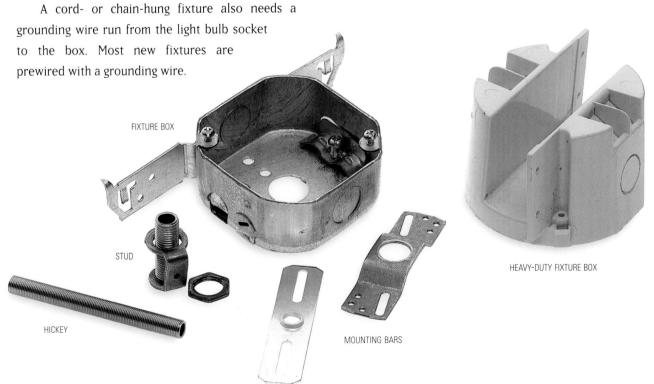

FIXTURE BOX

STUD

HICKEY

MOUNTING BARS

HEAVY-DUTY FIXTURE BOX

ATTACHING AN INCANDESCENT FIXTURE: Once you've routed cable and installed the box and switch, mounting the fixture itself is straightforward.

To connect the fixture, splice the box's black wire to the fixture's hot wire, and the box's white wire to the fixture's neutral wire. If the fixture has a grounding wire, connect it to the other grounding wires in the box and, if the box is metal, to the grounding screw or clip. Cap all splices with wire nuts. Mount the fixture with the hardware specified by the manufacturer.

Note: If the fixture is heavy, have a helper hold it while you work, or hang it from the box with a hook made from a wire coat hanger.

INSTALLING AN INCANDESCENT FIXTURE

1 Attach any mounting hardware

The fixture we're installing attaches to a grounding bar that's first screwed to the nonmetallic housing box. Mounting bolts are then loosely fastened to the bar.

2 Make the connections

Splice the black fixture wire to the circuit hot wire, and the white fixture wire to the incoming neutral wire. This fixture has its own grounding wire; secure it to the grounding screw on the grounding bar.

3 Secure the canopy

Carefully fold wires into the housing box, then secure the canopy to the box. This fixture has keyhole slots that slip over the mounting bolts. Push the canopy into place, then tighten the bolts.

4 Add the trim

Finally, screw in the light bulb or bulbs, and then add the diffusing globe atop the bulbs. This globe slips over the long center hickey and is held in place by a threaded end piece.

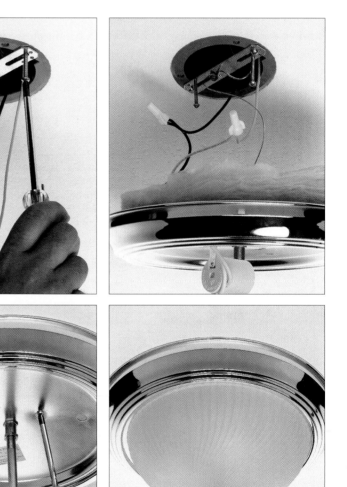

ATTACHING A FLUORESCENT FIXTURE: To mount a typical ceiling fixture, such as the one shown below, you first must feed cable through a knockout in the fixture's top or side. Secure cable to the fixture with a metal cable connector, then firmly anchor the fixture to the ceiling—with wood screws into joists or, if joists aren't accessible, with toggle bolts.

Make internal wire hookups as directed by the fixture manufacturer, using wire nuts for splices. You may also need to add pigtails and a grounding jumper to bridge the gaps between internal fixture wires and the point where cable enters the fixture.

INSTALLING A FLUORESCENT FIXTURE

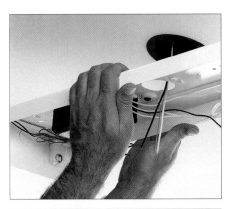

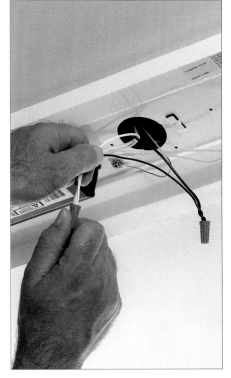

I Bring wires into the fixture

Open up a knockout in the fixture canopy, then feed incoming wires through the hole. This fixture is mounted directly below a ceiling box; if yours isn't, plan to secure cable to a smaller knockout with a metal cable clamp.

2 Fasten the fixture to the ceiling

When possible, drive screws through the fixture canopy and into ceiling joists. If joists don't align with the fixture, secure fixture to ceiling material with toggle bolts instead.

3 Make the connections

Splice the fixture's black wire to the circuit hot wire, and the white fixture wire to the cable's incoming neutral wire. Secure the circuit grounding wire to the fixture's grounding screw.

4 Add the trim

Finally, slip the ends of the fluorescent tubes into the tubeholders, then add the diffusing panel atop the tubes. Like this one, most diffusing panels simply snap into place.

INSTALLING TRACK SYSTEMS

Track systems mount to the wall or ceiling either directly or with mounting clips. Power is provided from a fixture box or, in some cases, through a cord plugged into an existing receptacle. For flexibility (and sometimes to distribute the load), tracks are often wired into two separate circuits controlled by two switches or dimmers.

ATTACHING THE CONNECTOR: A track system with a wire-in connector hooks up directly to a fixture box. You'll need as many wall switches as your track has circuits. The standard wire-in connector brings power to the end of the track. By using an optional in-line connector available with some track systems, you can bring power to the middle of a track run instead.

The fixture shown on the facing page uses a wire-in connector and a fixture box saddle to conceal the box and connections. Some connectors are held in place by the saddle, others by the track itself. Still others attach to an adapter plate that screws to the box. Mount the connector, according to manufacturer's instructions, and splice the wires using wire nuts.

MOUNTING THE TRACK: You attach a track to the ceiling or wall by installing mounting screws or toggle bolts through the track's predrilled holes. (Screws are preferable, but you'll need to use toggle bolts if you can't locate the joists or if the joist spacing is wrong.) Hold the track in place and mark the positions of the mounting holes. These marks will show you where to drill.

Because most connectors lie flush against the ceiling or wall surface, you can usually attach the track directly to the surface. Slip the two bare wire ends of the first length of track into the connector receptacles, then secure the track with screws or toggle bolts. Repeat to secure the remaining lengths of track.

However, you may need special clips to hold some types of track 1/4 to 1/2 inch away from the mounting surface. Screw or bolt the clips to the ceiling or wall, slip the first length of track onto the connector, then press the track and succeeding lengths into the mounting clips, as required.

ADDING UNDERCABINET FIXTURES

Kitchen designers frequently tuck task lighting under wall cabinets. One of the most common fixtures—and one of the easiest to install—is a shallow fluorescent unit housing one or two tubes. These lights can be powered in one of three ways: they can be wired permanently to a switch; wired without a separate switch (assuming the fixtures have their own switches); or, in some cases, plugged into nearby outlets. For greatest lighting efficiency, the fixture should span at least two-thirds of the area to be lighted and mount as close as possible to the front of the cabinet.

To wire undercabinet fixtures, route cable out through the wall just below the cabinet's bottom edge, where the fixture will hide it. This takes some careful measuring: if you come out too high, you can probably notch some extra wall material behind the cabinet; if you're too low, you'll probably need to move the cable up and patch the wall. Once you've routed the cable out properly, run it through a knockout in the fixture back and secure it with a cable connector. Screw the fixture to the cabinet bottom, then strip wires and make connections according to the manufacturer's instructions.

Adding a wood or metal valance (trim strip) hides the unit and eliminates glare. Some wall cabinets include this trim or at least a recessed area at the bottom where you can tuck a fixture; otherwise, plan to add your own trim.

SOME SAMPLE TRACK LAYOUTS

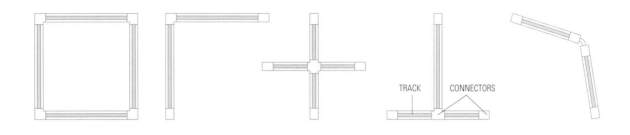

TRACK   CONNECTORS

HOOKING UP A WIRE-IN CONNECTOR AND TRACK

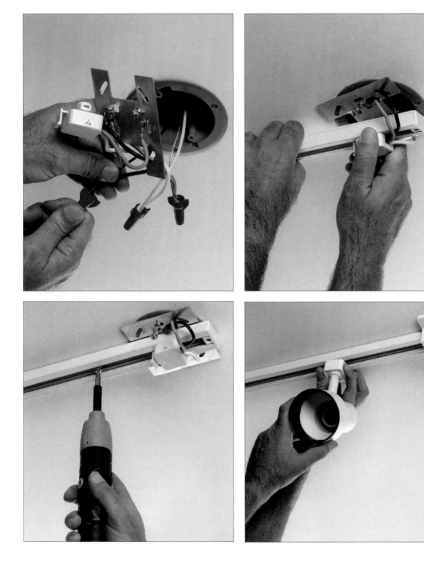

1 Wire the track connector

Fixtures vary, but with most, your first step is to splice the connector's black wire to the circuit hot wire, the white wire to the cable's neutral wire, and the green or bare wire to the circuit grounding wire.

2 Secure the connector to box and track

Again, installations differ—it depends on the exact pieces and the slack you have to work with. Here, we first screwed the adapter plate to the housing box; then, while holding the track in position, attach the connector by twisting it onto the track.

3 Fasten the track to the ceiling

When possible, drive screws through the track's mounting slots and into ceiling joists. If joists don't align with the fixture, secure fixture to ceiling material using toggle bolts.

4 Add the fixtures

Finally, position fixtures along the track where you want them; twist them into place like the track connector in Step #2. Add any remaining fixture trim that remains—for example, this design includes a saddle that covers both box and track connector.

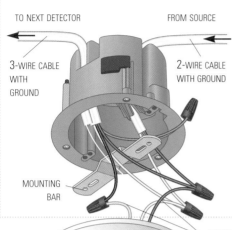

TO NEXT DETECTOR   FROM SOURCE

3-WIRE CABLE
WITH
GROUND

2-WIRE CABLE
WITH GROUND

MOUNTING
BAR

HOT WIRES

SMOKE
DETECTOR

ADDING SMOKE DETECTORS

In new construction, smoke detectors are required in each bedroom and in the adjoining hall. You'll also need at least one on every story, including the basement. Retrofits may be battery operated, but new installations must be hardwired models with battery backups.

You install a 120-volt smoke detector the same way you do a surface-mounted light fixture (see page 106). A detector doesn't weigh much, so you won't need any special brackets or studs to secure it. In new construction, however, units must be wired together so that any alarm signal will also be transmitted "downstream" and set off all the other alarms. Solution? Plan to run three-conductor cable between detectors, as shown at left. ✂

INSTALLING RECESSED DOWNLIGHTS

Today, recessed downlights are usually prewired and grounded to their own housing box; however, older-style downlights may require wiring into a junction box attached to a ceiling joist.

Many downlights produce a lot of heat, so you must either buy an IC-rated fixture for direct contact or plan to remove insulation within 3 inches of the fixture. You'll also need clearance above the unit (special low-clearance downlights are available for tight spaces). Make sure that no combustible materials are within 1/2 inch of the fixture, with the exception of joists or other blocking used for support.

If you have access from above, choose a standard new-work downlight; most of these fixtures simply fasten to ceiling joists with adjustable hanger bars. Fixture trim is added once the ceiling is in place and textured and/or painted.

NEW-WORK DOWNLIGHT WITH BOX

New-work downlights with adjustable hanger bars are easy to install from above—you probably won't even need a helper to do it. Simply nail the ends of the bars to joists on either side (left), then make wiring connections inside the unit's junction box. Replace the cover plate on the box. Once the ceiling material is in place, clip the fixture trim or baffle into place from below.

When you don't have access from above the ceiling, use an old-work fixture, which can be installed from below. Before wiring these fixtures, you'll need to cut a hole for the fixture housing in the ceiling between two joists. If there's no crawl space above the joists, locate the joists—and any obstructing wires or pipes—from below, using the bent-wire method described on page 63. Make sure to shut off power to any circuits that may be wired behind the ceiling before drilling exploratory holes.

WIRING AN OLD-WORK (REMODELING) DOWNLIGHT

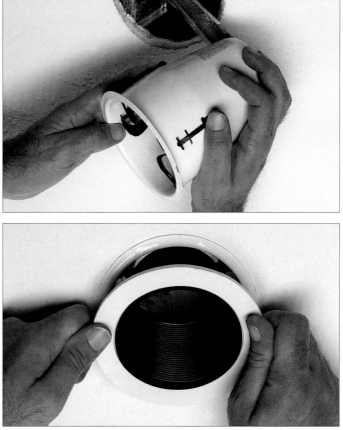

1 Make the connections
To install this fixture, first cut an access hole in the existing ceiling (most fixtures come with paper templates), then splice the fixture wires to the incoming circuit wires— black to black, white to white, and green or bare fixture wire to the circuit's grounding wire. Replace the cover plate on the box.

2 Slip the fixture into position
Thread the fixture, junction box first, into the ceiling. Attachment methods vary; this fixture has spring clips that, when locked into place, grab the ceiling material from above.

3 Add the trim
With the fixture secured to the ceiling, add the light bulb and baffle, diffusing panel, or other trim. The baffle shown clips onto the fixture, controlling light spread and masking the ceiling hole's rough edges.

INSTALLING CEILING FANS

A ceiling fan can reduce your dependence on an air conditioner if you regularly use one, or improve the comfort of a room if you don't. Ceiling fans can also help improve heat circulation in winter. They are easy to install, and because many models include light fixtures, you can benefit from the fan without giving up room brightness.

Ceiling fans are available in a variety of styles, sizes, shapes, and colors. Quality varies as well; better models have heavy motors that are quieter, run longer, and produce a better breeze than low-cost units. Most fans have components similar to those shown on the facing page. If you want the convenience of a switch without having to run wiring to a new or existing wall switch, shop for a ceiling fan with remote control.

MOUNTING THE FIXTURE BOX

Ceiling fans weighing up to 35 pounds can be attached to a heavy-duty fixture box that carries an approval label for ceiling fans. (One example is shown on page 105.) A fixture box with an attached flange can be nailed to a ceiling joist. If the joists aren't located where you want to hang the fan, add a 2x4 or 2x6 brace between them. Nail the brace to the joists on both ends, then nail a shallow pancake box to the brace.

When you don't have access to the ceiling from above, the best mounting choice is usually an expandable hanger bar that is approved for ceiling fans. For details, see page 71.

A ceiling fan that weighs more than 35 pounds can't be supported by a ceiling box alone. You must also use a J-hook screwed firmly into the framing or a special hanger bracket supplied by the manufacturer. These fasteners run right through the back of the fixture box into a ceiling joist or sturdy wood bridging between joists.

CHOOSING THE RIGHT SIZE

Ceiling fans come in different sizes for use in different-size areas. They're most efficient in rooms with 8-foot ceilings. The table below gives some general guidelines for choosing fan sizes. For example, in a typical 12-foot by 10-foot room (120 square feet), a 42-inch fan would be appropriate.

For adequate air movement, the blades should be at least 12 inches from the ceiling and 24 inches from any wall. For safety, the blades should be no lower than 7 feet high or they may hit a person's raised arm. You can buy fans that mount closer to the ceiling for rooms with low overhead. For high or sloped ceilings, down-rod extensions are available in lengths of up to 6 feet that put the fan close enough to the floor to provide the benefits of moving air where you'll feel them.

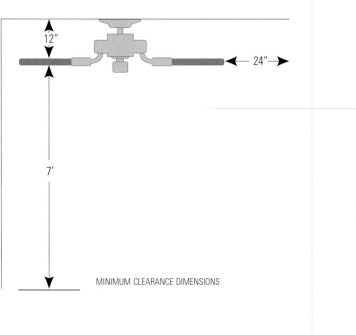

MINIMUM CLEARANCE DIMENSIONS

ROOM SIZE	FAN DIAMETER
Up to 64 sq. ft.	36 inches
Up to 144 sq. ft.	42 inches
Up to 225 sq. ft.	44 inches
Up to 400 sq. ft.	52 inches

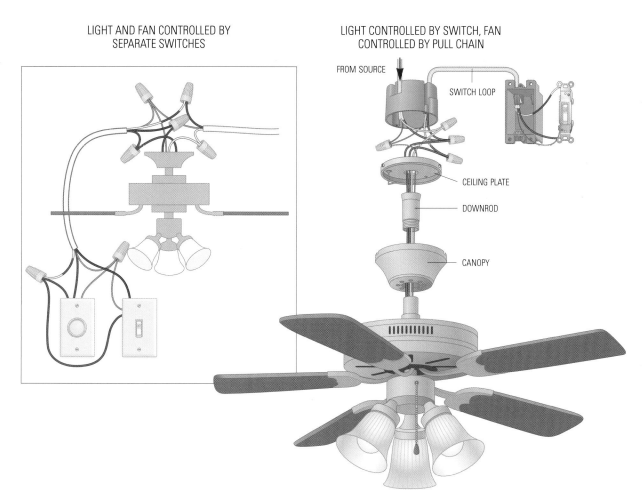

LIGHT AND FAN CONTROLLED BY
SEPARATE SWITCHES

LIGHT CONTROLLED BY SWITCH, FAN
CONTROLLED BY PULL CHAIN

FROM SOURCE

SWITCH LOOP

CEILING PLATE

DOWNROD

CANOPY

MOUNTING THE FAN

Each style of fan is mounted somewhat differently, so always follow the manufacturer's instructions. Although the parts may not look exactly the same, most fans go together as follows once the ceiling box is in place.

CONNECTING THE DOWNROD: First insert the downrod into the canopy. Feed the wires from the motor through the downrod and canopy. Tighten the screw or screws securing the fan to the pipe.

ATTACHING THE PLATE: Standing on a stepladder, feed the wires from the ceiling box through the ceiling plate and attach the plate to the box. Most ceiling plates have a hook for supporting the fan during installation. If yours doesn't, improvise one from a wire coat hanger.

WIRING THE FAN: A ceiling fan and its attached light can be turned on and off by several means. Each can be con-

trolled by a pull chain, each can be controlled by a wall switch, or the light can be controlled by a wall switch and the fan by a pull chain. Wiring differs for each method and depends on whether the power source first enters the switch box or the fixture box. The wiring patterns shown above should help you handle most typical situations.

Ceiling fans with attached lights can have a number of different-colored wires in them. Check the manufacturer's instructions for proper identification. Use wire nuts to secure the connections. Attach the canopy to the ceiling plate and tighten the screws.

WIRING A LIGHT: If your fan has a light fixture, connect the socket to the bottom of the switch housing following the manufacturer's instructions. Attach the fan blades, then test the fan and light.

PPLIANCES

Household appliances include everything from toasters and irons to built-in garbage disposals and water heaters. On the following pages, we explain how to wire the most common stationary appliances used in kitchens, bathrooms, living spaces, and utility rooms.

Many stationary appliances are wired directly into a circuit, without a receptacle (this is called hard-wiring). In these cases, you typically bring cable or conduit out of the wall or floor, then make the wire connections inside a splice box located on the appliance. Other installations simply require a receptacle and matching plug (for details, see pages 92–97).

Most of the following appliances require a dedicated circuit (which means that no other device can be hooked up to it). Exceptions are noted. Circuit requirements can vary, though, so be sure to check local codes.

KITCHEN RANGES

Most electric kitchen ranges require a dedicated 120/240-volt circuit rated for either 40 or 50 amps (depending on the range's wattage) and a receptacle that's either surface-mounted or flush-mounted on the wall or floor behind. To install a 120/240-volt receptacle, see page 97. Incidentally, even a gas range may need a 120-volt hookup to power its lights and/or a timer.

A range or cooktop (see below) may also require an adjacent vent hood. Fortunately, hoods don't draw much power; you can usually wire one into an adjacent lighting circuit.

OVENS AND COOKTOPS

In most cases, separate electric wall ovens and cooktops share a 120/240-volt circuit that's rated for 40 or 50 amps. Cable is first routed to a central junction box, as shown below; from there, smaller wires branch off to the appliances. Most ovens and cooktops come with their own flexible leads, or "whips"; if yours don't, plan to run individual wires inside flexible metal conduit.

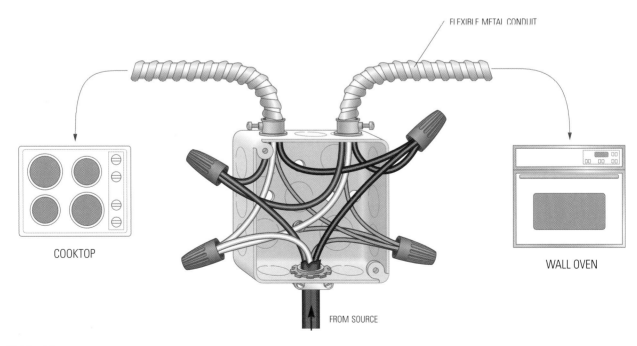

FLEXIBLE METAL CONDUIT

COOKTOP

WALL OVEN

FROM SOURCE

A microwave oven plugs into a nearby 20-amp, 120-volt receptacle. If the oven's nameplate rating is more than half the circuit's capacity, you may be required to place the microwave on its own circuit.

WARNING

Although 240-volt wiring is no more difficult to install than 120-volt wiring, the potential danger from shock or fire is far greater. If you're at all uncertain about your abilities, call in a professional to inspect your work and/or to make the final hookups.

DISHWASHERS AND DISPOSALS

Usually the dishwasher and garbage disposal each require a dedicated 20-amp, 120-volt circuit. The dishwasher may be a plug-in type (shown below) or may require direct wire hookups inside a splice box. Similarly, the disposal might come with a plug or be hardwired via a splice box on the disposal's bottom. The garbage disposal can sometimes share a circuit with a hot-water dispenser.

If both the dishwasher and the disposal are plug-ins, consider running a 120/240-volt "split-circuit" cable to a single duplex receptacle with its break-off fin removed (see pages 94–95). Place the receptacle inside the sink cabinet where it's adjacent to both appliances.

DISPOSAL
2-WIRE CABLE WITH GROUND
WHITE WIRES PAINTED BLACK
REMOVE BREAK-OFF FIN
DISHWASHER
3-WIRE CABLE WITH GROUND
FROM SOURCE

SEPARATE DISCONNECT?

Some stationary motor-operated appliances—such as garbage disposals, water heaters, and central air conditioners—require separate "disconnects." A disconnect is essentially a switch that allows power to be turned off before moving or servicing the appliance. The disconnect must be within sight of the appliance. (A plug-in appliance probably won't require a separate disconnect if the plug is readily accessible.) In some areas, on some installations, you may substitute a locking device, or "lockout," at the panel for the separate disconnect. A lockout is installed on the circuit breaker protecting the circuit to the appliance so that someone can't come along and inadvertently turn power back on.

So how can you know exactly what's required in your area? Be sure to check with your local inspector before finalizing your plans.

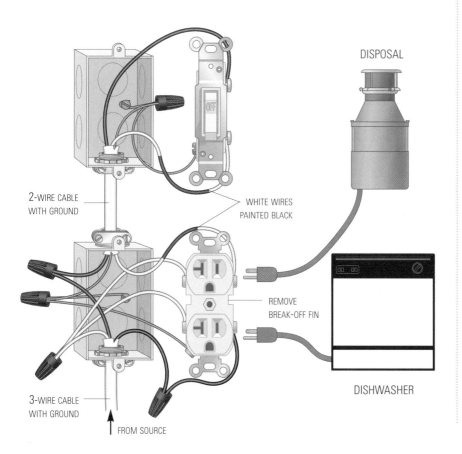

BATHROOM VENT FAN

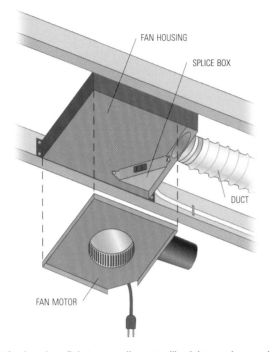

FAN HOUSING

SPLICE BOX

DUCT

FAN MOTOR

Most fan housings fit between adjacent ceiling joists; an inner unit slides into the housing and plugs into the housing's splice box (above). Vent the fan horizontally out the house wall or vertically through the roof (below).

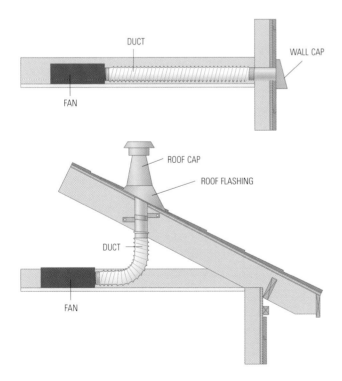

DUCT

WALL CAP

FAN

ROOF CAP

ROOF FLASHING

DUCT

FAN

BATHROOM FANS

Some fan-light-heater units may require a dedicated circuit, but normally you can wire a ventilation fan into the same general-purpose, 120-volt circuit that the bathroom lights are on.

Fan housings are easy to install—most models simply bridge the space between adjacent ceiling joists or wall studs. Typically, cable runs from a switch box to a knockout hole on the fan housing and is secured with a metal cable connector. You make wiring connections within a splice box, as shown at left, then plug the fan unit into a built-in receptacle in the box. Combination fan-light-heater units may require 3-conductor cable or even two or more cables, plus multiple wall switches or a manufacturer's special combination switch.

Sometimes a fan's ductwork presents more of a challenge than the wiring. You'll want the exhaust duct to be as short and straight as possible. You can run the duct either out an exterior wall or through an attic to the roof; both options are shown at left.

BATHROOM WALL HEATERS

Because electric wall heaters are easy to install and to operate, they're popular choices for heating a bathroom. Many models require a dedicated 120- or 240-volt circuit. Others allow you to wire them internally for either 120 or 240 volts; read the manufacturer's instructions for details, then be sure to configure the wires to match your circuit type.

To install a wall heater, bring the circuit cable into the heater housing via a knockout in the side or top; use a cable connector to secure the cable. Typically, wire connections are made inside a splice box, as shown for the bathroom fan, above left.

240-VOLT BASEBOARD HEATER

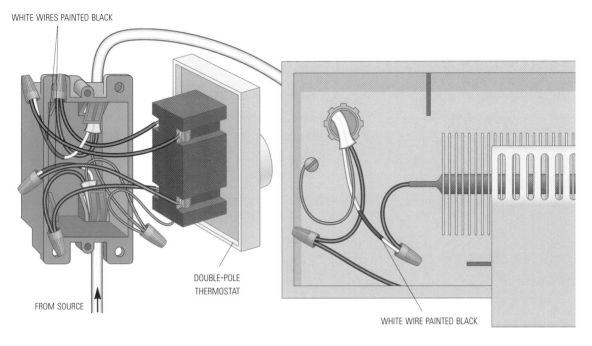

WHITE WIRES PAINTED BLACK

DOUBLE-POLE
THERMOSTAT

FROM SOURCE

WHITE WIRE PAINTED BLACK

BASEBOARD HEATERS

Electric baseboard heaters come in 120- and 240-volt versions and are either hard-wired types or plug-ins. A 240-volt, hardwired heater is the most efficient option. It will probably require a dedicated 240-volt circuit rated at either 20 or 30 amps.

You can buy a unit with a built-in thermostat or plan to install a separate two-pole wall unit, as shown above. Power runs to the "line" side of the thermostat, out the "load" side, and then on to the heater, where it enters via a knockout. Typically, heaters have a splice box at each end; use the box that's most convenient.

If a heater or any other appliance will be switched on for more than 3 hours straight, the circuit rating must be reduced to 80 percent of its normal value. A normal 20-amp circuit, for instance, is then rated for 0.8×20 amps = 16 amps.

PORTABLE AIR CONDITIONERS

Most window-mounted air conditioners are plug-in types, so you'll simply need a 240-volt receptacle of the appropriate amperage (typically 20 amps) to power one. Install the receptacle no more than 6 feet from the window unit.

WASHERS AND DRYERS

Most electric dryers require a dedicated 30-amp, 120/240-volt circuit. The National Electrical Code now requires you to wire this kind of installation with three-conductor cable that includes two hot wires, a neutral wire, and a separate grounding wire. The dryer plugs into a four-prong receptacle, either a surface-mounted or a flush-mounted model.

A washing machine simply needs a 20-amp, 120-volt receptacle. Note, however, that this is a dedicated circuit—fixtures, switches, and other receptacles in the area must be wired separately.

Washers, dryers, and other appliances in utility rooms may be wired with exposed conduit, as shown below. Note that the 120-volt circuit that feeds the washer travels in the same conduit as the dryer wires and first passes through the dryer's receptacle box, but the circuits are not spliced together.

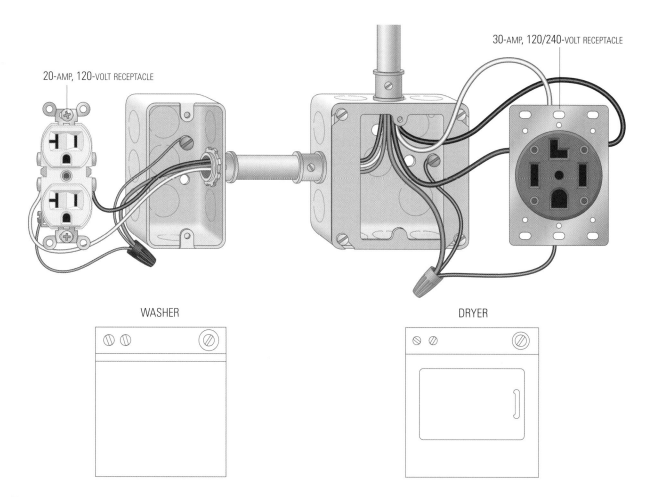

20-AMP, 120-VOLT RECEPTACLE

30-AMP, 120/240-VOLT RECEPTACLE

WASHER

DRYER

WATER HEATERS

An electric water heater requires a dedicated 240-volt circuit that can handle at least 125 percent of the heater's nameplate rating. A 30-amp circuit is typical. Typically, power runs first to a disconnect switch (see page 115) that's adjacent to the heater; then from the disconnect box to the heater's splice box via either AC or MC cable or individual wires inside flexible metal conduit, as shown at right.

STATIONARY POWER TOOLS

Large, powerful tools, such as stationary table saws, jointers, or planers, often require dedicated 240-volt circuits to drive them. Nameplate ratings can be deceptive, as the tool may "spike," or pull extra power, when it first starts up—enough to trip a "normal" breaker. Be sure to follow any manufacturer's recommendations for both circuit rating and tool grounding. For extra safety, consider a locking receptacle (see page 35) and a matching plug.

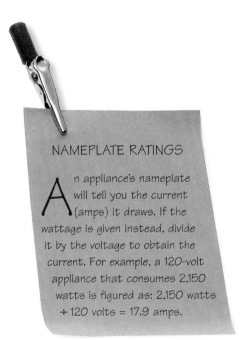

NAMEPLATE RATINGS

An appliance's nameplate will tell you the current (amps) it draws. If the wattage is given instead, divide it by the voltage to obtain the current. For example, a 120-volt appliance that consumes 2,150 watts is figured as: 2,150 watts ÷ 120 volts = 17.9 amps.

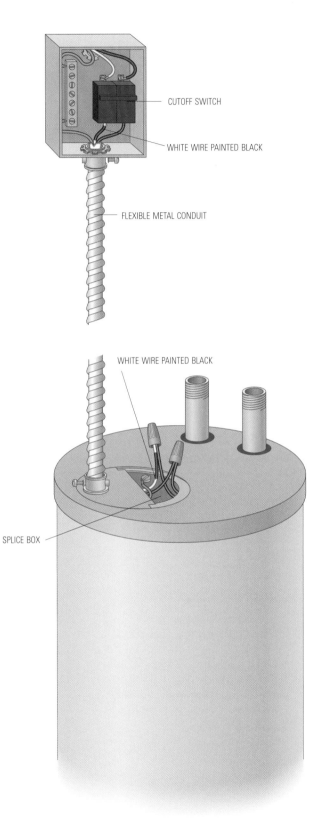

CUTOFF SWITCH

WHITE WIRE PAINTED BLACK

FLEXIBLE METAL CONDUIT

WHITE WIRE PAINTED BLACK

SPLICE BOX

WATER HEATER

FINAL CONNECTIONS

Once you've run cable and hooked up your new device or devices, you're in the homestretch: it's time to wire into the power source. If you're extending an existing circuit, that means splicing the new cable to the wires inside an existing housing box. If you've added a new circuit, you'll be making the hookup at the service entrance panel or inside a subpanel. Here's a close-up look at each procedure.

TAPPING AN EXISTING CIRCUIT

As discussed on page 62, you can tap power for a circuit extension at one of four sources: a receptacle, a light fixture, a switch box that includes a neutral wire, or a junction box where wires are simply joined. All four options are shown on the facing page.

CAUTION: Before wiring into any existing device, disconnect the circuit by removing the fuse or switching off the circuit breaker.

Peel back the outer sheath from the new cable, then cut off the sheath and any separation materials (see page 51). Then strip the insulation off the ends of the individual wires and splice them to the old wires, following the instructions on pages 52–55.

WARNING

You must shut off power to any existing device, entrance panel, or subpanel before beginning work. (For details, see pages 170–172.) If you're at all unsure of your abilities, have a professional electrician make the circuit connections and/or inspect your work.

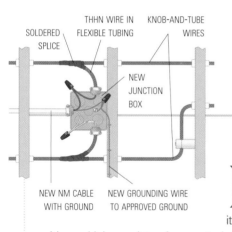

SOLDERED SPLICE — THHN WIRE IN FLEXIBLE TUBING — KNOB-AND-TUBE WIRES — NEW JUNCTION BOX — NEW NM CABLE WITH GROUND — NEW GROUNDING WIRE TO APPROVED GROUND

EXTENDING KNOB-AND-TUBE WIRING

If you live in an older home, you may discover that it has knob-and-tube wiring, which consists of separate hot and neutral wires threaded through porcelain knobs and tubes. No longer legal in new construction, knob-and-tube wiring may be retained only in existing installations.

The safest remodeling strategy is to replace the entire circuit run with NM cable. Another option is to extend the circuit with NM cable and single-conductor copper wires, as shown above. The THHN wires—one hot, one neutral—which run inside flexible tubing, or "loom," must be connected to the cable wires with wire nuts on one end and soldered to the old copper knob-and-tube wiring at the other

end. To do this, strip 2 inches of insulation from the knob-and-tube wire you want to splice and 1½ inches from the end of the THHN wire. Sand the wire ends with emery paper until shiny. Twist the bare end of the THHN wire tightly around the bare knob-and-tube wire, forming a coil ¾ inch long, and snip off the end of the THHN wire.

Heat the coil with a 250-watt solder gun, then touch the tip of a roll of rosin-core solder to the coil. You'll know that the coil has reached the proper temperature when the solder flows readily into the spaces within the coil and does not flow out again. Fill all the spaces.

When the liquefied solder has rehardened and the coil is cool, wrap the coil and the bare portion of the knob-and-tube wire with rubber insulating tape; seal it by wrapping it in the opposite direction with electrical tape.

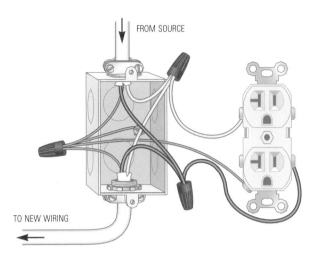

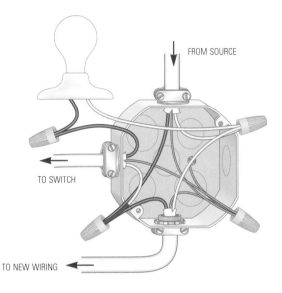

How to wire into a receptacle

Disconnect the circuit and gently pull the receptacle from the box. Hold the white (neutral) wires from the cables together, along with a white jumper wire attached to a silver screw terminal on the receptacle, and screw on a wire nut. Repeat the procedure for the black (hot) wires, attaching the jumper to a brass screw terminal. Splice the new grounding wire to any other grounding wires and a jumper wire to the box (if the box is metal).

How to wire into a fixture

Pull the fixture from the box and confirm that the power is off. Connect the wires in the new cable as shown above.

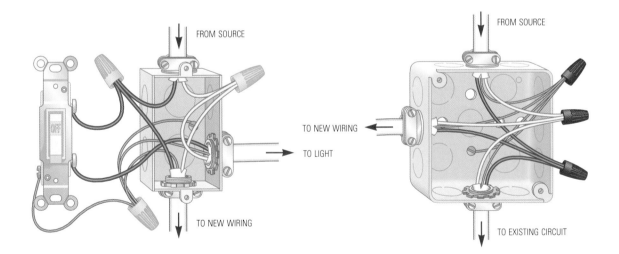

How to wire into a switch box

Note: This box must contain an unswitched neutral wire. Pull the switch from the box, then use a neon tester to locate the hot black wire (see page 175). Turn off power to the circuit. Follow the procedure for wiring into a receptacle, taking care to secure the black wire from the new cable to the hot wire.

How to wire into a junction box

Remove the cover from the junction box and confirm that the power is off. The drawing above shows a typical wiring extension from an existing junction box.

CONNECTING A 120-VOLT BRANCH CIRCUIT

1 Bring cable into the panel
First remove a knockout from the panel's side, top, or bottom, and bring about 2 feet of NM cable inside the panel. Secure cable to panel with a metal cable connector.

2 Hook up the neutral wire
Remove cable insulation and strip wire ends. Slip the end of the white neutral wire through a hole in the neutral bus bar, then tighten the setscrew.

BRANCH CIRCUIT CONNECTIONS IN THE SERVICE ENTRANCE PANEL

Although the sheer number of wires inside a service entrance panel can be intimidating, the actual work of connecting branch circuits is straightforward. Here's how to hook up 120-volt, 120/240-volt, and 240-volt circuits. For connections to a subpanel, see pages 124–125.

Before beginning, double-check that power inside the panel is dead. Using a neon tester, place one probe on a setscrew of a two-pole, 240-volt breaker and the other probe on the neutral bus bar. Repeat with the breaker's second setscrew. If the tester lights up either time, the panel is still live; if it doesn't light either time, the power is off.

CONNECTING NM CABLE TO A PANEL: Where nonmetallic sheathed cable (type NM) enters a service entrance panel, first remove the correct-size knockout for your cable, then use a metal cable connector to hold the cable (see page 81). The cable must then be stapled within 12 inches of the box.

Be sure to leave plenty of cable extending into the panel to be stripped back and connected to the overcurrent protection devices; 2 feet isn't too much for wiring a large panel.

CONNECTING CONDUIT TO A PANEL: Conduit is fastened to a service entrance panel the same way it's connected to any box (see pages 82–86). Outdoor installations require watertight fittings. Once the conduit system is installed, pull the circuit conductors into the panel.

CAUTION: If you're using metal fish tape inside a panel, you must be very careful to keep it away from potential live wires.

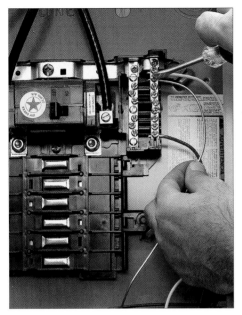

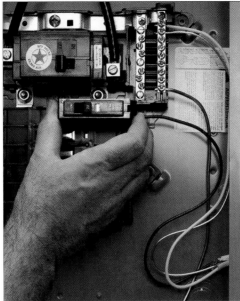

Connect the grounding wire

3 Next, fasten the circuit grounding wire to the neutral bus bar in the same way you secured the neutral wire.

Install the circuit breaker

4 Connect the hot wire to the circuit breaker's screw terminal. With most breakers, you simply strip the wire end, slide it inside a clamp, then tighten the setscrew. Install the breaker on a hot bus bar by pushing until the clip on the back of the breaker is firmly fastened. The breaker should snap into position.

CONNECTING A CIRCUIT: Connect cable or conduit to the panel as instructed on the facing page, then follow the steps as shown above. All circuit wires must go around the hot bus bars—if you loop the wires across them, the current might bypass the circuit breakers and cause a short circuit. Strive for neatness.

Balance your total house load so you have approximately the same amount on each hot bus bar. (If you're installing 120-volt circuit breakers consecutively, balancing is usually automatic: on most panels, every other breaker slot is assigned to a given bus bar.) Once installation is complete, remove the appropriate breaker knockouts in the cover plate and screw the plate back in place. Then replace the panel door.

Connecting a 240-volt circuit

A straight 240-volt circuit has two hot wires, a grounding wire, and no neutral wire. In the service entrance panel, use a common-trip, two-pole breaker to connect one hot wire to each of the hot bus bars. Connect the grounding wire to the neutral bus bar.

Connecting a 120/240-volt circuit

These circuits connect the same way as 120-volt circuits, except that two hot wires are used along with the neutral and grounding wires. Attach both hot wires to a common-trip, two-pole breaker; secure both the neutral wire and the grounding wire to the neutral bus bar.

HOW TO WIRE A SUBPANEL

1 Connect the subfeeds

First remove a knockout and bring the subfeed cable inside the panel. Secure cable to panel with a metal cable connector. Remove cable insulation and strip wire ends. Attach the hot subfeed wires directly to the hot bus bars, the neutral subfeed to the neutral bus bar, and the grounding wire to the grounding bus bar.

2 Hook up the circuit's neutral wire

Bring cable into the panel, clamp it, then remove cable insulation and strip wire ends. Slip the end of the white neutral wire through a hole in the neutral bus bar, then tighten the setscrew.

3 Connect the grounding wire

Route the grounding wire to its own grounding bus bar, then secure wire to bar by tightening the setscrew.

CIRCUIT CONNECTIONS TO A SUBPANEL

If your service entrance panel is centrally located, you'll probably want to run all branch circuits directly from it. But if it's in an out-of-the-way spot or if it's completely full of circuit breakers, adding a subpanel may be your best choice.

MOUNTING THE SUBPANEL: You can mount a subpanel by bolting it directly to a masonry wall, by screwing it to a larger plywood back and fastening the plywood to wall studs, or by recessing the panel in the wall and screwing it to the side of one or both studs.

The subpanel must be positioned in an easily accessible spot, not inside a closet or a bathroom. The breakers should be installed no more than 6 feet 7 inches off the floor (shoulder height is a good guideline). You must allow 36 inches clearance in front of the panel and 30 inches to each side.

SUBFEEDS: Think of a subpanel as a branch circuit; like any other branch circuit, the subpanel's ampacity must not be less than that of the breakers or fuses protecting it at the service entrance panel or in the subpanel itself.

The wires leading from the service entrance panel are called subpanel feeders, or just subfeeds. Add up the maximum ampacity of all planned branch circuits served by the subpanel, then choose your subfeed wire size from the chart on page 29.

In most subpanels, the hot subfeeds from the service entrance panel attach directly to the hot bus bars in the subpanel, requiring no subpanel main disconnect (the

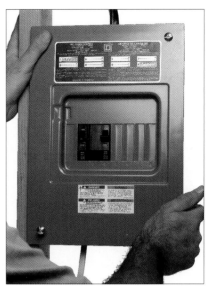

4 Install the circuit breaker
Connect the hot wire to the circuit breaker's screw terminal. With most breakers, you simply strip the wire end, slide it inside a clamp, then tighten the setscrew. Install the breaker on a hot bus bar by pushing until the clip on the back of the breaker is firmly fastened.

5 Adding 240-volt circuits
120/240-volt circuits connect the same way as 120-volt circuits, except than two hot wires are used along with the neutral and grounding wires. Attach both hot wires to a common-trip, two-pole breaker. A straight 240-volt circuit has two hot wires, a grounding wire, and no neutral wire.

6 Secure the cover plate
Once wiring connections are complete, remove the appropriate breaker knockouts in the subpanel's cover plate and screw the plate back in place. Your subpanel may also include a separate door atop the cover plate.

circuit breaker protecting the subfeeds doubles as a disconnect).

Where NM cable enters a subpanel, first remove the correct-size knockout for your cable, then use a metal cable connector to hold the cable (see page 81). The cable must then be stapled within 12 inches of the box. Plan to leave about 18 inches of cable inside the panel for final wiring connections. If the subfeeds run inside conduit, see pages 82–86.

BRANCH CIRCUIT CONNECTIONS: We assume here that you're installing a new subpanel, where subfeed connections to the service entrance panel are not yet made. If, instead, you are connecting a branch circuit to an existing subpanel, be sure to shut off power to the subpanel before beginning work.

Unlike a main panel, a subpanel has separate bus bars for neutral and grounding wires, so you'll need to attach the subfeed neutral wire to the so-called floating neutral bus bar, and run the subfeed grounding wire to the grounding bus bar (see above). Then connect the hot wires to the circuit breakers or fuses just as you would in a service entrance panel (for details, see page 123). Fold wires neatly around the outsides of the panel—don't cross over the hot bus bars.

Once installation is complete, remove the appropriate breaker knockouts in the subpanel's cover plate and screw the plate back in place.

MAKING THE FINAL HOOKUP: At the service entrance panel, connect the subfeeds just like any other 120/240-volt branch circuit (see page 123).

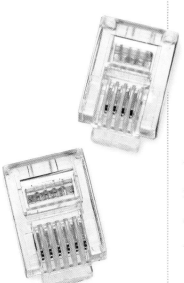

TELEPHONE SYSTEMS

Since the advent of modular telephone plugs in the mid-1960s, installing a new telephone has been almost as simple as plugging in a lamp. Today, with home-based communication needs on the increase, the question is, "Where?" Many, if not most, older homes are wired for only one or two telephone jacks: one traditionally in the kitchen, and perhaps an extension jack in the master bedroom.

The good news is that upgrading your home telephone wiring is remarkably simple. A wide selection of do-it-yourself products is designed for fast home installation. A screwdriver and a Saturday afternoon may be all you need to upgrade or completely rewire your telephone system. And because the electric current it carries is small, you don't have to take some of the precautions that are essential when working with standard electrical wiring.

This chapter will acquaint you with the basics of home telephone installations: how to route exposed wiring or runs that are concealed behind walls, and how to install new modular jacks. This information is adapted from *The Telephone Book,* available from AT&T Corporation. In addition, you'll learn how to add new lines for modern multiple-line phones, computer modems, faxes, and answering machines. For other ideas and information on today's home communications systems, see Chapter Eight, "Low Voltage, High Tech," on pages 138–155.

CORDS, WIRES, AND JACKS

When it comes time to purchase materials for a telephone system or to ask for advice at your home center or hardware store, it helps to know the nuts and bolts of telephone wiring. The following components are the building blocks of home systems.

LINE CORD: Line cord is flat, multi-conductor cord that plugs into a jack to connect a telephone or other accessory, such as a fax or modem. Long extensions can be created by using a small coupling that allows you to plug two line cords together (you should never splice line cords); but if you want to place a telephone more than 25 feet from an existing jack, it's better to run more-permanent station wire to a new jack and plug the phone into that.

COUPLING

LINE CORD

HANDSET CORD: This cord connects the handset to the telephone. It can't be used as line cord to connect a phone to a jack; it's wired differently, and its modular plug is a different size. Some telephones (usually models with the dial in the handset) require special handset cords; when replacing a handset cord, be sure to buy the type you need.

HANDSET CORD

TELEPHONE STATION WIRE: Station wire is the telephone equivalent of NM cable; it connects to the phone company's network interface jack, which is the box or block where the phone company wires enter the house. Standard station wire is intended for indoor installation and should never be used outdoors without special protection, such as conduit. A solid-core version is available for outdoor use.

Station wire can contain four, six, or even eight conductors, each sheathed in distinctive color-coded insulation. In a typical installation, only one pair of wires—the red and the green—is for basic telephone service; the others can be used to connect additional phone lines, for grounding, or as spares if a problem develops in the pair used for basic service.

STATION WIRES

2-PAIR WIRE
(4 CONDUCTORS)

3-PAIR WIRE
(6 CONDUCTORS)

4-LINE WIRE JUNCTION

42A BLOCK

WIRE JUNCTIONS: Think of these as junction boxes for telephone wires. The traditional 42A block, shown at left, is one option; a 4-line wire junction is another. You could also make phone connections using a standard junction box and wire nuts (see pages 136–137).

MODULAR JACKS: Phone jacks are connection points between the line cord and the station wire. You'll find a whole slew of single, double, and combination jacks at hardware and electronics stores. A representative selection is shown below.

Basically, you can choose between flush-mounted and surface-mounted designs. New construction usually calls for flush-mounted jacks; these install atop standard housing boxes (see pages 32–33) that are fastened to wall studs before wall coverings are put in place. When remodeling, you can bring station wire to a cut-in housing box or simply slip a special bracket atop an opening in the wall (see page 135), then screw the jack's cover plate to the bracket. Even simpler to install are surface-mounted jacks; these mount to baseboards and other existing surfaces with short screws or adhesive tape.

A dual-outlet adapter lets you add a fax, a modem, or an answering machine to a single phone jack. A triplex adapter connects three devices on either one, two, or three separate telephone lines.

HOW MANY JACKS DO YOU NEED?

Today, we want telephones within easy reach, and we need convenient jacks for answering machines, fax machines, and computers with modems. What's more, security systems and satellite entertainment systems also often require the use of a phone line. To satisfy the needs of typical families, builders now routinely install 15 to 20 jacks in new homes. You may not need that many telephone connections in your home, but a useful rule of thumb is one jack per room, with two or more in large rooms or those with special needs, such as home offices.

SURFACE-MOUNTED JACK

ADAPTERS

FLUSH-MOUNTED JACKS

TELEPHONE WIRING: AN OVERVIEW

Once you're familiar with the basic components of home telephone wiring systems, take time to acquaint yourself with some routing logistics before you begin stringing wire. Sketch a floor plan of your home, showing the location of each existing jack and where you want to put the new ones. This plan will help you choose the simplest type of system to install and the shortest routes for the new wires.

TWO WIRING SYSTEMS

You can wire a phone system in one of two basic ways. Each has its advantages, so consider which one best meets your needs.

Daisy-chain wiring (shown at left) connects many telephone outlets on one wiring circuit. The wiring begins at a wire junction connected to the phone company's network interface jack, then simply runs from jack to jack. The advantage of this system is quick, easy installation.

Home-run wiring connects each telephone jack to a common point (usually a wire junction or splice box adjacent to the interface jack). This type of system is recommended for larger homes and for homes in which an office is installed or planned. Home-run wiring requires a little more time and hardware to install, but it provides several advantages. If a wire breaks or shorts, for instance, the damage is confined to one jack, and the problem can be quickly identified and repaired. In addition, the system can be upgraded easily for more complex communications needs.

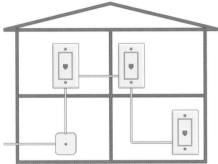

DAISY-CHAIN WIRING

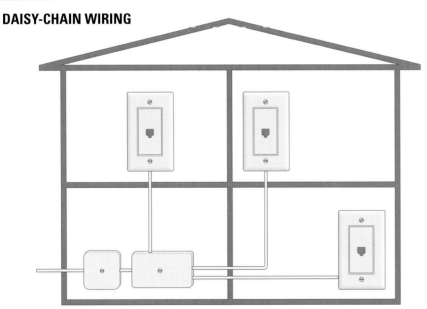

HOME-RUN WIRING

PLANNING YOUR WIRING ROUTES

You can extend wiring from existing jacks or from a wire junction located near where the wiring enters your home, or you can combine methods if that will produce the shortest runs of wire. Distance is the only major limitation on your work: jacks should be installed no more than 200 feet from the point where the wiring enters your home.

Since telephone station wire is thin, it's relatively easy to route along baseboards or through or inside walls. However, some situations are best avoided. To prevent corrosion, route wires away from steam or hot water pipes and air ducts. To reduce interference, separate telephone wiring and jacks from electrical receptacles by several inches. For safety, never let phone jacks and electrical outlets share a conduit or junction box: a short in the line-voltage wire could transfer excess current to the phone wire.

Also, never install jacks in locations that would permit someone to use a telephone near water: stay clear of bathtubs, laundry tubs, wash bowls, kitchen sinks, and swimming pools, and wet areas such as damp basements. Jacks installed in a kitchen should be located a reasonable distance from grounded surfaces such as sinks, refrigerators, and ranges.

WIRE COLOR CODING

STANDARD 2-PAIR WIRE	ALTERNATE TYPES
Red	Blue (white bands) Blue
Green	White (blue bands)
Yellow	Orange (white bands) Orange
Black	White (orange bands)
STANDARD 3-PAIR WIRE	
Red	Blue (white bands)
Green	White (blue bands)
Yellow	Orange (white bands)
Black	White (orange bands)
Blue	Green (white bands)
White	White (green bands)

PHONE CIRCUIT BASICS

A telephone circuit requires that at least two wires be used at all times. This basic pair consists of a "tip" wire (usually green) and a "ring" wire (usually red). It is very important that you maintain the continuity of this color-coding throughout your home. Always connect red to red, green to green, and so forth.

Some types of wire have a different color coding than standard station wire. However, the two types can be easily integrated by connecting the color-coded conductors shown at left.

SOME SAFETY TIPS

Although telephone lines conduct low-level electrical current that's unlikely to cause any harm, you should take the following precautions when working with any telephone wiring.

✓ Never work with an active telephone line. Since a higher current is used to ring the telephone, an incoming call could produce a small but unpleasant shock if you're touching any bare wire. Before you begin any work, disconnect the wiring at the interface jack or take a telephone handset off the hook. (Some telephones with lighted dials draw power from a low-voltage transformer instead of the telephone line. Check the electrical outlets near your phone; if you see a small, cube-shaped transformer, unplug it.)

✓ Never handle bare wires or screws. Always hold the insulated portion of wires and use insulated tools.

✓ Never work with telephone wiring during a thunderstorm. A lightning strike could send a strong, dangerous surge down the phone line.

✓ Never work with telephone wiring if you have a pacemaker.

EXTENDING YOUR SYSTEM

Whether you're simply adding a jack to your present phone line or doing major wiring, the basic steps are the same: tapping into the phone system, routing wire to new jack locations, and installing new modular jacks. Here's a closer look at all three steps.

MAKING CONNECTIONS

The easiest way to extend a modular system is to route new station wire from an existing modular jack or wire junction using daisy-chain wiring (see page 130). Special screw terminals inside both types of junctions allow you to connect station wire quickly and easily. No wire stripping is necessary; the conductors insert directly into slots that pierce the wire insulation when the terminals are tightened with a screwdriver.

If no jack or junction exists where you want to install new wiring, a nearby station wire may be used as the starting point for a new wire route. Often you can find an existing wire on a baseboard, in a closet or cabinet, or attached to joists in an attic or basement. If you obtain at least 3 inches of slack, you can cut the wire and attach it to either a modular jack or a wire junction. Additional station wire can then be routed from the jack or junction to another location. If no slack can be gained, an alternative is to cut the wire and install two wire junctions (or a jack and a junction) at least 2 inches apart. Each end of the cut wire can be attached to a junction, then the junctions can be bridged with a separate length of wire.

ROUTING NEW WIRES

When extending a phone line, you can save a great deal of time and trouble by leaving the new wiring exposed. However, routing wiring beneath a floor, above a ceiling, or in a wall requires less wire, is more attractive, and provides better protection. It's definitely the way to go in new construction.

INSTALLING EXPOSED WIRING: Choose a route where the wire will be inconspicuous and well protected. If possible, run it inside cabinets and closets or beneath shelving. In paneled rooms, you can conceal wire under panels, hollow corner trim, and baseboard molding. Wire also can be routed along baseboards, around door and window frames, and along picture molding or chair

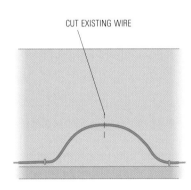

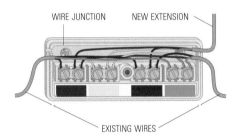

Tapping into existing station wire
If you can find—or make—at least 3 inches of slack (top), you can cut an existing station wire and install a wire junction. Additional wire can then be routed from the junction to another location (bottom).

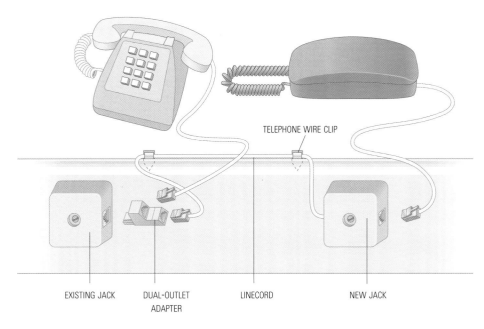

TELEPHONE WIRE CLIP

EXISTING JACK   DUAL-OUTLET   LINECORD   NEW JACK
                ADAPTER

Routing along a baseboard

To add a new jack near an existing jack, simply plug a dual-outlet adapter into the old jack, then run line cord along the baseboard as shown at left. For a more permanent installation or for distances over 25 feet, plan to hard-wire new and old jacks together with station wire.

rails. If you do the work carefully and use telephone wire clips or staples to anchor the wiring in place, it won't attract much attention at all.

Wire can also be run beneath carpeting, where the carpet meets the wall. If the carpet edges are tacked down, remove tacks with pliers or a screwdriver tip, or use pliers to lift up a tack strip.

ROUTING WIRE THROUGH WALLS: Drilling through a wall is often the easiest way to route wire from room to room. In homes with typical gypsum wallboard walls, this is usually a simple job. Find a hollow spot between wall studs (for tips, see pages 62–63), then use a ¹/₄-inch drill bit at least 5 inches long to drill through the wallboard just above the baseboard.

Feeding the wire through the wall is easier if you push a soda straw through the hole first, as shown at right.

FLOOR-TO-FLOOR WIRING: Running wire horizontally within walls is nearly impossible without cutting holes in the wall surface. However, running a line vertically is somewhat simpler, and a route from floor to floor is often the most practical path for taking a phone line from one room to another—even when both rooms are on the same floor. Usually, you'll be running the wire through one wall into the attic or basement, and from there into the wall of another room. Adapt the same wire-routing and fishing strategies detailed for electrical cable on pages 64–69.

Feeding wire through a wall

Since telephone wire is limp and difficult to fish through a hollow wall, push a soda straw through first, then insert the wire through the straw. Once the wire is through, remove the straw. Holes can be sealed with putty or a paintable caulking compound.

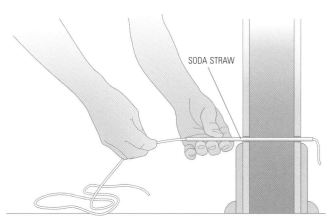

SODA STRAW

INSTALLING MODULAR JACKS

Installing your new modular jacks is the last step in extending or rewiring your home telephone system. It takes a matter of minutes and requires only a screwdriver. Three of the most common types—the flush-mounted jack, the wall-phone jack, and the surface-mounted jack—are shown at right. Jacks with swivel covers, jacks that team up with a cable outlet, and outdoor jacks are also available.

Always read the installation instructions provided with each jack, and make sure all color-coded wires are attached to the correct terminals. Better-quality jacks have special terminals that can accommodate extra station wire or line cord, allowing you to route wire to another jack in a daisy-chain extension. Never insert more than one conductor into each slot of a terminal.

After installing any new jack, conduct the tests described on page 188 to make sure you've connected it correctly.

FLUSH-MOUNTED JACK

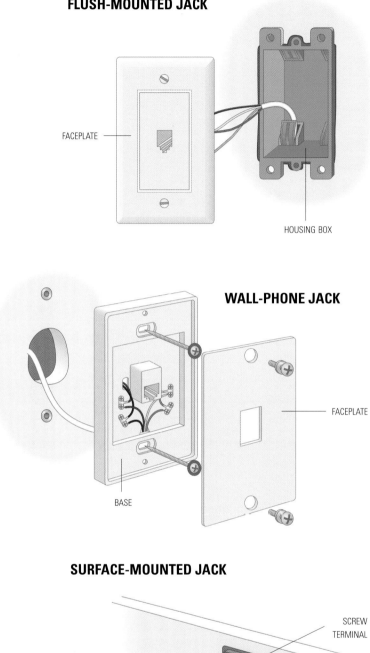

FACEPLATE

HOUSING BOX

WALL-PHONE JACK

FACEPLATE

BASE

SURFACE-MOUNTED JACK

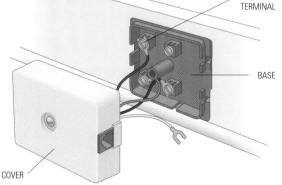

SCREW TERMINAL

BASE

COVER

CONVERTING TO MODULAR

Since all new telephones and accessories are designed for use with modular jacks, you may have to convert to modular connections before adding new phone lines and jacks.

HARD-WIRED JACKS: The most common type of telephone connection installed before 1974 is referred to as "hard-wired," since the telephone cannot be unplugged. There are two kinds of hard-wired connections: the block, which is attached directly to the wall or baseboard; and flush-mounted connections, which are actually in-the-wall housing boxes and can have either round or rectangular faceplates.

A hard-wired block connection can be converted to a modular one simply by removing its existing cover and replacing it with a modular jack converter, as shown below. Like most modular phone products, the package contains complete instructions for installation.

As shown below center, flush-mounted connections are also easy to change, using a slightly different converter.

FOUR-PRONG JACKS: A type of non-modular outlet that was often used for portable extension telephones is called a "four-prong jack." This type of jack may be mounted on a wall or baseboard, or flush-mounted in a housing box covered by a plastic faceplate. You can change four-prong jacks over permanently with the modular jacks shown on the facing page, or you can use a plug-in adapter, as shown at bottom left.

HARD-WIRED PHONES: Hard-wired telephones are ones with a permanent, non-modular connection between the line cord and the body of the phone itself. Hard-wired desk phones are easy to spot, and you can quickly convert them for a modular line cord by removing the phone housing and installing a line cord converter.

Old, hard-wired wall phones can't be converted; you'll have to remove the telephone and install a new modular jack. Most older wall phones have a small U-shaped hole where the coiled handset enters the phone. Inside this hole is a tab. To remove the housing, use the eraser end of a pencil to push the tab up while pressing the bottom of the phone toward the wall with your other hand. The housing should pop free easily.

Wall phones that don't have these U-shaped holes are attached with screws, usually concealed beneath the telephone number card. To expose these screws, use a bent paper clip to remove the clear plastic cover, then lift out the number card.

After the housing is removed, remove the screws securing the telephone base to the wall and lift off the phone, exposing the wires. These can be cut, but don't let the loose wires fall down inside the wall—you'll need them to connect a new modular jack.

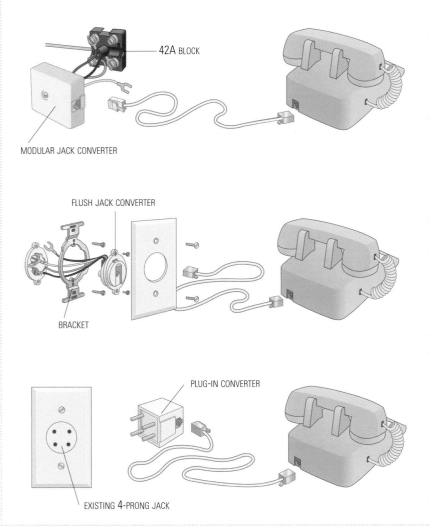

42A BLOCK

MODULAR JACK CONVERTER

FLUSH JACK CONVERTER

BRACKET

PLUG-IN CONVERTER

EXISTING 4-PRONG JACK

ADDING NEW LINES

4-CONDUCTOR
PLUG

6-CONDUCTOR
PLUG

Today's communication needs have made two, three, and even four separate phone lines commonplace—especially in a home office.

INSTALLING A SECOND LINE: If you're thinking of adding one new line, you may need only to call the telephone company and sign up for the service. Because standard phone wire has four conductors, and only two are typically used, the other two may be prewired to existing jacks as a backup pair or to allow for future needs. If not, you need to connect the additional wires to existing jacks or add new jacks. To plug in a multiple-line phone, you'll need a so-called RJ-14 (two-line) jack instead of an RJ-11 (single-device) version. If the jack is already wired for two lines but has only one outlet, you can plug in a multiline adapter (see page 129) that supplies access to both lines.

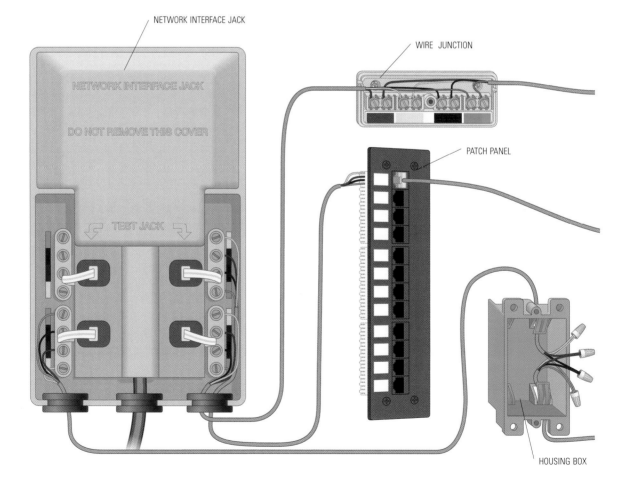

NETWORK INTERFACE JACK

WIRE JUNCTION

PATCH PANEL

NETWORK INTERFACE JACK

DO NOT REMOVE THIS COVER

TEST JACK

HOUSING BOX

ADDING MULTIPLE LINES: What about adding even more phone lines? You'll first need to have the phone company make the connections at the network interface jack; if necessary, the service person will install a new, larger interface. Then you must run station wire to a wire junction, housing box, or patch panel (all three options are shown below). New wires branch out from there, in home-run fashion.

Remember that you can buy standard station wire with at least three pairs of conductors. Or look for so-called Category 5 communications cable (see page 152), which comes with four twisted pairs of wires. If you need even more conductors, you'll need to run multiple station wires or Cat-5 cables side by side.

Modular jacks and line cord that handle six conductors—or three phone lines—are readily available, but standard wire junctions can accommodate only four conductors. Installations that call for four or more phone lines may require you to carefully orchestrate which station wire, line cord, and jack goes where.

PHONE WIRE FOR THE FUTURE

Category 5 wire (see page 152) handles standard phone conversations; but, unlike phone wire, it also handles computer data transmissions at speeds up to 100 megabits per second.

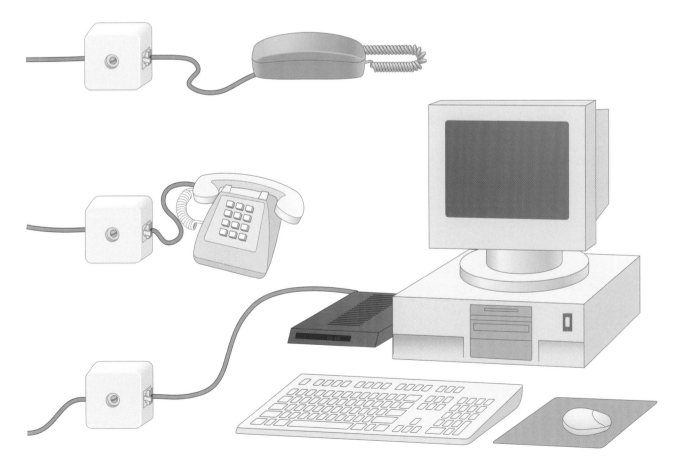

LOW VOLTAGE, HIGH TECH

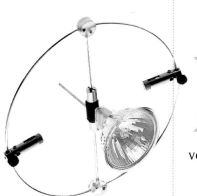

Low voltage is simply a catchall term for any wiring system that uses less power than traditional house wiring. Such a system involves use of a transformer, which steps down 120-volt household power to much lower levels—typically 12 to 24 volts.

Because there's little threat of shock or fire, low-voltage wires and cables have less insulation, making them easier to route, both because they're more flexible and because you don't have to drill big holes through framing members. Also, interior circuits typically don't need a separate grounding wire.

We've seen low-voltage lighting and doorbell circuits for years now. Some other familiar low-voltage systems, like cable and telephone lines, are taking on expanded roles. Other low-voltage applications are brand new. You'll now find many of these materials in well-stocked lighting showrooms, home centers, and hardware stores. Other late-breaking items may require some additional sleuthing: try home electronic stores and computer outlets—both retail and mail-order. Because some of these technologies are changing by the minute, it's also a good idea to consult your supplier for updates and advice.

FIBER-OPTIC
CABLE

WHAT ABOUT FIBER OPTICS?

It's the wave of future, perhaps, but experts are skeptical about the need for fiber-optic cable in the home. It's pricey, and the cable can be tricky to connect. Its primary advantage is its ability to transmit large amounts of data long distances; the short-distance needs encountered at home suggest that fiber will be unnecessary for some time to come.

On the other hand, it's the fiberoptics terminations, not the cable, that are unduly expensive. You might simply run the cable now, when wiring routes are exposed. Just leave it loose inside the wall, awaiting future technologies.

GEARING UP

The changing world of low-voltage wiring has its own emerging hardware and logistics. Here's a brief introduction.

THE LOW-VOLTAGE PLAYERS

The perfect time to get wired for the information superhighway is when new construction or a remodel is under way and the crucial walls and ceilings are still opened up. But what exactly should you bury in the walls to meet future phone, video, and computer needs? Here's a shopping list.

CATEGORY 5 CABLE: Think of this "twisted pair" cable as phone line for the future. Inside the cable are four pairs of wires—each pair twisted together so it doesn't interfere with the others while transmitting data. There are several different levels of cabling, designated categories 2, 3, 4, and 5. (There is no category 1.)

Category 2 is what cabling contractors call plain old telephone service, or POTS. Category 3 (which transfers data at 10 megabits per second) is used for voice and low-speed data transmission. Category 4 is no longer used because the difference in bandwidth—the space available for transmitting data—between Category 3 and Category 4 was not very significant. Category 5 cable, which transfers data at up to 100 megabits per second, is used for telecommunications and computer networks. It is downwardly compatible, which simply means that it can replace lower-capacity cables. So even if all you're going to do for now is run a basic phone, you can still use one pair of wires in a Cat-5 cable. For a closer look at working with this kind of cable, see page 152.

COAXIAL CABLE: Experts recommend installing coaxial cables along with the Category 5 cables. There are two basic types: video cable, which is rated at 75 ohms; and data cable, rated at 50 ohms. Some developing technologies use paired coaxial cable for the interactive connections of future two-way datatransmission links. See page 146 for details on video cable. For a closer look at network cable, turn to page 154.

AUDIO CABLE: This cable, also known more prosaically as speaker wire, contains a pair of polarized wires; two cables add up to stereo. Not only is running audio cable behind walls, floors, and ceilings neater than snaking it across the floor or along the wall, it also allows you to "network" sound throughout the house. For installation guidelines, see page 149.

ROUTING STRATEGIES

Experts are emphatic about installing all wires "home run," with each wire starting at the same point. As discussed on page 130, old phone installations were wired in a "daisy chain" from phone to phone rather than back to a central location. With home-run wiring (also called star topology in the communications trade), you'll use more wire, but all rooms will be networked together, enabling you to link computers and such peripherals as a printer, modem, and storage disk (for details, see page 155). It also lets a television share a signal from a cable or satellite (see page 148). And, if you add in audio cable, you can tap into a sound system located elsewhere in the house.

Where is the "command center," or main distribution point, for these wiring runs? Often it's in a new or existing closet that has easy access to wiring corridors in a basement or attic crawl space. If necessary, the distribution point can be in the garage or basement proper; but be sure to protect the spot from wide swings in moisture or temperature.

Keeping future needs in mind, many professionals run empty conduit vertically between floors or horizontally along walls, allowing easy-to-access paths for future wiring needs. Consider running a thin piece of twine or rope with new wires or through empty conduit. If you need to add a wire or cable later, you can attach it to this pull cord at one end and draw it through to the other end.

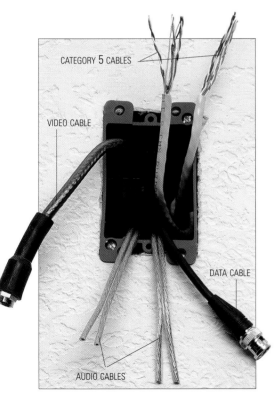

CATEGORY 5 CABLES

VIDEO CABLE

DATA CABLE

AUDIO CABLES

The future in a faceplate

At left, a standard plastic wall box houses low-voltage cables for voice, data, audio signals, and video communications. At right, six modular jacks snap into a multi-port faceplate and connect to incoming cables.

LOW-VOLTAGE LIGHTING

Because they're smaller, safer, and more energy-efficient than standard 120-volt systems, low-voltage light fixtures have become popular indoors as well as out. These systems use a transformer to step down household current to 12 volts. You can buy packaged low-voltage systems or create your own system with individual fixtures.

INTEGRAL OR REMOTE TRANSFORMER?

Low-voltage downlights may include an integral transformer, or you can use one remote (external) transformer to serve a number of fixtures. Both options are shown below.

REMOTE TRANSFORMER

INTEGRAL TRANSFORMER

Like their recessed counterparts, some low-voltage track fixtures have built-in transformers, while others fit a standard track with adapter transformers. Another option is to use an external transformer mounted away from the track that can serve several tracks and lights.

Which wiring arrangement is best? Both have plusses and minuses. Integral transformers are convenient, especially when only one or two fixtures are involved. But the built-in unit makes the fixtures bulkier and more expensive; some integral units may also hum, especially when coupled with dimmers. A remote transformer housed inside a nearby closet, basement, or ceiling can serve a number of fixtures; but you'll have to hassle with more routing and calculate your needs on the low-voltage side. The size of the transformer limits the total wattage of the lamps hooked up to it. For instance, you could use as many as six 50-watt lamps or fifteen 20-watt lamps with a 300-watt transformer. For added safety, a transformer should have an internal circuit breaker or be fused on the transformer's secondary (or fixture) side.

You'll need beefier conductors for low-voltage fixtures than you might expect. The lights may operate at only 12 volts, but wire size is determined by amperage (see page 29). Remember that amps = watts ÷ volts. So although voltage is much lower than household current, amperage must be much higher to serve the same amount of wattage. For example: A 120-volt circuit that feeds a group of fixtures rated at 1,200 watts requires only 10 amps—or #14 NM cable. A group of 12-volt fixtures that pulls only 300 watts would require at least 25 amps—or #10 THHN conductors.

CABLE LIGHTS

These low-voltage lights have illuminated shops and showrooms for years; now they're gaining popularity with homeowners. Minimalist, futuristic, fantastic, or whimsical, the diminutive fixtures are designed to be noticed.

The basic components of a cable light system break down into four categories: fixtures, power source, cables, and hardware. Because all the parts can be surface mounted, you won't have to open up walls or cut holes in ceilings. Some manufacturers offer basic kits that can be installed by homeowners; more elaborate systems may require professional installation.

At the heart of each fixture is the light source: a tiny MR-16 halogen bulb (see page 39).

Transformers are offered with capacities that commonly range from 250- to 500-watt loads. Some can simply be plugged into a wall receptacle or wired into an exposed junction box; others are located remotely, with wires run to the room.

Most cables are tin-plated copper wires that are bundled around a core of synthetic material called Kevlar, which prevents stretching. The cables run in parallel pairs spaced 1 inch to more than 6 inches apart, depending on the fixtures used.

The amount of hardware that supports and tensions the cables varies with the complexity of the installation. A straight run requires a pair of anchors at one end and a second pair with adjustable turnbuckles to draw the lines tight at the other. For straight runs of more than 25 feet, you must add midspan support brackets.

Things get more interesting once you start changing direction or adding more than one circuit. Wall- or ceiling-mounted brackets or metal wands let you weave the cables through overhead space while maintaining the required spacing. Line separators (or insulators) allow a pair of cables to have more than one circuit or transformer hooked to it.

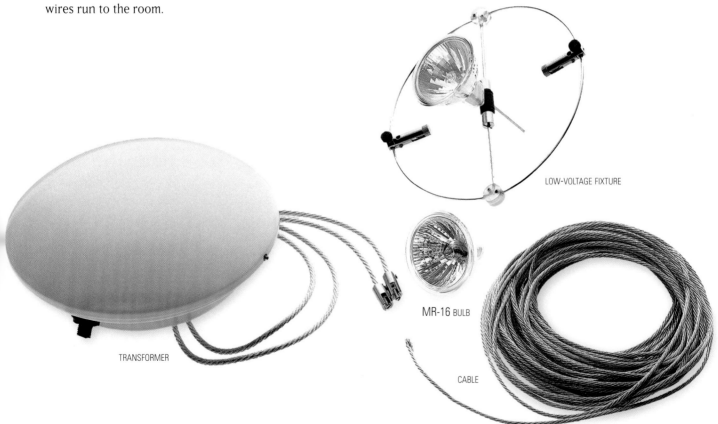

LOW-VOLTAGE FIXTURE

MR-16 BULB

TRANSFORMER

CABLE

Doorbells and Chimes

The parts of a typical doorbell system are the push button, the bell (or chimes or buzzer), and the transformer. The transformer allows the doorbell to operate on low voltage. You can buy doorbell kits or purchase the transformer, bell unit, and push button separately.

Plan to install components with bell wire—either 18-gauge or 20-gauge, depending on what your unit requires. Bell wire is available in many colors; buy several different ones so you'll be able to color-code the various wire connections.

The transformer you buy must match the system. Doorbells typically require 6 to 12 volts or so; chimes may need up to 18 volts. Connect the transformer to an existing 120-volt branch circuit at a junction box, as shown on the facing page. Most transformers attach to the knockout of a standard metal housing box; secure the transformer to the box with the furnished locknut. Caution: Before installing the transformer, first turn off power to the 120-volt circuit you're wiring into. Splice the transformer wires on the so-called primary (120-volt) side to the circuit wires with wire nuts.

PUSH BUTTONS

TRANSFORMER

BELL WIRE

CHIME UNIT

WIRING A CHIME WITH TWO PUSH BUTTONS

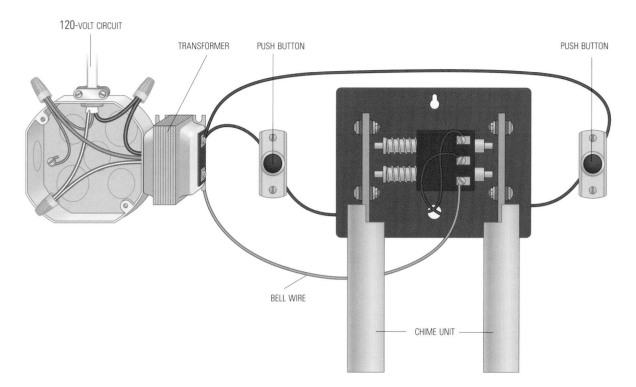

120-VOLT CIRCUIT

TRANSFORMER

PUSH BUTTON

PUSH BUTTON

BELL WIRE

CHIME UNIT

To wire a single-button system, run one wire from the transformer's secondary (low-voltage) side to the push button and another from the button to the bell unit; then run a wire from the bell unit back to the transformer. The button serves as a switch—when it's depressed, you complete the circuit, sounding the bell.

To wire a system with two push buttons (for example, one at both front and back doors), first run one wire from the screw terminal on the secondary side of the transformer directly to the bell unit. Then run switch loops to both push buttons, as shown above.

GOING REMOTE

Want a shortcut when installing a new doorbell or replacing a broken one? Consider one of the many remote systems now available. These radio-frequency devices don't require wires at all.

Audiovisual Systems

Low-voltage audiovisual wiring is the connecting link for cable TV and radio, satellite TV, stereo components and speakers, and a combination of all the above: home theater. Here's an overview of each system.

A CABLE CLOSE-UP

That familiar flat, black lifeline that drives both TV and FM signals is called coaxial cable. Cable comes in several varieties, but all types have similar components: an insulating core surrounds a thin copper conductor; woven shielding goes around the core to block radio interference; then an outer, rubberized sheath wraps everything up. Some cable types include solid foil wraps or multiple insulating/shielding layers to cut interference further.

Cable for audiovisual use is rated at 75 ohms (coaxial used for data transmission is rated at 50 ohms). There are two main types: RG-59 and RG-6. The latter is fatter—with an 18-gauge core instead of RG-59's 22-gauge—so there's less resistance over long distances. So-called quad cable (RG-6 quad cable) has four times the normal shielding for minimal interference; it's popular outdoors for satellite feeds (see page 148) and, to an extent, indoors for high-end home theaters (pages 150–151).

RG-59 CABLE

CABLE SPLITTER

CRIMP CONNECTORS

COUPLING

CABLE STAPLES

TWIST-ON CONNECTORS

ROUTING LOGISTICS: Coaxial cable may be routed through walls, floors, and ceilings, just like standard NM cable (for techniques, see Chapter Five, "Rough Wiring," beginning on page 56); or it can be strung atop baseboards, along carpet edges, or even down a wall (you can paint it to match). Use insulated cable staples to secure coaxial without damaging its insulation. Run the cable a minimum of 2 inches away from electrical wires; whenever possible, increase this distance to several feet.

When roughing-in new wiring, some professionals make a practice of running NM cable down the face of one wall stud and low-voltage cable down the facing surface of the adjacent stud. When crossing NM cable or conduit, try to do so at right angles. Don't place cable inside a housing box that has standard electrical wires—that's not only a source of interference, but it's also dangerous.

RG-6 CABLE

MAKING CONNECTIONS: Cable splices, or terminations, as they are sometimes called, are made with male couplings and female F-connectors. It's simplest to buy set lengths of coaxial cable with integral F-connectors. However, if you need a nonstandard length or have to make repairs, you can also add your own connectors—either by crimping (see below) or by using twist-on models (although they aren't as reliable as crimp-ons). Note that RG-59 and RG-6 cables require different connectors.

Cable junctions are handled with "splitters," which come in two-way, three-way, and four-way versions. A splitter with a built-in amplifier boosts the signal, which would otherwise drop with each new splice. The amplifier is best placed where cable enters the house.

ATTACHING A CABLE CONNECTOR

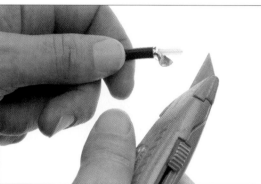

1 Remove the sheath
First cut back about ½ inch of the cable's outer, rubberized sheath, exposing the insulating core. Score the sheath with a utility knife; then simply twist the sheath off the cable, leaving the core intact.

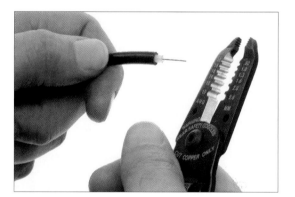

2 Strip the core
Some connectors require you to fold back the inner foil wrap or woven shielding; with others (like this one), simply remove the shielding. Then strip about ⅜ inch of the inner core off the copper conductor as shown. A wire stripper makes a clean cut.

3 Position the connector
Next, slip the cable connector over the exposed cable end, twisting as necessary until about ¹⁄₁₆ inch of conductor protrudes past the connector's end.

4 Crimp the connector
Finally, squeeze the connector onto the cable as shown. A cable crimper works best, but in a pinch you could also use a multipurpose tool or lineman's pliers.

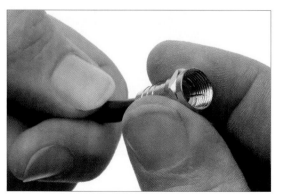

DIGITAL SATELLITE DISHES

Just a few years ago, state-of-the-art satellite dishes that allowed you to bring in long-distance TV channels were about 7 feet in diameter. Now they're an unobtrusive 18 inches and can be conveniently mounted to a house wall, eave, or chimney (depending on the model) with the appropriate installation kit. The only firm requirement is that the dish must have an unobstructed line of sight to the southern sky, where the sending satellite is located.

COMPONENTS: As shown at right, the key parts of a digital satellite system (DSS) are the dish and a DSS receiver located inside the house. The dish meets the receiver by way of coaxial cable—preferably RG-6 quad cable, which has four times the shielding of standard cable.

The quad cable runs from the dish to a wall-mounted, exterior grounding block, as shown, then from the block to the inside receiver. Exterior drip loops keep water from running directly down the cable and into either the connectors or the house. A solid copper grounding wire connects the grounding block to your home's grounding electrode conductor at the service entrance panel.

Inside, you'll need a 120-volt receptacle to power the receiver and a phone jack (this is how ordering and billing are done). If you want to hook up more than one TV to the satellite, the simplest way is via a cable splitter (see page 146) between the receiver and the first TV (you can't split the cable before it reaches the DSS receiver).

WARNING

Antennas are extremely efficient conductors. When working with any satellite dish or off-the-air antenna, you must not contact any electrical wires in the area. Do not work when there is any threat of lightning.

The drawback is each TV will receive the same channel. If you'd like the flexibility to watch a different channel on the second TV, installation gets a little messy: you'll need a second LNBF feedhorn (a signal receiver) at the dish, a second RG-6 quad cable, and an additional DSS receiver.

LOCAL PROGRAMMING: If local programming is important to you, you may need an additional off-the-air antenna wired with coaxial cable. This roof-mounted antenna follows a separate path into the house and, depending on the components, connects to either the DSS receiver, a VCR, or the "antenna in" port on your TV. (For a closer look at these connections, see pages 150–151.)

If an off-the-air antenna is already installed, it's likely to be wired with flat, twin-lead wire; if that's the case, you'll need to add an impedance-matching transformer inside, connecting the twin-lead and 75-ohm coaxial, then run coaxial to one of the components listed above.

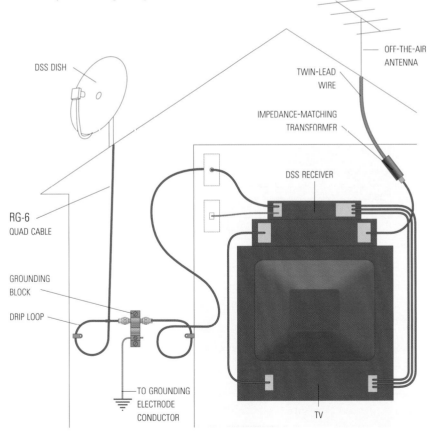

DSS DISH

OFF-THE-AIR ANTENNA

TWIN-LEAD WIRE

IMPEDANCE-MATCHING TRANSFORMER

DSS RECEIVER

RG-6 QUAD CABLE

GROUNDING BLOCK

DRIP LOOP

TO GROUNDING ELECTRODE CONDUCTOR

TV

INSTALLING A BUILT-IN SPEAKER

1 Cut a hole, fish wire

First cut a hole in the ceiling or wall for the speaker body; most speakers come with hole-cutting templates. Fish speaker cable through the hole and attach wires to speaker terminals (be sure each wire goes to the correct terminal).

2 Secure the speaker

This speaker comes with integral clamping wings; simply slip the speaker into the hole and tighten the mounting screws—which in turn secure the wings to ceiling or wall material. Some speakers may require toggle bolts or plastic anchors instead.

3 Add the grill

The hard work is done. To complete the job, simply push the speaker grill onto the speaker—it's much like securing a recessed downlight's trim ring or baffle (see page 111).

AUDIO ADVICE

When talking about stereo wiring, two terms matter: impedance and polarity.

Impedance, measured in ohms, is the resistance a speaker offers to the signal passing through it. Speakers are rated for a certain impedance—most are rated at 8 ohms, but the available range is 4 to 16 ohms. AV receivers often have specific sets of ports, or terminals, for different impedance ratings.

If your receiver supports multiple channels—such as A, B, and A+B—you can wire two sets of speakers directly from the receiver in home-run fashion. You simply wire the speakers to the correct ports. However, if you choose to run multiple speakers in series fashion, the impedance rating becomes the sum of the individual speakers' ratings. Two 8-ohm speakers are now a 16-ohm load. If you wire the speakers in parallel, the impedance is the speakers' individual ohm ratings divided by the number of speakers. Two 8-ohm speakers become a 4-ohm load.

Polarity refers to the direction that current flows through a device. The ports or terminals on a receiver, speakers, and other components are polarized: each set should have one input marked "+" or "L" and one marked "–" or "R." Your wiring hookups must match up at both ends; that is, if a wire is connected to a negative terminal on a speaker it should also be connected to the negative terminal on the receiver. Most audio and speaker cables are color-coded or otherwise marked (ribbing is common): be sure that the red connector or the ribbed leg is connected to the same polarized terminal on both ends.

Speaker cable comes in several grades and gauges—commonly #10 to #16. Generally, the bigger the cable the better. For stereo, you'll need two cables—one to each speaker—each with two wires. Keep wire runs as short as possible.

HOME THEATER BASICS

What transforms a TV, a VCR, and a pile of other black boxes into a formal home theater? It's the systematic relationship between several key devices, all tied together with the same cast of low-voltage wires and cables we've met already.

Typical home theater components are shown on the facing page. The TV and speakers are obvious stars, but it's the audiovisual receiver that's really "command central." A plethora of media signals may be routed to the AV receiver from components both inside and outside the home: a cable box, satellite dish, off-the-air antenna, VCR, or DVD player. The receiver allows you to choose which of these input sources you want, and then encodes and outputs signals to the TV and speakers. Consider the AV receiver as the axis of whatever wiring scheme you're planning.

VIDEO OPTIONS: TVs are available with a choice of features: direct view, rear-projection, front-projection, flat-screen, high-definition. You'll need some showroom help unraveling your options; and, just as important, you'll need the right cable and wiring connections that are compatible with your AV receiver.

Whenever possible, use shielded cable rather than coaxial cable to make hookups between your TV and receiver. Coaxial cable transmits RF (radio frequency) signals, while shielded cable sends cleaner baseband signals. Most connectors are RCA types (shown at left); newer video-S and composite jacks, which divide the video signal into multiple facets, may use 4-pin connectors.

To keep wire runs as short as possible, plan to cluster home theater components in a central location or nearby closet. Be sure to maintain at least 6 inches of clearance between audiovisual cables and standard electrical wires. Don't make loops in cable to take up wire slack; loops add interference.

AUDIO ASPECTS: Surround sound is the heart of the home theater experience. A battery of at least five and sometimes six speakers is driven by digital encoding supplied by the AV receiver. Matching speakers at front left and front right provide "stereo." A shielded center speaker, mounted above the TV or placed right on top, fills in the middle. (You could also use the TV's built-in speaker, but a separate center speaker usually sounds better.) Left-rear and right-rear speakers create the surround-sound effect. In addition, a sixth speaker—a specialized subwoofer—is often placed at rear center (although technically, it could be placed anywhere, as these low-frequency sounds have no clear "direction").

LABEL THAT CABLE

Because of the sheer number of interwoven cables coming and going throughout a home theater installation, it's essential to keep some sense of order—as well as a firm sense of polarity. Be sure to mark all cables at both ends—either by using a permanent marker and masking tape or by purchasing specific cable labels, available at home electronics stores.

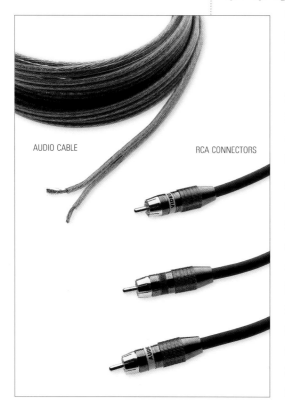

AUDIO CABLE   RCA CONNECTORS

So how do you organize this potential tangle of speakers and speaker wires? If walls are open, simply run wires through house framing to wall jacks with stereo speaker inputs. In existing homes, you can use the same fishing tricks used for standard electrical wiring (see pages 64–69). If other avenues are closed, you can also route cable along baseboards, inside carpet tack strips, or through surface raceways (see page 69).

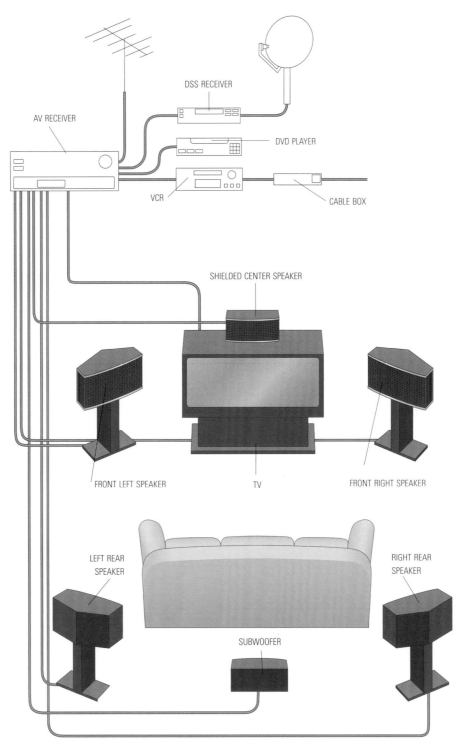

DSS RECEIVER

AV RECEIVER

DVD PLAYER

VCR

CABLE BOX

SHIELDED CENTER SPEAKER

FRONT LEFT SPEAKER

TV

FRONT RIGHT SPEAKER

LEFT REAR
SPEAKER

RIGHT REAR
SPEAKER

SUBWOOFER

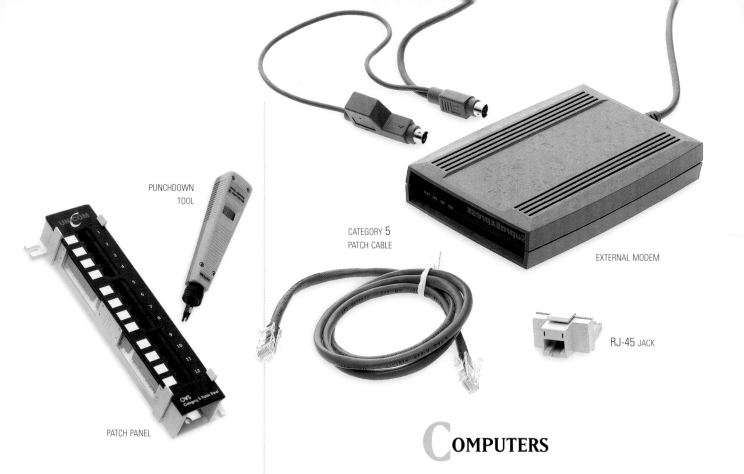

PUNCHDOWN
TOOL

CATEGORY 5
PATCH CABLE

EXTERNAL MODEM

RJ-45 JACK

PATCH PANEL

CATEGORY 5
CABLE

COMPUTERS

Telecommunications began, of course, with the humble phone line, as described in Chapter Seven, "Telephone Systems," beginning on page 126. But it has quickly grown into e-mail, Internet access, and home computer networking. The jargon can be confusing, but the actual cabling and connections are straightforward. Here's how to get wired.

PHONE ADD-ONS AND UPGRADES

Typically, to jump into cyberspace, you'd simply plug one end of your modem—either an external model or a built-in—into a standard telephone jack, which is hooked up to standard 2-pair or 3-pair telephone wire. Installation gets a little more challenging when you're linking phone, answering machine, fax, and modem together, but it's still a relatively simple matter, involving the addition of a multi-line jack and perhaps an adapter or two to your present POTS (plain old telephone service) wire. For an overview of basic telephone systems, see pages 128–130.

If, however, you're wiring from scratch or adding a new phone line for a home office, it's a good investment to wire the new run with 4-pair, Category 5 cable. Even if you need only one phone line now, you can eventually run up to four lines off it; whereas you may not be able to wire any future devices off the POTS wire. Category 5 cable comes in several versions, including interior, exterior, and fire-rated.

Bring the Cat-5 cable into a standard wall box as shown on page 141. Don't make splices inside walls; make them where accessible, using RJ-45 couplings. Avoid sharp bends when routing cable. When making connections, strip off as little insulation as possible, and untwist only as much wire as necessary.

Wire an 8-pin, RJ-45 jack (used for computer hookups) to the cable, using a screwdriver or a specialized punchdown tool (shown on the facing page) to press the conductors into the slots on the back of the jack. Although a standard 4- or 6-pin telephone connector will fit the wider RJ-45 jack, the RJ-45 connector won't fit the traditional jack.

If you're adding a standard phone, fax, or answering machine, negotiate your way around the room with either 2- or 3-pair line cord (see page 128); or, if your device calls for it, use a Cat-5 patch cable (available in different lengths) with RJ-45 connectors at both ends.

SURGE SUPPRESSION

SURGE ARRESTOR

Lightning strikes, power spikes, and even daily voltage fluctuations can potentially travel right into your home on electrical or phone lines and make "toast" of your expensive audiovisual gear, phone equipment, and home computer networks. To protect both your investment and important data, it makes sense to add surge protection to your wiring scheme.

There are two main types of surge arrestors: point-of-use and whole house. Both are designed to block excess voltage from reaching your expensive electronics. Instead, the arrestors divert excess voltage back through the grounding system to the grounding electrode conductor and into the earth. Note: You must have an adequate grounding system for the arrestor to do its job.

Point-of-use devices, like the one shown above right, resemble multi-outlet power strips, and, unfortunately, many cheaper versions are little more than that. When shopping, compare joule ratings (the higher the better); maximum voltage the unit will let pass through (the less the better); and the maximum spike the unit can sustain without failing. Many protectors come with insurance policies in case of failure. Good units have an internal fuse and a reset button. Many come with telephone jacks, as well as 120-volt outlets. Check whether the strip has room for all your large plugs and/or transformers.

Whole-house arrestors reside either inside or just outside the service entrance panel, clamped to a knockout. They are usually wired to a double-pole, 240-volt circuit breaker and to the neutral bus bar.

You can also help protect a computer by placing it on its own dedicated circuit and installing a so-called isolated

ISOLATED GROUND RECEPTACLE

ground receptacle (shown below). If you're using a plastic housing box, wire this device like any other receptacle (see pages 92–95). For a metal box, wire the circuit with 3-conductor cable. Make hot and neutral connections as usual, but attach the grounding wire to the box only. Then, run the extra red wire from the neutral bus bar to the receptacle's grounding screw, and tape the wire green to identify it as a second uninterrupted grounding wire.

There's an extra step you can take to protect your equipment during a lightning storm or power outage: unplug it. This advice applies not only to equipment plugged into receptacles on household voltage, but also to phone lines that may be connected to a lone computer or, worse yet, to a computer network. In either case, detach the phone line from its jack.

NETWORKING

Multicomputer families and home businesses may feel the need to access data, share peripherals such as printers and scanners, share Internet connections, or simply play computer games against each other from different rooms. Home computer networks come in two basic flavors: coaxial cable and twisted pair.

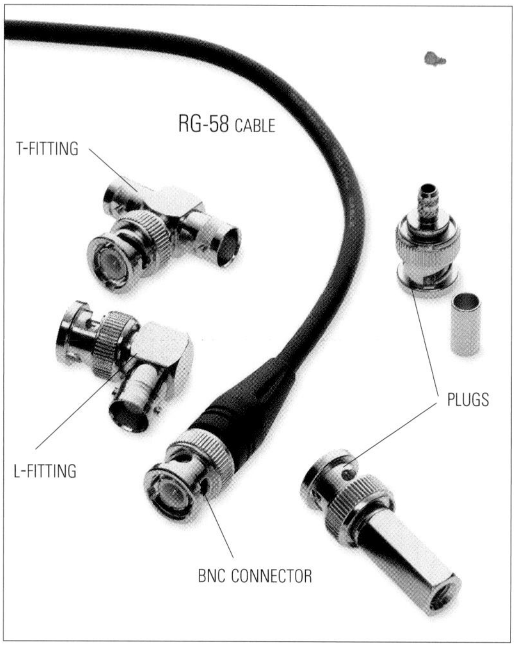

CABLE NETWORK: This is not the same cable that serves your TV or video: it's RG-58 coaxial, also called thinnet, which is smaller in diameter, is rated for 50 ohms rather than 75 ohms, and takes knurled BNC (bayonet) fittings like those shown at left.

Coaxial networks have their pros and cons. On the positive side, cable networking is fairly inexpensive—there's no hub or distribution center (see below) required, just cable, couplings, and network interface cards for your computers or other devices. On the down side, cable networking is limited to 10-base (10-megabit) transmission, which means it will be slow. Devices must be wired in series or "daisy-chain" fashion, so if one leg fails, the whole system goes kaput.

Make cable connections between cable and computer with BNC T-fittings and standard F-connectors. At the end of the line, close the unused end with a plug. You can buy cable with ready-made F-connectors at both ends or buy cable in bulk and add your own F-connectors, as shown on page 147.

UTP NETWORK: This is a techy-sounding acronym for "unshielded twisted pair"—in other words, a network that travels via Category 3 or Category 5 cable. Cat-3 cable can handle only 10-base transmission speeds, so opt for the faster 100-base (100-megabit) Cat-5 cable instead.

The heart of a UTP network is the central distribution center, or "hub." You'll need a hub with enough input and output ports to handle all your computers and shared peripherals, such as printers and hard drives. Plug the hub into a nearby 120-volt receptacle.

You'll also need some other items: a network interface card (NIC) for each computer (unless your computers offer built-in support for Ethernet), some Cat-5 patch cables, and networking software "drivers" for each machine.

RG-58 CABLE

T-FITTING

L-FITTING

BNC CONNECTOR

PLUGS

CAT-5 PATCH CABLE

NETGEAR ...Fast Ethernet Hub ...FE-104

HUB

NETWORK
INTERFACE CARD

Networking pieces are available as kits, which include a hub, two or more NICs, patch cables, and software. However, if your computers don't have the same expansion slots or internal hubs (either PCI or ISA versions), you'll need to buy the pieces individually.

Plan to connect devices as shown below with home-run wiring (also called star topology). Drill and fish wires between rooms as necessary; for tips, see pages 64–69.

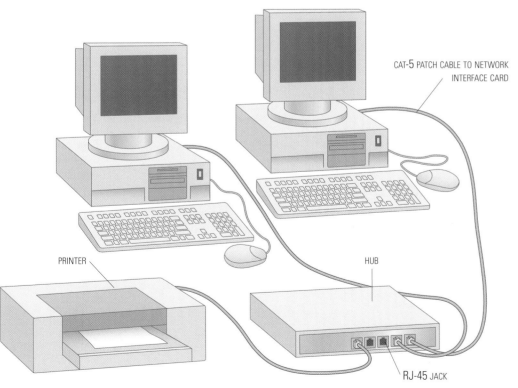

CAT-5 PATCH CABLE TO NETWORK
INTERFACE CARD

PRINTER

HUB

RJ-45 JACK

THE GREAT OUTDOORS

You learned the basics of installing indoor wiring in the preceding chapters. But chances are you'll also become involved with outdoor wiring—whether for security, recreation, or to enhance your landscape. Although the principles are the same for both indoor and outdoor wiring, many of the materials used outside are specially designed to resist the weather (and your garden hose). Outdoor housing boxes are either driptight or watertight. Underground feeder cable has a thick, solid plastic covering that makes it watertight when buried underground. Other wires are typically routed through rigid conduit for more protection from the weather, as well as accidental damage from digging.

You can bring electricity outdoors in two ways: by tapping into an existing device and extending an inside power source, or by running a circuit directly from the service entrance panel to an outdoor housing box or subpanel. These sources in turn can feed new outdoor receptacles and both 120-volt and low-voltage light fixtures.

When working with electricity outdoors, be extra careful. Always de-energize the circuit before working on it. Make sure that outdoor circuits are properly grounded by running a copper grounding conductor the same size as the circuit conductors from source to load. To be on the safe side, use ground fault circuit interrupters—either receptacle or circuit-breaker types—on all outdoor circuits.

UTDOOR MATERIALS

The concepts and basic techniques for wiring are the same inside and outside—it's the materials that make the difference. Because outdoor wiring must survive the elements, materials are stronger and more resistant to corrosion. Also, the components must fit together exactly to prevent water from entering them, so heavy-duty gaskets or special fittings are often used to seal boxes. Shown here are many of the devices you'll need for outdoor wiring projects.

OUTDOOR BOXES

Exterior housing boxes come in two types: so-called driptight boxes that deflect vertically falling water, and watertight boxes that keep out water coming from any direction.

DRIPTIGHT: This type of box is usually made of painted sheet metal and often has a shroud or shield that sheds rain falling from above. A typical driptight subpanel is shown below left. These units are not waterproof and must be mounted where floods, or even "rain" from sprinklers below, can't touch them, such as under an eave.

WATERTIGHT: For any place that is likely to get wet, a watertight box is best. These boxes are made of cast aluminum, zinc-dipped iron, or bronze, and have threaded entries to keep out water. All covers for watertight boxes are sealed with gaskets, and many switch boxes are equipped with an exterior on/off lever that enables you to operate the switch without opening the cover. The outdoor fixture box and switch box shown are typical watertight boxes.

DRIPTIGHT SUBPANEL

EXTENDER RING

GASKET

COVER PLATE

LAMP SOCKET

WATERTIGHT FIXTURE BOX

EXTERIOR SWITCH PLATE

"WHILE-IN-USE" COVER

WATERTIGHT SWITCH BOX

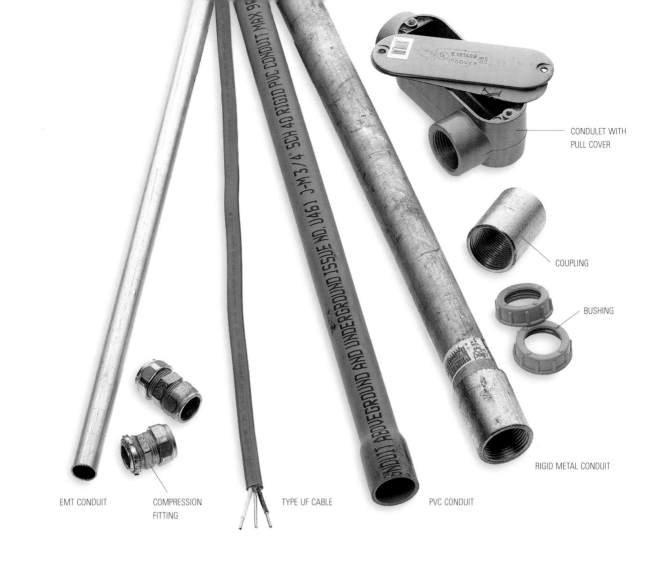

CONDULET WITH PULL COVER

COUPLING

BUSHING

RIGID METAL CONDUIT

EMT CONDUIT   COMPRESSION FITTING   TYPE UF CABLE   PVC CONDUIT

CABLE AND CONDUIT

In most situations when you're running cable outside, you'll be burying it underground. Underground feeder cable (type UF) is waterproof and can be buried directly in the ground, although it's sometimes housed in conduit for additional protection from water, as well as from physical damage. The National Electrical Code permits direct burial as shallow as 12 inches deep if the feeder cable is used for a 120- or 120/240-volt residential branch circuit. Any cable that is aboveground must be covered with some kind of conduit.

Conduit shields conductors—usually THWN/THHN wires—from moisture and physical harm. Different types of conduit are rated for underground or aboveground use, depending on their construction. Common sizes range from 1/2 inch to 3 inches, based on inside diameter. The size you need depends on the number and size of conductors the conduit will be holding. For guidelines, see page 30.

Rigid nonmetallic (PVC schedule 40) is the most popular type of outdoor conduit and the best choice for direct burial because it's lightweight and it doesn't corrode. Schedule 80 PVC is even sturdier. Cut and connect lengths of PVC conduit as outlined on page 86.

Rigid metal conduit isn't as popular because it's pricey and it requires threaded fittings for assembly. One advantage, however, is that it can be buried as little as 6 inches deep.

Thinwall conduit (EMT), detailed on pages 84–85, can't be buried because it isn't rigid enough or corrosion resistant, but it is acceptable for exposed locations above ground level, such as on the side of a house. Outdoors, EMT must be used with watertight compression fittings (shown above).

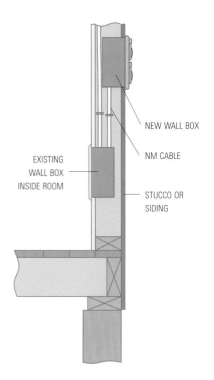

BACK-TO-BACK BOXES

NEW WALL BOX

NM CABLE

EXISTING
WALL BOX
INSIDE ROOM

STUCCO OR
SIDING

EXTENDING WIRING OUTDOORS

Routing a circuit to the outside of your house requires the same procedures as extending an indoor circuit (see pages 62–81). Once outside, the wiring techniques are similar, but you'll be working with outdoor-rated materials. Here's a closer look at what's involved.

SELECTING A POWER SOURCE

You can tap into any existing switch, fixture, receptacle, or junction box that is in the middle or at the end of a circuit run. CAUTION: Be sure to de-energize the circuit before tapping into it.

The four diagrams on this page illustrate how to extend a circuit outside to a new device. Two diagrams show the addition of a watertight extender ring to an existing outdoor receptacle (lower left) and a porch light (lower right). In each case, the extender adds space to the housing box for splicing the new wires, which run through conduit to the new device.

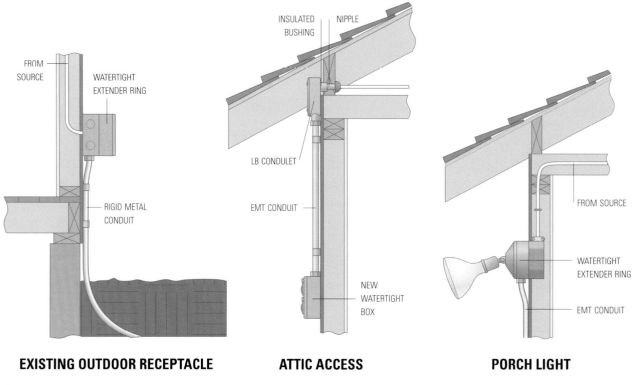

FROM SOURCE

WATERTIGHT EXTENDER RING

RIGID METAL CONDUIT

EXISTING OUTDOOR RECEPTACLE

INSULATED BUSHING   NIPPLE

LB CONDULET

EMT CONDUIT

NEW WATERTIGHT BOX

ATTIC ACCESS

FROM SOURCE

WATERTIGHT EXTENDER RING

EMT CONDUIT

PORCH LIGHT

The other two diagrams show how to bring cable from inside the house. The easiest way is to install a new receptacle box back-to-back with an existing box in an interior room, feeding the cable from the existing box to the new box location. NM cable can be used because the cable isn't exposed to the weather. Another option is to tap into a junction box in the attic and run cable outside through an LB condulet fitting to a new device.

You can, of course, plan one or more dedicated circuits for outdoor use. Run circuit cable directly from the service entrance panel or route subfeeds (page 124) to a driptight subpanel outdoors. It's fine to use NM cable while indoors, but you must switch to exposed conduit or buried UF cable once outside.

ROUTING CONDUIT AND CABLE

The drawing below illustrates some typical uses of three types of conduit and UF cable.

If covered with a layer of concrete, rigid nonmetallic (PVC) conduit can be buried just 12 inches deep. Otherwise, bury it at least 18 inches deep. Rigid metal conduit may be buried as little as 6 inches deep, with or without a concrete cap.

When burying UF cable, dig as deep as possible, but to 12 inches minimum. Lay a rot-resistant (redwood or cedar) or pressure-treated board on top of the cable before covering it with dirt. This reduces the danger of spading through the cable later.

Thinwall (EMT) conduit can't be used underground, but it may be used to protect aboveground wiring runs, as shown.

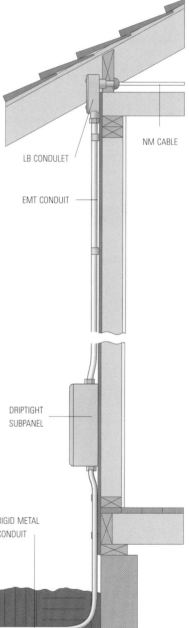

NM CABLE

LB CONDULET

EMT CONDUIT

DRIPTIGHT SUBPANEL

RIGID METAL CONDUIT

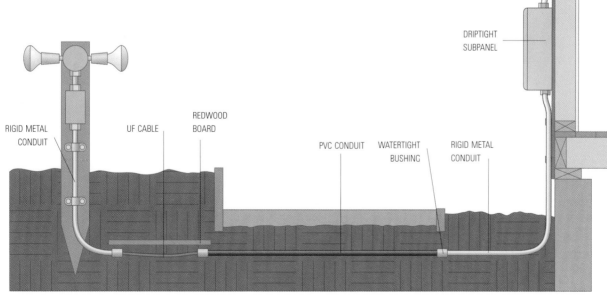

RIGID METAL CONDUIT

UF CABLE

REDWOOD BOARD

PVC CONDUIT

WATERTIGHT BUSHING

RIGID METAL CONDUIT

OUTDOOR IMPROVEMENTS

Outdoor wiring additions most often include GFCI-protected receptacles and light fixtures—either 120-volt or low-voltage or both.

WIRING AN OUTDOOR RECEPTACLE

According to present electrical codes, any new outside receptacle (such as one used to plug in a patio charcoal starter, a patio heater, or a radio) must be protected with a GFCI. For installation pointers, see page 96. To make your job easier, you can buy a complete kit consisting of a cast aluminum outdoor box and cover and a GFCI receptacle.

A pump or filter for an aboveground pool, a hot tub, or a garden pond or fountain is also usually cord-connected to an outdoor receptacle. You should use these devices only on a GFCI-protected circuit, even if your home was built before GFCIs were required. If the device isn't already equipped with a locking plug, it's recommended that you install one; then wire a matching locking receptacle (see page 35) that's protected by a GFCI-type circuit breaker (see page 18).

After wiring an outdoor receptacle, install a gasket in combination with a plastic shield to keep out any moisture. The cover, shown below, called a while-in-use cover, flips up to admit a plug.

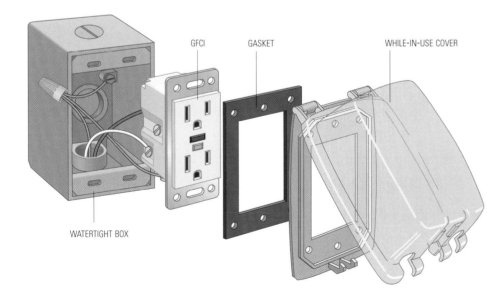

GFCI   GASKET   WHILE-IN-USE COVER

WATERTIGHT BOX

WIRING A TIMER

By wiring in an indoor switch and timer to an outdoor lighting circuit, as shown below, you can turn on outdoor lights or devices from inside the house or let the timer turn them on automatically. (If you wire the switch to the automatic timer in a switch loop, you can bypass the timer and turn the lights on or off right away.) Connect the incoming black hot wires to the "line" terminal of the timer and the outgoing hot wire and switch wire to the "load" terminal. Some timers may have wire leads instead of screw terminals. Connect the leads to the wires of the cable with wire nuts. Set the timer according to the manufacturer's instructions.

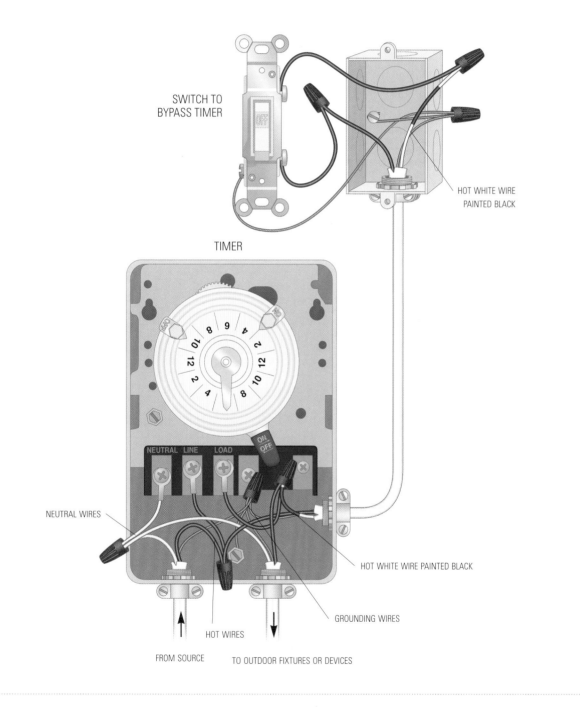

SWITCH TO
BYPASS TIMER

HOT WHITE WIRE
PAINTED BLACK

TIMER

NEUTRAL WIRES

NEUTRAL   LINE   LOAD

HOT WHITE WIRE PAINTED BLACK

GROUNDING WIRES

HOT WIRES

FROM SOURCE   TO OUTDOOR FIXTURES OR DEVICES

MOTION SENSOR

DAYLIGHT SENSORS

AUTOMATIC ILLUMINATORS

How can you set up landscape or security lights to take care of themselves? A timer, like the one shown on page 163, is one solution. Other options include daylight-sensitive photocells and motion-sensor fixtures, both detailed below.

DAYLIGHT SENSORS: These are simply photocells that react to daylight. When it's dark, the photocell sends power to the light fixture it's connected to; when dawn comes, the sensor opens the circuit, shutting down the fixture. You can install fixtures with built-in photocells or buy sensors separately.

Several retrofits are shown at left. Most common is a large photocell that's mounted directly onto a knockout in an outdoor fixture box. You can also buy a simple screw-base adapter with built-in sensor that fits a standard A-bulb socket; the fixture bulb screws into the adapter. Or opt for a discreet photo eye that's designed to fit a hole drilled in a lamppost.

I2O-VOLT LIGHTING

A 120-volt outdoor lighting system offers several advantages over a 12-volt system (see pages 166–167). For starters, 120-volt fixtures usually illuminate larger areas than 12-volt fixtures can—especially useful for security and for lighting trees from the ground. A 120-volt system also offers flexibility: power tools, patio heaters, and electric garden tools can be plugged into 120-volt circuits.

A 120-volt outdoor system consists of a set of light fixtures and type UF cable (if allowed by local code) or THWN/THHN wires in conduit. Several standard fixture arrangements are shown at right.

You may want to connect the system through an indoor switch and timer to an existing electrical source or circuit, as described on page 163.

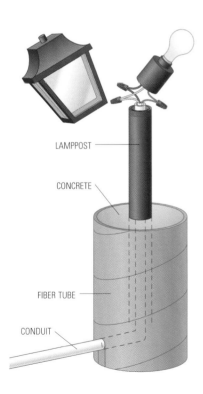

LAMPPOST

CONCRETE

FIBER TUBE

CONDUIT

MOTION SENSORS: These "remote eyes" are handy for both security and for unloading a batch of groceries after dark. Motion sensors come in two basic versions: infrared and microwave. Some units combine both wave types. Like daylight sensors, you can buy motion sensors alone or integrated into a fixture that houses one or more floodlights (as shown on the facing page).

Plan to install the motion sensor on a house wall, eave, or freestanding post, no higher than about 12 feet off the ground. Mount the fixture like any other outdoor floodlight (see "120-Volt Lighting," below), and follow the wiring instructions included with the unit. The trick is aiming the sensor's detection lobes or waves. Don't align the lobes so they're parallel to the most likely traffic path (for example, a front walkway); there are "dead" spots between the parallel detection bands. Instead, place the sensor so the lobes will cut across the traffic area, as shown at right.

Some motion sensors have adjustable ranges of sensitivity and can be set to remain on for varying amounts of time. The right combination of aim, response level, and duration will probably take some trial and error to achieve.

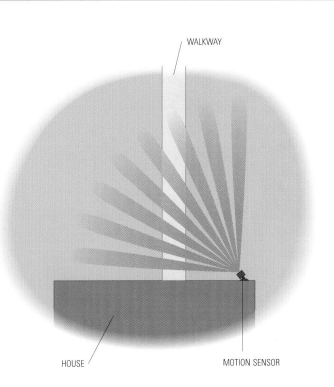

WALKWAY

HOUSE

MOTION SENSOR

When mounting a motion sensor, aim the unit's detection lobes so they cut across the most likely traffic path.

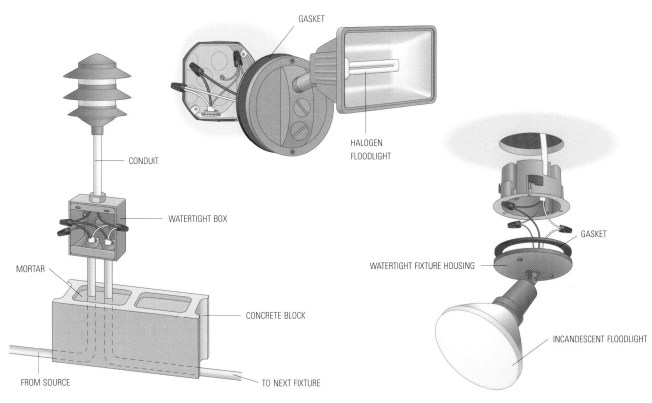

GASKET

HALOGEN FLOODLIGHT

CONDUIT

WATERTIGHT BOX

MORTAR

CONCRETE BLOCK

FROM SOURCE

TO NEXT FIXTURE

GASKET

WATERTIGHT FIXTURE HOUSING

INCANDESCENT FLOODLIGHT

LOW-VOLTAGE LIGHTING

Although low-voltage fixtures lack the "punch" of line-current fixtures, their output is sufficient for most outdoor applications. Because it carries only 12 volts, low-voltage wiring doesn't present the dangers of 120 volts; nor does it require the special conduit and boxes of other outdoor wiring. All you need is a plug-in transformer, 12-volt cable, and low-voltage fixtures.

NUTS AND BOLTS: The transformer, usually housed in an integral driptight box, steps down the household current of 120 volts to 12 volts. Plug it into a nearby receptacle, then run the 12-volt cable from the low-voltage side of the transformer to the desired locations for your lights. The cable can be buried a few inches deep in the ground or simply covered with mulch in a planting area; however, to avoid accidentally spading through it, consider running the cable alongside structures, walks, and fences where you won't be likely to cultivate.

A low-voltage system often comes in a kit with lights, cable, and transformer. Some light fixtures simply clip onto the wire, others require a clamp connector, while still others must be spliced into the system and connected with wire nuts. Be sure to use the wire and connections specified in the instructions. If you don't already have a receptacle to plug the transformer into, install a GFCI-protected receptacle, as discussed on page 162.

LOW-VOLTAGE
FIXTURE

LOW-VOLTAGE
CABLE

CLAMP
CONNECTOR

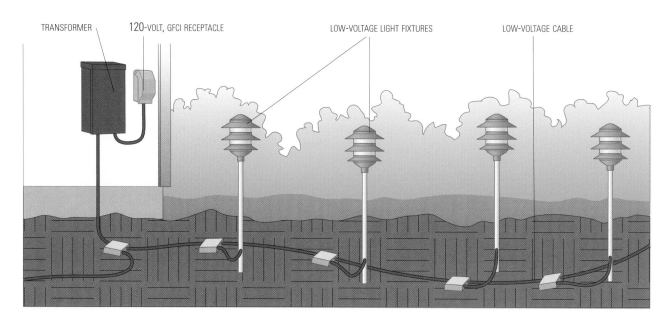

TRANSFORMER 120-VOLT, GFCI RECEPTACLE   LOW-VOLTAGE LIGHT FIXTURES   LOW-VOLTAGE CABLE

SIZING YOUR SYSTEM: Most 12-volt transformers are rated for loads from 100 to 300 watts. The higher the rating, the more light fixtures you can connect to the transformer. In most cases, you simply add up the wattages of all the light fixtures you wish to install, then choose a transformer and cable size that can handle the load.

For long cable runs, however, you must de-rate the circuit to account for "voltage drop"—the accumulated resistance in all that wire. A voltage drop up to 10 percent (1.2 volts) is considered acceptable—more than that, and you'll see noticeably less light output.

How can you combat voltage drop? For starters, simply try a larger wire size. Or plan to run two or more shorter cables in a "split-load" pattern, as shown below. You can also install multiple transformers and/or circuits. Two transformers don't need to be placed side-by-side—one might be pole-mounted in a remote location that's fed by 120-volt cable or wires, allowing a much shorter low-voltage run.

LOW-VOLTAGE ROUTING OPTIONS

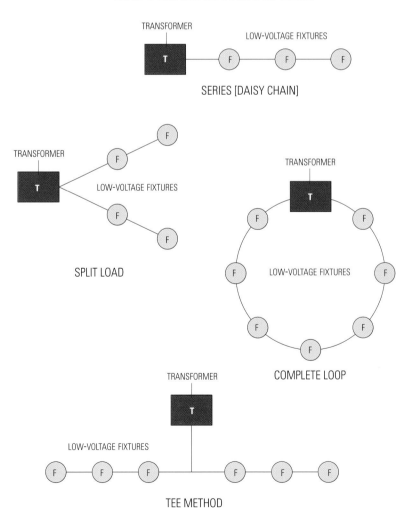

SERIES [DAISY CHAIN]

SPLIT LOAD

COMPLETE LOOP

TEE METHOD

FIGURING VOLTAGE DROP

There are a number of ways that professional designers and electricians figure voltage drop. Probably the simplest method is to multiply your wattage by the distance the cable will travel—then divide that figure by the cable's so-called "cable constant," which takes the product's inherent resistance into account. Cable constants for typical low-voltage gauges are as follows:

#16 wire	2,200
#14 wire	3,500
#12 wire	7,500
#10 wire	11,920

For example, a string of six 20-watt fixtures served by a 60-foot run of #12 cable would be calculated as follows: 120 (6 x 20 watts) x 60 (feet) ÷ 7,500 (the cable constant of #12 wire) = .96 volts. This is less than the allowable voltage drop of 1.2 volts, so all is well. But a 150-watt load that runs 50 feet on #14 cable computes as: 150 x 50 ÷ 3500 = 2.14. This voltage drop is too high. Subtract a fixture or two, plan a shorter cable run, or increase wire size—then try again.

TROUBLESHOOTING AND REPAIRS

Y ou would get quite a charge—financially, that is—if you had to call in an electrician every time the lights went out. This chapter will help you move toward electrical independence by explaining what to do when things go wrong.

With the right safety precautions (see pages 18–19) and some basic diagnostic tools (page 45), even novice do-it-yourselfers can replace plugs, cords, cables, switches, and receptacles; repair light fixtures and lamps; and diagnose circuit problems when these devices break down.

Understanding the electrical system in your home will help you solve many of the problems you may encounter. So before you turn to the repair instructions on the following pages, make sure you've read the information in Chapter One, "An Introduction to the Basics," beginning on page 6.

Electrical repair work is safe as long as you make sure the current is off before working on any wiring. This means first unplugging the troublesome device or shutting off the circuit at the service entrance panel or subpanel (see page 172).

SHUTTING OFF THE MAIN POWER SUPPLY

Most service entrance panels have a switch or fuse that enables you to disconnect your entire electrical system instantly. This shut-off feature, called the "main disconnect," is important whenever you work on existing wiring or make major repairs—or in case of an emergency, such as a fire.

Look at your main disconnect (usually identified as "Main") to see if it's one of the following types.

Lever switch

A handle on the outside of the panel controls two main fuses in the cabinet. To shut off power, pull the lever to the "off" position.

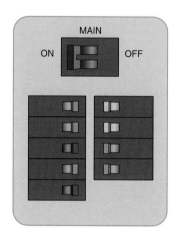

Single main circuit breaker

A single main breaker controls power to the service entrance panel; normally, it's located above the branch circuit breakers. To shut off power, push the main breaker handle to the "off" position.

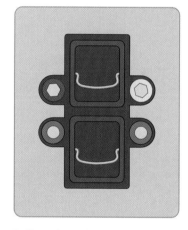

Pull-out fuse block

The main cartridge fuses are mounted on one or two nonmetallic pull-out blocks inside the panel. Pull firmly on the handgrips to remove the blocks and shut off power.

WHAT IF THE LIGHTS GO OUT?

It's easy to feel overwhelmed when you lose power to all or part of your home. But a few guidelines will help you isolate the cause of the problem.

If your entire home is without electricity, you either have a local power outage or a blown main fuse or tripped main circuit breaker. If you're in partial darkness, the first possibility to consider is an overloaded circuit. When a lamp or appliance doesn't work, the source of the problem may be the device itself, faulty wiring connections, or an overload or a short circuit.

To begin troubleshooting the cause of your problem, large or small, first consult the chart on the facing page.

TROUBLESHOOTING ELECTRICAL PROBLEMS

PROBLEM	POSSIBLE CAUSE	REMEDIES	PAGES
Entire home is without electricity and there are no blown fuses or tripped circuit breakers	If neighboring houses seem to be in the dark too, your area probably has a local power failure	Telephone your utility company	—
Your home is the only one in your area without electricity	Main fuse has blown or main circuit breaker has tripped	Check your service panel for a blown fuse or tripped circuit breaker If the main is intact, call your utility company; you may have a downed line	170
Some lights on circuit won't work	Loose wiring	Tighten connections at switch or fixture Replace switch Replace receptacle	185, 180–183 185 184
All lights on circuit won't work	Overloaded circuit Short circuit Loose wiring Faulty switch	Test for overload; adjust if needed Test for short circuit; repair if needed Tighten connections at switch Replace switch	174 174 185 185
Light fixture won't work (check first for burned-out bulb or fluorescent tube)	Defective fluorescent starter Faulty switch Loose wiring	Replace fluorescent starter Replace switch Tighten connections at switch or fixture Replace socket	182–183 185 185, 180–183 178–183
Appliance or lamp won't work (check first for burned-out bulb or fluorescent tube)	Overloaded circuit Damaged plug Damaged cord Loose wiring Defect in appliance or lamp	Test for overload; shift appliance or lamp to another circuit Replace plug Replace cord Tighten connections at switch or receptacle Test in another circuit; repair if faulty	174 176–177 176 184–185 178–179
Appliance or lamp won't work in one circuit but works in others	Overloaded circuit Loose connection at receptacle Short circuit	Test for overload; shift appliance or lamp to another circuit Tighten connections at receptacle Test for short circuit; make necessary repair	174 184 174
Appliance or lamp won't work in one receptacle or circuit	Loose wiring Faulty receptacle Short circuit	Tighten connections at receptacle Replace receptacle Test for short circuit; make necessary repair	184 184 174
Appliance or lamp won't work in switch-controlled receptacle	Loose wiring Faulty switch Faulty receptacle	Tighten connections at switch or fixture Replace switch Replace receptacle	185, 180–183 185 184

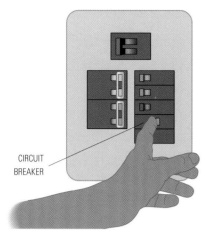

CIRCUIT
BREAKER

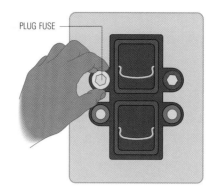

PLUG FUSE

CARTRIDGE
FUSE

Tripping a circuit breaker

Locate the circuit breaker protecting the circuit you wish to shut off, then push the toggle
to the "off" position. (Note: Switching a circuit breaker may require more force than it
takes to flip an ordinary household switch.)

Removing a plug fuse

In the service panel or subpanel, locate the
plug fuse controlling the circuit you wish to
work on. Grasp the fuse by its insulated rim
and unscrew it. Next, check that devices on
the circuit are dead. If they aren't, return to
the panel and repeat the procedure.

Removing a cartridge fuse

In the service panel or subpanel, locate the
fuse block protecting the circuit you wish
to shut off. Grasp the handle firmly and pull
out the fuse block. Use a fuse puller (as
shown) or your hand to release the cartridge fuse from the spring clips.

SHUTTING OFF A BRANCH CIRCUIT

When you're going to work on a switch, receptacle, or
fixture that can't simply be unplugged, you need to shut
off power to the branch circuit. Either trip the breaker
for the circuit; or, for a circuit with a fuse, turn off the
main power supply, remove the fuse for the circuit you're
working on, then turn the main power supply back on.
Both techniques are described in more detail above. See
page 20 for how to identify which circuit breaker or fuse
protects a particular circuit.

EVALUATING CIRCUIT BREAKERS

All circuit breakers are rated for a specific number of
amps. Single-pole breakers protect 120-volt circuits; double-pole breakers—typically twice as thick—handle
120/240- and 240-volt circuits.

When a breaker is installed in a service entrance
panel or subpanel, a bimetallic strip becomes a link in
the circuit. Heat from excessive current will bend the
metal strip, causing a release to trip and break the cir-

cuit. (When this happens, the toggle goes to "off" or to an
intermediate position between "on" and "off.") Unlike
fuses, which work on the self-destruct principle, circuit
breakers can be reset (turned back on) once they've
tripped.

The procedure for resetting a tripped breaker varies.
Directions are often embossed on the breaker. Many of
the modern circuit breakers go to an intermediate position between "on" and "off" when they trip. To reset a
breaker of this type, push the toggle firmly to "off" before
returning it to "on." (Note: Switching a circuit breaker may require more
force than it takes
to flip an ordi-
nary household
switch.)

DOUBLE-
POLE CIRCUIT
BREAKER

SINGLE-POLE
CIRCUIT BREAKER

EVALUATING FUSES

Fuses have a thin metal strip through which current passes into a circuit. If too much current starts to flow, such as when the circuit is overloaded or it shorts, the metal melts and cuts off the current. When this happens, the fuse is ruined and must be replaced.

Fuses may be one of two basic types: plug or cartridge. Replacement fuses must be the same type as the original, and the fuse size must match the circuit rating. For example, if the circuit is rated for 15 amps, use a 15-amp fuse; never replace it with one rated higher.

GOOD FUSE

BLOWN FUSE (OVERLOAD)

PLUG FUSES: These fuses come in two basic styles: Edison base and type S. Edison base fuses, which are equipped with screw-in bases like those of ordinary light bulbs, come in ratings up to 30 amps. According to the National Electrical Code, Edison base fuses are now permitted only as replacements in 120-volt circuits. (This restriction is meant to encourage use of the safer type S fuse.)

BLOWN FUSE (SHORT CIRCUIT)

Before using a type S fuse, you must install an adapter with the correct rating in the fuse socket. Each adapter is constructed so that it is impossible to install a fuse with a higher rating. Fuses can be replaced as needed, but once an adapter is installed, it can't be removed. Plug fuses usually provide a clue to what made them blow: an overload melts the bridge; a short circuit blackens the glass.

CARTRIDGE FUSES: Cartridge fuses also come in two styles: ferrule and knife blade. A ferrule-type fuse, which comes in ratings of 10 to 60 amps, is most commonly used to protect the circuit of an individual 120/240-volt appliance, such as a kitchen range. The knife-blade fuse, available in ratings of 70 amps or more and suitable for 240 volts, is generally used as the main overcurrent protection in fused service entrance panels.

A fuse pulling tool (see page 43) is best for removing cartridge fuses from their fuse holders. Check a suspect fuse for continuity as shown at right.

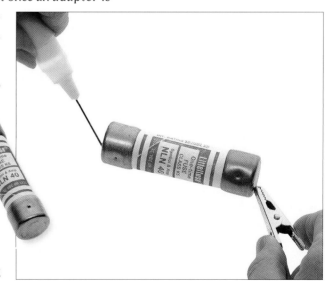

Test a cartridge fuse with a continuity tester. If the tester lights or buzzes, the fuse is okay; if it doesn't, buy a replacement.

TRACING A SHORT CIRCUIT OR OVERLOAD

A tripped breaker or blown fuse is a signal that you may have either a short circuit or an overload in the electrical system.

Often when a circuit shorts, the source of the problem is easy to spot. Look for black smudge marks on switch or receptacle cover plates, or for frayed or damaged cords or damaged plugs on lamps and appliances connected to the dead circuit. Replace the damaged cord or plug (see pages 176–177), then replace the fuse or reset the breaker (see pages 172–173).

If the circuit goes dead after an appliance has been in use for a short time, you probably have an overloaded circuit. Plug some of the lamps and appliances into receptacles on another circuit and replace the fuse or reset the breaker for the first circuit.

If you find none of these signs of trouble, you'll have to trace your way through the circuit following the steps below. If that doesn't identify the source of the problem, and your fuse or circuit breaker still blows or trips, your wiring is faulty. See the facing page and/or call a licensed electrician to correct the problem.

Turn off all wall switches and unplug every lamp and appliance on the dead circuit. Then reset the tripped breaker or install a new fuse (see pages 172–173).

If the breaker trips or the fuse blows right away, the problem may be a short circuit in a switch or receptacle. With the circuit dead, remove each faceplate and inspect the device and its wiring. Look and smell for charred wire insulation, check whether a loose wire end is touching a metal box, and inspect the device for defects (see pages 184–185); replace the faulty wiring or defective device.

If the breaker doesn't trip or the new fuse doesn't blow right away, turn on each wall switch, one by one, checking each time to see whether the circuit breaker has tripped or the fuse has blown.

If turning on a wall switch causes a breaker to trip or the fuse to blow, there's a short circuit in a light fixture or receptacle controlled by that switch, or there's a short circuit in the switch wiring. With the circuit dead, inspect the fixture, receptacle, and switch for charred wire insulation or faulty connections. Replace the faulty switch, fixture, or wiring as necessary.

If turning on a wall switch doesn't trip the breaker or blow a fuse, the trouble is in the lamps or appliances. Test them by plugging them in, one at a time. If the circuit doesn't go dead, the circuit was overloaded; move some of the lamps or appliances to another circuit. If the circuit goes dead just after you've plugged in a lamp or appliance, then you've found the offender.

If the circuit went dead as soon as you plugged in the lamp or appliance, the plug or cord is probably at fault and should be replaced.

If the circuit went dead as soon as you turned on the lamp or appliance, the appliance or lamp or its switch is probably defective and should be replaced or repaired.

TESTING YOUR NEW WORK

Circuit testing should first be done at the "rough wiring" stage. At this point no receptacles, switches, or light fixtures are installed. However, all hot, neutral, and grounding wire splices should be made up, so that each circuit is continuous up to the last box. Test again after installing walls, ceilings, and floors, because occasionally a nail will penetrate the wiring and cause a short.

MULTITESTER

WARNING

Shut off the power before checking resistance or continuity.

CONTINUITY TESTER

TESTING FOR SHORT CIRCUITS: So that your test will run the entire length of a circuit, temporarily join the hot wires each place you'll have a switch. This simulates the "on" position and thereby extends your circuit test to include the wiring from the switch to whatever it will control.

At the service entrance panel, test your circuits as follows: hook one alligator clip of your continuity tester or multitester to the neutral bus bar; then touch the hot wire of each circuit to the tester probe one at a time. The circuits should check out as open (no buzzer or light). If the light comes on or the buzzer rings, you have a short in that circuit.

When testing circuits at a subpanel, you must run the same test described above twice. First, hook your clip to the neutral bus bar to check the hot wire/neutral wire circuits. Second, hook your clip to the grounding wire terminal to check your fault-current circuits.

TRACKING DOWN A SHORT: First, check that the free device wires at boxes are not inadvertently touching each other or the metal box. This might save you some time in tracking down a nonexistent short.

If your wiring is exposed, a careful visual check of the circuit should turn up the problem. If you still can't find the problem, or if wiring has already been covered, proceed as follows: undo the wire splices at the next-to-last box on the circuit to open the circuit there. Then retest the circuit at the distribution center. Continue this procedure if necessary, moving closer to the source each time until the circuit tests out open. You have now isolated the short between the box where the circuit checked out open and the previous box (or at one of those boxes).

WHICH WIRE IS HOT?

When two or more wires or cables enter the electrical box you're working on, it isn't always obvious which wire carries the electrical load. White wires are usually—but not always—neutral wires. White wires can be hot, so you should always assume they are until you test them. Older woven wires may all be black.

To identify the hot wire, use the neon tester. Use caution: you're working near live wires. Touch one tester probe to the grounding wire or metal box, then touch the other probe to the other wires, one at a time. The tester will light when the second probe touches the hot wire.

REPLACING CORDS

Cords on lamps and appliances are often subject to pulling and twisting that can sever the wires inside and break down the insulation, resulting in a short circuit. You should always replace (rather than repair) any electrical cord with broken wires or brittle, worn insulation.

Detach the cord from the lamp or appliance and take the old cord with you to an electrical supply store. Buy a length of replacement cord with the same size wires and the same insulation as the original. (The inventory below shows typical flexible cord for lamps, appliances, and power tools.) Do not use a long lamp cord or extension cord on an ongoing basis; if you find you're relying on one, extend the existing circuit and install a new receptacle with NM cable. As a matter of course when you're replacing a defective cord, also replace the plug, as detailed at right.

LAMP OR FIXTURE CORD (TYPE SPT)

HEATER CORD (TYPE HPN)

VACUUM CLEANER CORD (TYPE SVT)

POWER TOOL CORD (TYPE SJT)

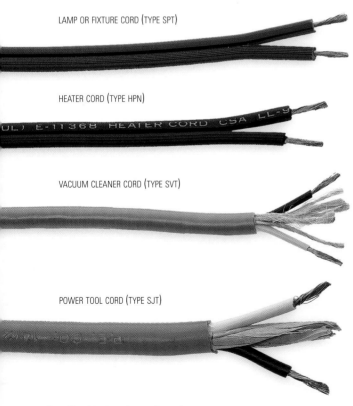

REPLACING PLUGS

Any plug with a cracked shell or with loose, damaged, or badly bent prongs should be replaced. Also replace plugs that transmit power erratically or get warm when used. If a plug sparks when it's pushed into or pulled out of a receptacle, examine the wires. If they're not firmly attached to the terminal screws, tighten the connections.

The two common kinds of plugs are screw-terminal and self-connecting plugs. In plugs with screw terminals, the wires attach to screws inside the plug body. Self-connecting plugs clamp onto wires, making an automatic connection. These plugs, as well as two-prong plugs with screw terminals, are commonly used for lamps and small appliances. Three-prong grounding plugs are used for larger appliances and power tools. Detachable cords for small appliances have "female" plugs with screw terminals.

Note: Many old-style plugs with screw terminals have a removable insulating disk covering the terminals and wires. The NEC now requires "dead-front" plugs; such plugs have a rigid insulating barrier.

To replace a plug, cut off the old one with at least an inch of cord. Then proceed as follows:

For plugs that have screw terminals, split the cord insulation to separate the wires, then strip the insulation from the ends.

When replacing a two-prong plug, connect the identified conductor (it's often ribbed) to the silver-colored screw.

When wiring a polarized plug, connect the marked wire of the cord (indicated by a thin band of color, ribbing, or a colored strand visible in the wire ends) to the wide prong and the unmarked wire to the narrow prong.

For a three-prong grounding plug, attach the wires to the screw terminals as follows: white neutral wire to silver screw, black hot wire to brass screw, and green grounding wire to green grounding screw.

WIRING A PLUG WITH SCREW TERMINALS

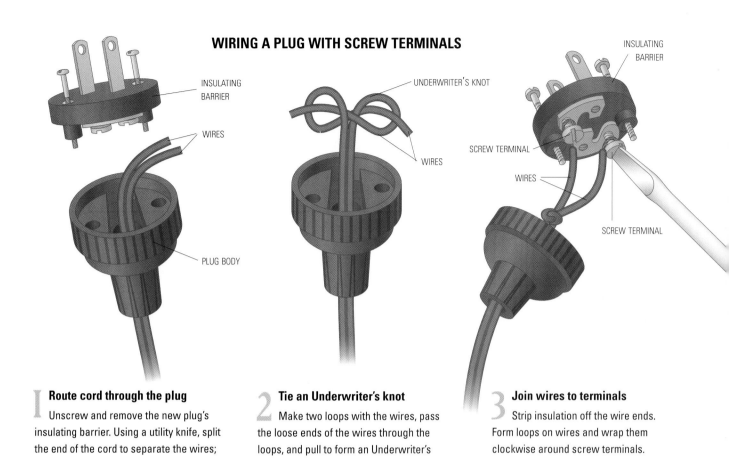

INSULATING
BARRIER

WIRES

PLUG BODY

UNDERWRITER'S KNOT

WIRES

INSULATING
BARRIER

SCREW TERMINAL

WIRES

SCREW TERMINAL

1 Route cord through the plug

Unscrew and remove the new plug's insulating barrier. Using a utility knife, split the end of the cord to separate the wires; push the cord through the plug body.

2 Tie an Underwriter's knot

Make two loops with the wires, pass the loose ends of the wires through the loops, and pull to form an Underwriter's knot (to prevent strain on connections).

3 Join wires to terminals

Strip insulation off the wire ends. Form loops on wires and wrap them clockwise around screw terminals. Tighten the screws, then reattach the barrier to the body.

REPLACING THREE SPECIALTY PLUGS

PRONGS

TERMINAL BLOCK

CORD

SHELL

INSULATING
BARRIER

SCREW
TERMINALS

CORD

SHELL

SCREW TERMINALS

SPRING
GUARD

CORD

To attach a self-connecting plug, push the cord (don't strip it) through the shell and into the terminal block; squeeze the prongs together to grip the cord and slide it into the shell.

To install a three-prong grounding plug, first unscrew the insulating barrier; push the stripped wires through the plug body into the correct terminal slots. Tighten the screw terminals and reassemble the plug.

To replace a female appliance plug, first unscrew the plug shell, then feed the cord through the spring guard. Strip the wire ends, wrap them clockwise around the screw terminals, and tighten; then reassemble the plug.

REPAIRING LAMPS

Most plug-in incandescent lamps have a socket, switch, cord, and plug. (In a simple lamp like the one shown at left, the switch is built into the socket.) Any one of these parts may wear out and have to be replaced.

If a lamp isn't working, first check the light bulb to make sure it isn't loose or burned out. Next, plug the lamp into another receptacle to be sure the receptacle isn't at fault. (If it is, see page 184.)

WARNING

Before working on any lamp, be sure it's unplugged.

Check the plug and cord for wear. (To replace the plug, see pages 176–177; to inspect and replace the cord, see 176.) If the bulb, cord, and plug are in good shape, use a continuity tester (page 45) to test the socket. To replace the socket and built-in switch, see the facing page. (If the lamp's switch is attached to the cord, inspect it and replace it if it's faulty.)

Low-voltage lamps have a transformer that also may need to be replaced. On some low-voltage models, you may be able to unscrew the defective transformer and install a new one.

A lamp assembled with rivets instead of nuts and bolts can't be taken apart for repair, so you'll have to replace it.

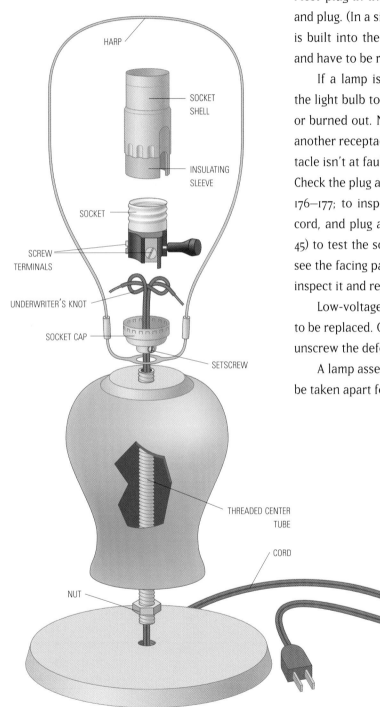

HARP

SOCKET SHELL

INSULATING SLEEVE

SOCKET

SCREW TERMINALS

UNDERWRITER'S KNOT

SOCKET CAP

SETSCREW

THREADED CENTER TUBE

CORD

NUT

REPLACING A LAMP SOCKET AND CORD

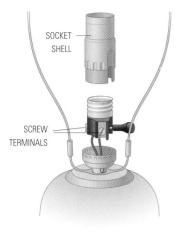

SOCKET SHELL

SCREW TERMINALS

1 Remove the old socket

To detach a socket, first loosen the socket shell by pushing in on the area where the word "press" is embossed. Lift off the shell and insulating sleeve. Unfasten the wires from the socket's screw terminals and inspect the cord insulation. If it's okay, test the socket and replace as necessary. If the cord is damaged, go to Steps 2 and 3.

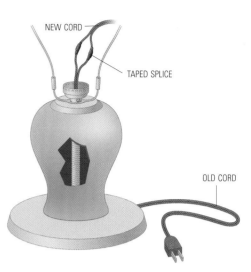

NEW CORD

TAPED SPLICE

OLD CORD

2 Replace the cord

If the old cord is faulty, first untie the knot. Splice the new cord to the old by twisting the wires' bare ends together and taping them. Pull both cords through; detach the old cord.

UNDERWRITER'S KNOT

SOCKET CAP

3 Tie an Underwriter's knot

Split the new cord to 2½ inches from one end. Make an Underwriter's knot by forming two loops and passing the loose wire ends through the loops. Pull the knot snug.

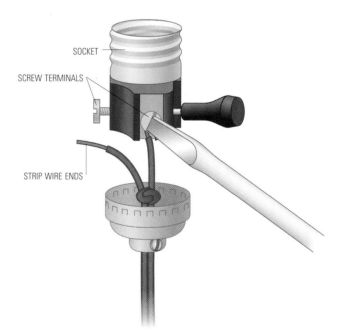

SOCKET

SCREW TERMINALS

STRIP WIRE ENDS

CLEANING AND ADJUSTING THE SOCKET TAB

If a lamp doesn't work, check to make sure it's plugged in, and that the bulb isn't loose or burned out. If you still haven't identified the problem, unplug the lamp, unscrew the bulb, and inspect the socket tab. If the tab is too flat, it won't make contact with the base of the bulb. To raise the socket tab, use a standard screwdriver to gently pry it up, as shown. Also use the tip of the screwdriver to scrape dirt from the tab. If the lamp still doesn't work, replace the socket.

4 Join wires to terminals

Loop the wires clockwise around the screw terminals of the new socket and tighten the screws (be sure to observe correct polarity). Push the insulating sleeve over the socket, then push in the shell until you hear it click. Attach a polarized plug to the new cord (see page 177).

CEILING FIXTURE

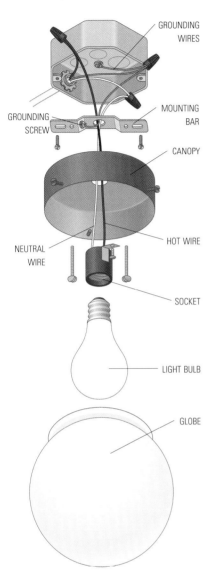

GROUNDING WIRES

GROUNDING SCREW

MOUNTING BAR

CANOPY

NEUTRAL WIRE

HOT WIRE

SOCKET

LIGHT BULB

GLOBE

REPAIRING INCANDESCENT LIGHT FIXTURES

When a fixture doesn't work, first check the light bulb to make sure it isn't loose or burned out. Then check the circuit and the light switch (see pages 172 and 185). If those are fine, the problem may be in the fixture wiring or in the socket. Detach the fixture from the ceiling box and check for a loose connection. Tighten it if necessary. Also use a continuity tester (page 45) to check the socket. If the fixture still doesn't work, you'll have to either replace or repair it.

CAUTION: Before you work on any fixture, shut off the power to the entire circuit and use a neon tester or multitester to make sure that it's off.

REPAIRING A FIXTURE: Repair involves removing and replacing the sockets and/or wiring. Sockets in all types of fixtures may have screw terminals like a lamp socket (see page 179), or they may have permanently attached wires as shown at left. When you replace a socket, ensure polarity by connecting wires of the same color.

On a chandelier, the sockets and socket wires in the arms connect to a main cord running up the center. Usually the connections are hidden inside the fixture body; you may have to remove a cap or nut on the bottom to reach them. Replace the main cord as you would a lamp cord (see page 177). To replace a prewired socket, first disconnect the socket wires from the circuit wires, then unclip the faulty socket from the fixture. Attach the new socket by reversing these steps.

WALL SCONCE

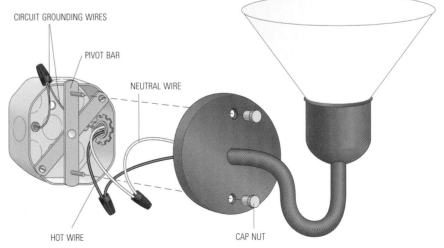

CIRCUIT GROUNDING WIRES

PIVOT BAR

NEUTRAL WIRE

HOT WIRE

CAP NUT

TRACK FIXTURE

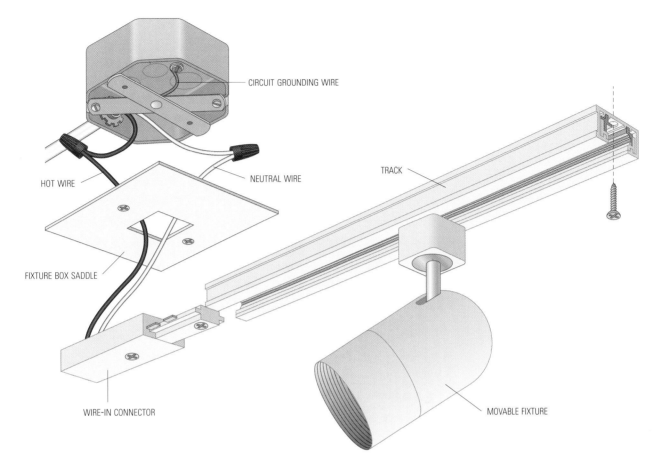

CIRCUIT GROUNDING WIRE

HOT WIRE

NEUTRAL WIRE

TRACK

FIXTURE BOX SADDLE

WIRE-IN CONNECTOR

MOVABLE FIXTURE

REPLACING A FIXTURE: The replacement procedure is basically the same for all types of fixtures. You simply detach the old fixture and undo the wiring connections, then make new connections and attach the new fixture, as shown on pages 106–111. Wiring connections should be made with wire nuts; if there are more than two black and two white wires, label all wires and make a sketch before undoing them.

Note: If the fixture is heavy, have a helper hold it while you're working on it or hang it from the box temporarily with a hook made from a wire coat hanger.

You may have to buy mounting hardware to hang the new fixture. If the ceiling box has a metallic stud (see page 105), the fixture may be attached to it with a nipple and hickey, a reducing nut, or a strap. If there's no stud in the right location, a strap may be attached to the ceiling box ears. A fixture heavier than 10 pounds should be hung from a box that's nailed to the ceiling joists.

SHOPPING FOR REPLACEMENT PARTS?

Replacement parts for a fluorescent lamp must be carefully matched to the fixture. Tubes and ballasts for one type of fixture (i.e., instant-start, rapid-start, or preheat) can't be interchanged with those of another, and the starter—if there is one—and ballast must match the wattage of the tube. You'll find most of the information you need printed on the parts themselves.

Parts are available in most home centers. Tubes come in a range of temperature ratings; the lower the rating, the warmer the light. To get the most use out of a tube, leave the fixture on for several hours rather than switching it on and off frequently.

FIXING FLUORESCENT LIGHTS

Unlike incandescent lights, which operate on house voltage (120 volts), fluorescent fixtures require a high-voltage current to produce light. The working parts of a fluorescent light fixture consist of fluorescent tubes; a ballast (transformer) that steps up household voltage; a tubeholder (socket); and, on some fixtures, a starter that assists the ballast in the initial start-up process.

The three types of fluorescent light fixtures are preheat, rapid-start, and instant-start. On a preheat fixture—an older style—the starter is visible; it looks like a miniature aluminum can. On a rapid-start fixture, the starter is built into the ballast. An instant-start fixture has no starter and is distinguished by a tube with a single pin on each end.

You can easily make most repairs on a faulty fluorescent light fixture. Use the chart on the facing page to help pinpoint the cause of the problem.

REPLACING A FLUORESCENT TUBE: Before you remove a fluorescent tube, be sure to turn off the wall switch to the fixture.

To remove a double-pin tube, rotate it a quarter turn in either direction and gently pull it out of the tubeholders. Install the new tube by pushing it into the tubeholders and then giving it a quarter turn to lock it into place.

Remove a single-pin tube from the fixture by pushing the tube against the spring-loaded tubeholder until the other end of the tube can be removed. To install the new tube, put the tube pin into the spring-loaded tubeholder and push until the other end can be inserted.

REPLACING A STARTER: Before you replace a starter, turn off power to the circuit and test to make sure it's off. To replace the starter on a preheat fixture, first remove the fluorescent tube or tubes. Rotate the starter a quarter turn counterclockwise to pull it out of its socket. Place the new starter in the socket and rotate it a quarter turn in either direction.

FLUORESCENT FIXTURE

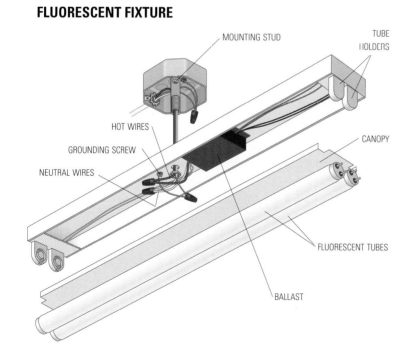

MOUNTING STUD

TUBE HOLDERS

HOT WIRES

GROUNDING SCREW

NEUTRAL WIRES

CANOPY

FLUORESCENT TUBES

BALLAST

REPLACING A TUBEHOLDER OR BALLAST:
Before you replace a tubeholder or ballast, shut off power to the circuit and test
to make sure it's off.

Unscrew or unsnap the old part, then
cut or disconnect the old wires between
the tubeholder or ballast and the fixture. Attach the
replacement part. To reconnect the wires, you'll have to
strip insulation from the end of each wire and use wire

W A R N I N G

Should you accidentally
break a tube, handle the
broken pieces carefully; the coat-
ing on the inside is dangerous.

nuts to connect the ballast or tubeholder wires to the fixture wires. If
your new tubeholder has push-in connections or screw terminals instead of
permanently connected wires, connect
the fixture wires to them directly
rather than using wire nuts. A new ballast will have permanently connected wires. Install the cover plate and
tube; turn on the power.

TROUBLESHOOTING A FLUORESCENT FIXTURE

PROBLEM	POSSIBLE CAUSE	REMEDIES
Lamp won't light	Circuit breaker tripped or fuse blown	Reset circuit breaker or replace fuse*
	Tube burned out (ends blackened)	Replace tube
	Improper tube installation	Take out and install again
	Dirty tube (rapid-start only)	Remove tube; wash, dry, and reinstall
	Fixture too cold	Raise room temperature to at least 50°F
	Oxide film buildup on tube pins	Rotate tube in tubeholder once or twice
	Starter burned out	Replace starter on preheat type, ballast on rapid-start
	Tubeholder broken	Replace tubeholder
Lamp flickers (NEW TUBES MAY FLICKER FOR A SHORT TIME AFTER INSTALLATION)	Improper tube installation	Take out and install again
	Tube nearly worn out (ends blackened)	Replace tube
	Oxide film buildup on tube pins	Rotate tube in tubeholder once or twice
	Fixture too cold	Raise room temperature to at least 50°F
	Poor contact with tubeholders	Realign tubeholders; straighten and sand, if needed
Ends of tubes are discolored (DARK BANDS ABOUT TWO INCHES FROM ENDS ARE NORMAL)	Tube nearly worn out	Replace tube
	Defective starter (preheat type with new tubes)	Replace starter on preheat type, ballast on rapid-start
	Temperamental tube (discolored on one end only)	Remove tube; turn end for end
	Defective starter	Replace starter
Ends glow, center doesn't	Defective ballast	Replace ballast
	Ballast incorrectly installed	Check wiring diagram printed on ballast and correct
Lamp fixture hums	Wrong type of ballast	Check wattage rating and type; replace
	Defective ballast	Replace ballast

*IF CIRCUIT BREAKER TRIPS OR FUSE BLOWS AGAIN, YOU HAVE A SHORT CIRCUIT (PAGE 174); CHECK WIRING OR CALL AN ELECTRICIAN.

To troubleshoot a 120-volt receptacle, plug in a circuit analyzer. The analyzer's lights can tell you whether wiring is normal or whether the device is ungrounded, has hot and neutral wires reversed, or some other problem.

REPLACING RECEPTACLES

If appliances or lamps that work properly elsewhere don't work when plugged into a certain receptacle, and you've determined that there's no loose wiring or short circuit (page 174), the receptacle needs to be replaced.

You'll find receptacle details on pages 34–35. Receptacles are rated for a specific amperage and voltage; be sure to buy the correct replacement. If your wiring is aluminum, you must use a receptacle designed for use with aluminum wire (it should have "AL-CU" imprinted on it).

Newer receptacles are grounding types. Always replace an older, ungrounded receptacle with a grounding type unless there's no grounding wire in the box or unless the box isn't grounded. A grounding receptacle can be installed in an ungrounded box only if you ground the receptacle independently; for help, see below.

To remove a faulty receptacle, first shut off the power to the circuit and test to make sure it's off. Then unscrew the cover plate and set it aside. Unscrew the receptacle from its box and carefully pull it out. Note which wire is connected to which screw terminal; then disconnect the wires from the screws. To wire the new receptacle, see pages 92–97. Replace the faceplate.

GOING FROM A TWO- TO A THREE-HOLE RECEPTACLE

Many portable appliances and tools have a grounding wire that eliminates the possibility of an electrical shock. A three-prong plug indicates the presence of a grounding wire. This wire connects to the circuit grounding wire through the third hole of a grounding-type receptacle. What do you do with a three-prong plug when your receptacles are the two-prong variety? You can either use an adapter plug or change the receptacle.

An adapter plug is effective only if the receptacle box is grounded and if you connect the screw lug properly, as shown at right. If your circuit wiring runs in conduit or is armored cable or nonmetallic sheathed cable with ground, chances are the box is grounded. Don't assume so, however; test to be sure: after removing the receptacle's faceplate, place one probe of a neon tester in a receptacle slot and the other probe on a mounting screw. If you get a strong light in the tester, the box is grounded and you can use an adapter plug.

If your box isn't grounded, you must replace the receptacle with a grounding type and run a grounding wire to the closest cold-water pipe and/or another approved ground (check local code). Use #14 copper wire for a 15-amp circuit and #12 copper wire for a 20-amp circuit.

Grounding a receptacle independently isn't always the most convenient thing to do. You'll need to run wire out from the box through a partially opened knockout, then fish wire (see page 65) behind the wall to the nearest approved ground. As an alternative, some codes allow you to replace the two-prong receptacle with an ungrounded, three-prong GFCI receptacle.

REPLACING SWITCHES

When a switch fails, it's usually because the internal contact points are worn or have oxidized. When this happens, the switch must be replaced. You can replace it with an exact duplicate, with another toggle style, or with a dimmer. You'll find shopping pointers on pages 36–37; for wiring instructions, see pages 98–103.

It's easy to troubleshoot an existing switch. First, shut off power to the circuit. Before you touch any wires or terminals, use a neon tester or multitester to make sure the circuit is dead. Then disconnect the switch from the wires. Use a continuity tester as shown at right, or a multitester, to determine whether the switch is functional. If it is, then check out the circuit, as described on page 175. Fortunately, switches are inexpensive, so if there's any doubt about one's viability, simply replace it.

Note: Many new switches have grounding terminals; chances are an older switch will not. If the existing wiring includes a grounding wire inside the box, you can pigtail (see page 55) a grounding wire from the replacement switch's green grounding screw to the circuit grounding wire. If the circuit has no grounding wire, it's simplest to replace the switch with a model that has no grounding terminal.

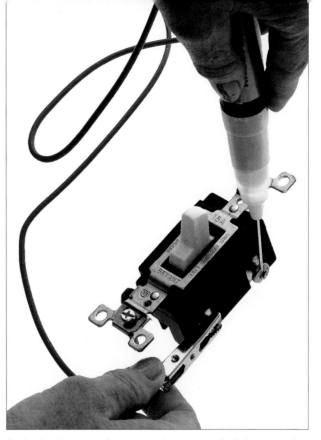

To check a faulty switch, use a continuity tester. Hook the tester clip onto one of the switch's hot terminals, then touch the probe to the other hot terminal. Flip the switch to the "on" position: if the tester lights up or buzzes, the switch is good.

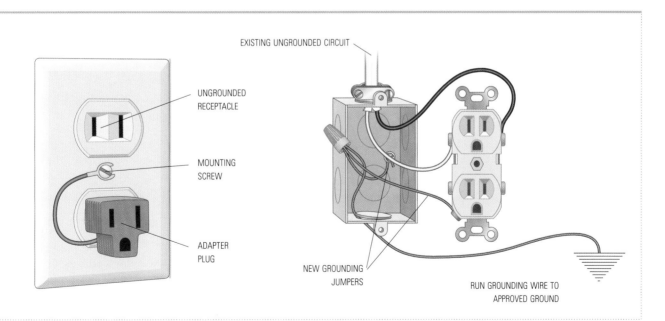

UNGROUNDED RECEPTACLE

MOUNTING SCREW

ADAPTER PLUG

EXISTING UNGROUNDED CIRCUIT

NEW GROUNDING JUMPERS

RUN GROUNDING WIRE TO APPROVED GROUND

REPAIRING DOORBELLS

The parts of a typical doorbell system are the push button, the bell (or chimes or buzzer), and the transformer. The transformer steps down the voltage from a regular 120-volt circuit to somewhere between 6 and 24 volts. The transformer is wired into the doorbell circuit at a junction box.

WARNING

To diagnose most doorbell problems, you'll need to have the power source connected. But if you're going to work on the transformer or the wire in the junction box, be sure to shut off the power to the circuit. The input side of the transformer carries a full 120 volts.

CURING SILENT DOORBELLS: Any of a variety of problems—including a faulty transformer, push button, or bell; dirt in the mechanism; or poor wiring—can cause your doorbell not to sound. The first place to check is the source of power. Make sure a circuit breaker hasn't tripped or a fuse hasn't blown (see pages 172–173). Once you're certain that the 120-volt side of the transformer is getting power, check the low-voltage side.

The best and safest way to test the transformer is to use a multitester. If the transformer is working correctly, the meter reading should match the secondary (low-voltage) level marked on the transformer or bell. If the meter reads significantly higher, the transformer is defective and should be replaced. If the reading is close to the correct secondary voltage, test again by setting the voltage range on the meter to a lower value. If the new reading doesn't match, replace the transformer.

To check the push button, disconnect the two wires connected to it and short them by touching their bare ends together. If this makes the bell sound, the push button is defective and should be replaced. If the bell doesn't sound, the problem is either in the bell mechanism itself or in the wiring.

Test a doorbell's transformer with a multitester. The meter reading should match the low-voltage level marked on the transformer or bell.

To test the bell, have a helper ring the doorbell while you listen. If the bell hums or buzzes, it may be gummed up with dirt. Check the mechanism and clean it if necessary. Use fine-grade sandpaper to remove corrosion from any contacts. If the bell still hums or buzzes after cleaning, replace it.

If the bell didn't make any noise at all when the button was pushed, disconnect the bell and, using new wire, hook it up directly to the transformer. If the bell works, inspect the old wiring for breaks or frayed insulation that may be causing the wires to short out. Repair any breaks and wrap the repairs with electrical tape. If the bell doesn't sound, replace it.

A CONSTANTLY RINGING DOORBELL: If a doorbell won't stop ringing, either the button is stuck or the wires going to the button are shorted together.

To isolate the problem, first turn off the power to the transformer. Unscrew the button from the door frame and disconnect one of the two wires connected to it. Turn the power back on. If the bell doesn't ring, the button should be replaced. If the bell rings, then the problem is a short between the two wires.

To find the short, turn the power off and examine the wires for frayed insulation or bare wires that are touching. Use electrical tape to wrap them where necessary. If you can't find the short, replace the wires.

TROUBLESHOOTING A THERMOSTAT

A thermostat is a temperature-sensitive switch that in turn activates the switch controlling the operation of a boiler, furnace, electric heater, air conditioner, or other heating or cooling device. Low-voltage and millivolt thermostats are the most common types.

The three principal parts of a thermostat are the heat sensor; the switch; and, in low-voltage types only, the heat anticipator. The sensor contracts as it cools, turning the switch on, and expands as it warms, tripping the switch off. The switch may have open contacts (in older models) or a mercury-type contact enclosed in an airtight glass tube. The anticipator prevents the living area from overheating by shutting off the boiler or furnace just before the desired temperature is reached.

Thermostats for heating or air conditioning systems rarely break down. The only maintenance required is an occasional cleaning with a soft brush. If your thermostat is equipped with switch contacts, brush them clean with a cotton swab moistened with alcohol. Don't attempt to make a major repair on a defective thermostat; just replace the unit.

TROUBLESHOOTING: To test whether your thermostat is good or bad, first switch the thermostat to "auto" and "heat," then take a short piece of insulated wire with stripped ends and bridge the W and R screw terminals (shown below). If the heater turns on, the thermostat is defective and should be replaced. If the heater does not respond, turn the power off and check for loose connections at the heater's transformer. Then turn power back on and test the transformer's screw terminals for current with a multitester. If there's no current, the transformer is the culprit.

INSTALLING A NEW THERMOSTAT: First, remove the thermostat cover and detach the wires from their lettered terminals (see below). Label each wire to ensure you hook them up to the correct terminal and so they don't slide back into the hole.

Attach the new base plate to the wall with screws, checking to ensure its level. Strip the wire ends, if needed, or scrape them clean; wrap the ends clockwise around the terminal screws and tighten the screws.

Finally, mount the thermostat cover on the base plate following manufacturer's instructions.

ANATOMY OF A THERMOSTAT

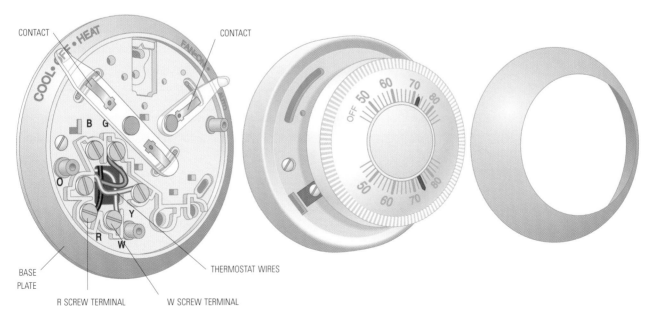

CONTACT · CONTACT · COOL · OFF · HEAT · FAN·ON · B · G · O · Y · R · W · BASE PLATE · R SCREW TERMINAL · W SCREW TERMINAL · THERMOSTAT WIRES

TESTING TELEPHONES

After making any modifications to your telephone wiring, you should conduct a simple test to make sure everything is working properly. The most reliable way to check your wiring installation is by using a telephone line tester, shown below. These are available in most hardware and home-electronics stores that stock telephone wiring components.

If you don't have a line tester, you can use a telephone to check wiring integrity. First make sure the telephone is working properly. Plug it into a functional jack and dial a number to check. (If you can, use the jack closest to the point where telephone wiring enters your home.)

Perform the following tests at newly installed jacks, or at any jack that may not be working properly.

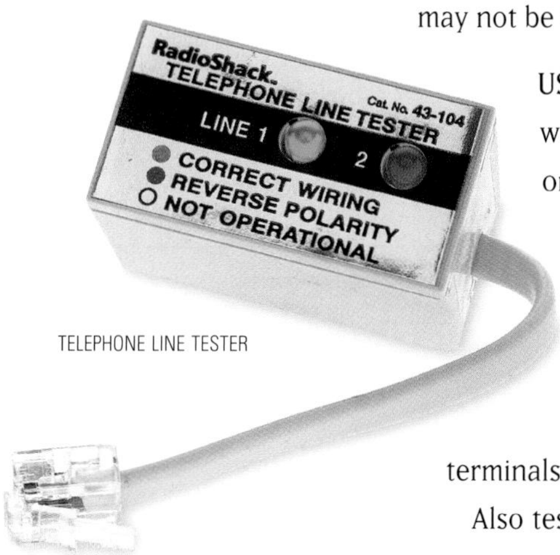

TELEPHONE LINE TESTER

USING A LINE TESTER: First test the integrity of the red and green wire connections, the circuit that carries basic telephone service, or service for line one in a two-line home. A green light indicates that wiring is correct. A red light indicates that the wires are reversed. To correct the problem, open the jack and reverse the red and green wires, then test again.

If the tester does not light, open the jack and check to make sure the red and green wires are connected securely to the terminals.

Also test the integrity of the yellow and black wire connections. This circuit may not be needed if you have only one line, but should be checked; it could be useful later to add another line, or to provide an alternate path for basic telephone service if the red/green circuit is damaged.

USING A TELEPHONE: Plug the telephone into the jack, lift the handset, and listen for a dial tone. If you hear nothing, you have a bad contact or a wrong connection. Open the jack and check to make sure all wires are connected firmly to wire terminals.

If you hear a dial tone, dial a telephone number. If you continue to hear a dial tone during and after dialing, the red and green wires are reversed. Open the jack and switch the red and green wire connections. If you have two telephone lines and the same problem occurs on the second line, the yellow and black wires should be reversed.

LOW-VOLTAGE LOGISTICS

Troubleshooting data-network and audiovisual problems is often a matter of determining whether the connecting cables are routed correctly and whether they're functioning properly. Often the testing method of choice depends on whether you can easily get to both ends of the cable or not.

Some basic diagnostic tools can help. A tone generator (shown below) helps you identify which wire at one end of a long, covered cable run corresponds to one of a slew of wires at the other end. The UTP cable tester has twin RJ-45 jacks: plug one end into one jack and the other into the second jack to see if a Cat-3 or Cat-5 patch cable is good or bad. The multi-cable tester shown performs the same trick on phone cords, UTP cables, coaxial cables, and computer connections.

Or run some basic tests with your trusty multitester or continuity tester. To test a cable where you can access both ends, place probes or clips at opposite ends; the tester should indicate zero ohms resistance (multitester) or register continuity. If you can't reach both ends, try bridging the inner conductor and outer shielding, as shown at right. This time around, continuity is a bad thing; a zero reading or continuity buzzer or light indicates a faulty cable.

Perform one more test to track down a hidden short: place one probe on the cable's center conductor, and the other on a nearby ground. Again, continuity, or zero resistance, is bad, and indicates a short somewhere along the line. Also try connecting one wire to another at the end of a cluster of wires; again, continuity means a short.

To check a coaxial cable for shorts, place one probe of a multitester or continuity tester on the cable's center conductor, and the alligator clip on the outer shield. If the tester indicates continuity, the cable is defective and should be repaired or replaced.

TONE GENERATOR

UTP CABLE TESTER

MULTI-CABLE TESTER

GLOSSARY

ALTERNATING CURRENT: Abbreviated as AC. Electrical flow that cycles—or reverses direction—60 or so times per second (in the case of "60-hertz" current).

AMPACITY: Coined word combining ampere and capacity. Expresses in amperes the current-carrying capacity of electrical conductors.

AMPERE: Unit used in measuring electrical current, based on the number of electrons flowing past a given point per second. Many elements of a wiring system are rated in amperes for the greatest amount of current they can safely carry. Abbreviated amp.

ARMORED CABLE: Flexible, metallic-clad cable (also known as BX cable) used for residential wiring. MC cable is an updated version.

BONDING: Connecting metal components of an electrical system to form a continuous conductive path capable of handling any current likely to flow.

BRANCH CIRCUIT: Any one of many separate circuits distributing electricity throughout a house from the last overcurrent device protecting the circuit.

CABLE: Two or more insulated wires or conductors bundled together and covered with an integral insulating sheath. Most commonly NM cable.

CIRCUIT: Two or more wires providing a path for electrical current to flow from the source through some device using electricity (such as a light) and back to the source.

CIRCUIT BREAKER: Safety switch installed in circuit to break electricity flow automatically when current exceeds a predetermined amount.

CONDUCTOR: Technical term for electrical wire.

CONDUIT: A metal or PVC pipe that is designed to shield conductors from moisture and physical harm.

CONTACT: The point or points inside a device where electrical conductors meet.

CONTINUITY: An electrical pathway—in a circuit, device, or fuse—that's unbroken, or "continuous."

CURRENT: Movement or flow of electrons through a conductor; measured in amperes.

DIRECT CURRENT: Continuous flow from one electrical pole to another, as in a battery.

FUSE: Safety device installed in circuit that stops the flow of electricity when current exceeds a predetermined amount.

GROUND: Any conducting body, such as a metal rod driven solidly into the earth, that provides electrical current with a path to the ground. Sometimes called "grounding electrode." Also, to connect any part of an electrical wiring system to the ground.

GROUND FAULT: Occurs when a bare hot wire accidentally touches a grounded object, providing a shorter path to ground than intended. This leakage is also known as "fault current."

GROUNDING ELECTRODE CONDUCTOR: Conductor that connects neutral bus bar of service panel to ground. Sometimes referred to as a "ground wire."

GROUNDING WIRE: Conductor that grounds a metal component but does not carry current during normal operation. Returns current to source in order to open circuit breaker or fuse if metal component accidentally becomes electrically alive.

HOT BUS BARS: Solid metal bars connected to main power source in service panel and subpanel. Branch circuit hot wires are connected to them.

HOT WIRE: Ungrounded conductor carrying electrical current forward from the source. Usually identified by black or red insulation, but may be any color other than white, gray, or green.

IMPEDANCE: The sum of resistance that's found inside an electronic component—like a speaker, for example. Measured in ohms.

INSULATION: Material that does not carry current, such as the color-coded thermoplastic insulation on wires.

JOIST: Horizontal wooden framing member placed on edge, as in a floor or ceiling joist.

JUMPER: Short piece of wire connected to the electrical box or to an electrical device, such as a switch or receptacle.

KILOWATT: Unit of electrical power equal to 1,000 watts. Abbreviated kw.

KILOWATT-HOUR: Unit used for metering and selling electricity. One kilowatt-hour equals 1,000 watts used for one hour (or any equivalent, such as 500 watts used for two hours). Abbreviated kwh.

KNOCKOUT: Prestamped circular impression in metal electrical boxes that is removed so that cable can enter the box.

NEUTRAL BUS BAR: Solid metal bar in service panel or subpanel which provides a common terminal for all neutral wires. In service panel, neutral bus bar is bonded to metal cabinet and is in direct contact with earth through grounding electrode conductor. All neutral and grounding wires are connected to this bus bar. In subpanel, only neutral wires are connected to neutral bus bar, which "floats" in metal cabinet (it is not bonded).

NEUTRAL WIRE: Grounded conductor that completes a circuit by providing a return path to the source. Except for a few switching situations, neutral wires must never be interrupted by a fuse, circuit breaker, or switch. Always identified by white or gray insulation.

OHM: The unit of measurement for electrical resistance or impedance.

OVERLOAD: A circuit that's passing more current than it's designed for and overheating—causing a circuit breaker to trip or fuse to blow.

OVERCURRENT PROTECTION DEVICE: Fuse or circuit breaker that shuts off electricity flow when a conductor carries more than a predetermined amount of current.

PIGTAIL SPLICE: When three or more wires are connected together, the connection is referred to as a pigtail splice.

POLARIZATION: Plugs and matching receptacles with different-size prongs for hot and neutral wires, preventing them from being reversed.

RESISTANCE: Property of an electric circuit that restricts the flow of current. Always measured in ohms.

SCREW TERMINAL: Threaded screw found on sockets, switches, and receptacles; used to make wire connections.

SERVICE ENTRANCE CONDUCTORS: Wires connecting terminals of service entrance equipment to either the service drop (if service is overhead) or the service lateral (underground service).

SERVICE ENTRANCE PANEL: Main power cabinet through which electricity enters a home wiring system. Contains main disconnect breaker or fuse and grounding connection for entire system; sometimes called a fusebox, panel box, or main panel.

SPLICE: To join wires by twisting and soldering or with solderless connectors such as wire nuts.

SHORT CIRCUIT: Occurs when a bare hot wire touches a bare neutral wire, providing a shorter path than the intended circuit.

STUD: Vertical wooden framing member; also referred to as a wall stud.

SUBPANEL: A distribution center that's remote from the main service entrance and from which some or all branch circuits are routed. Wires that connect main panel and subpanel are called subfeeds.

TRANSFORMER: Electrical device that raises or lowers voltage in a circuit.

TYPE NM (NONMETALLIC) SHEATHED CABLE: A multiconductor cable, consisting of three or more wires that are contained within the same nonmetallic outer sheathing; used for interior wiring only.

TYPE UF (UNDERGROUND FEEDER) CABLE: A multiconductor cable, consisting of three or more wires that are contained within the same nonmetallic outer sheathing; used for exterior wiring only.

UL: Stands for Underwriters Laboratories, an independent agency that tests electrical products for safety. A UL-listed item is approved for its intended use.

UNDERWRITERS' KNOT: Type of knot that relieves strain on the screw terminal connections on lamp sockets and some plugs.

VOLT: Unit of measure denoting electrical pressure. Abbreviated V.

VOLTAGE: Pressure at which a circuit operates, expressed in volts.

WATT: Unit of measurement for electrical power. One watt of power equals one volt of pressure times one ampere of current. Many electrical devices are rated in watts according to the power they consume. Abbreviated W.

WIRE: Single electrical conductor, usually made of solid-core or stranded copper and wrapped in a non-conducting, color-coded insulation.

WIRE NUT: Plastic or plastic-and-metal connector used to splice two or more wires without solder.

INDEX